The Results Facilitator

The Results Facilitator

EXPERT, MANAGER, MENTOR

Marvin T. Howell

CRC Press
Taylor & Francis Group
Boca Raton   London   New York

CRC Press is an imprint of the
Taylor & Francis Group, an **informa** business

CRC Press
Taylor & Francis Group
6000 Broken Sound Parkway NW, Suite 300
Boca Raton, FL 33487-2742

Library of Congress Cataloging-in-Publication Data

Howell, Marvin T., 1936-
  The results facilitator : expert, manager, mentor / Marvin T. Howell.
      pages cm
  Includes bibliographical references and index.
    ISBN 978-1-4822-5235-4
  1. Teams in the workplace--Management. 2. Group facilitation. 3. Performance. 4. Workflow. 5. Organizational effectiveness--Management. 6. Total quality management. I. Title.

HD66.H696 2015
658.4'022--dc23   2014021770

Visit the Taylor & Francis Web site at
http://www.taylorandfrancis.com

and the CRC Press Web site at
http://www.crcpress.com

This book is dedicated to all the part-time and full-time facilitators all over the world who have made meetings bearable and productive, processes more efficient, and outcomes that include high customer satisfaction.

Contents

Preface xvii

Acknowledgments xix

1   **Facilitation by Facilitators** 1
    1.1   Facilitator Definition 1
        1.1.1   Structure 1
        1.1.2   Process 2
        1.1.3   Groups 4
        1.1.4   Function Effectively 4
        1.1.5   Decision Making 4
        1.1.6   A Helper and Enabler 5
        1.1.7   Supports Others 5
        1.1.8   Group Achievement 5
    1.2   Roles and Responsibilities of a Facilitator 6
    1.3   Core Practices for a Facilitator 6
        1.3.1   FNS 4D Facilitation Model and Core Practices 7
    1.4   Neutral Is a Must 7
    1.5   Benefits of a Neutral Facilitator 9
    1.6   What Can Go Wrong in Facilitation? 10
    1.7   A Hypothetical Company: Quality Value Systems (QVS) 11
    1.8   IAF and INIFAC Core Values/Competencies 11
    1.9   Facilitator's Exercises 11

2   **Becoming and Sustaining Being an Excellent Facilitator** 13
    2.1   Becoming an Excellent Facilitator Takes Continuous Learning 13
    2.2   The Facilitator's Checklist 15
        2.2.1   Prior to the Meeting 15
            2.2.1.1   UNIFAC's Core Competency B Assessment 15
            2.2.1.2   Using OAR and/or PAL 20

  2.2.2 Just Prior to the Meeting 22
  2.2.3 During the Meeting 22
    2.2.3.1 The Process 22
    2.2.3.2 Establishing the Ground Rules 23
  2.2.4 After the Meeting 24
2.3 Self-Evaluation after Each Meeting 27
2.4 Using TOTs to Get Team Back on Track....................................28
2.5 Tool to Use When the Team and/or the System Needs
  Jumpstarting...30
2.6 Facilitator's Exercises 33

3 Different Types of Facilitators 35
3.1 Types of Facilitators..35
  3.1.1 Business Facilitators..36
  3.1.2 Training Facilitators 36
  3.1.3 Conflict Resolution Facilitators...37
  3.1.4 Wraparound Facilitators..37
  3.1.5 Small Group Facilitation 37
3.2 The Results Facilitator 44
3.3 The Hendecagon Model: The Skill Set of an Experienced
  Facilitator 47
3.4 Facilitator's Exercises 53

4 Ability to Influence..55
4.1 Be Able to Influence 55
4.2 Knowing You...56
4.3 Know Your Client...58
  4.3.1 IAF Core Competencies in this Area 58
    4.3.1.1 Create Collaborative Client Relationships................58
4.4 Facilitator and Team Leader Interface: Keys to Their Success........60
  4.4.1 Share Responsibility 60
  4.4.2 Work Together 61
  4.4.3 Keeping Focused 61
4.5 Know Your Team Members 61
4.6 Coaching...62
  4.6.1 Introduction 62
  4.6.2 Guidelines and Coaching Process..63
    4.6.2.1 Coaching Method 68
  4.6.3 Coaching: Toyota Kata 70
4.7 Facilitator's Exercises 74

5 Understanding Group Dynamics, Handling Difficult Behaviors, and Managing Conflict...**77**

5.1 Teams and Groups 77

5.2 Tuckman's Four Stages of Group Development 78

    5.2.1 Form 78

    5.2.2 Storm 78

    5.2.3 Norm 78

    5.2.4 Perform 79

    5.2.5 New Stage Needed for the "Never-Ending, on a Journey" Group 80

5.3 IAF Facilitator Core Competencies 82

    5.3.1 Create and Sustain a Participatory Environment 82

    5.3.2 Cultivate Cultural Awareness and Sensitivity 83

5.4 Group Members' Behavior 83

5.5 Intervention Approaches 86

5.6 Managing Conflict 88

    5.6.1 IAF Facilitators' Core Competencies 88

        5.6.1.1 Create and Sustain a Participatory Environment ... 88

5.7 Observing Group Dynamics 90

5.8 Group Guidance and Self-Awareness 95

    5.8.1 Guide Group to Appropriate and Useful Outcomes ... 95

        5.8.1.1 Facilitate Group Self-Awareness about Its Task 95

    5.8.2 Model Positive Professional Attitude 95

        5.8.2.1 Trust Group Potential and Model Neutrality 95

5.9 Facilitation Engagement Processes 96

5.10 Group Building, Teamwork, and High-Performing Groups 101

    5.10.1 Groups 101

    5.10.2 Group Building 102

    5.10.3 Teamwork and High-Performance Results 102

    5.10.4 Quick Check on Whether a Group Is High-Performance or Not? 106

5.11 Facilitator Exercises 107

6 Know the Technical Area or Process (Four Key Examples)..... 109

6.1 Introduction 109

6.2 Example 1: ISO 50001 Energy Management System (EMS) 110

6.3 Example 2: ISO 14001 Environmental Management System 112

6.4 Example 3: Construction Partnering 113

6.5 Example 4: Problem Solving 114

6.6 What Is CAPDO (Check–Act–Plan–Do)? 117
6.7 Tools and Techniques Needed for PDCA and CAPDO 119
6.8 Facilitator Exercises 120

7 Facilitation Tools and Techniques 121
7.1 Introduction 121
7.2 Facilitator's Toolkit 121
    7.2.1 Objective and Problem Definition 122
    7.2.2 Generation of Ideas and Collection of Data 122
    7.2.3 Evaluation of Ideas/Data 123
    7.2.4 Analysis of Data 123
    7.2.5 Countermeasures 124
    7.2.6 Implementation 124
7.3 Generating Ideas 126
    7.3.1 Brainstorming and Nominal Group Technique 126
7.4 Strategic Planning 129
    7.4.1 Headlight Teams 129
    7.4.2 Environmental Scan 129
    7.4.3 SWOT Analysis 130
    7.4.4 Affinity Diagrams 130
7.5 Gathering Data 133
    7.5.1 Check Sheets 133
    7.5.2 Company's Information Systems 134
    7.5.3 Research Internet 134
    7.5.4 Surveys 135
    7.5.5 Focus Groups 136
7.6 Evaluating Ideas 137
    7.6.1 Multivoting 137
    7.6.2 Pareto Analysis 137
    7.6.3 Metrics 140
    7.6.4 Criterion Matrix and Ranking 140
    7.6.5 Flow Chart 140
7.7 Analyzing 141
    7.7.1 Fishbone Diagram 141
    7.7.2 Root Cause Matrix 143
    7.7.3 Benchmarking 145
7.8 Selling Your Solution 147
    7.8.1 Rate of Return or Payback Period 147
    7.8.2 The Solution Matrix 147

7.9   Facilitator Exercises 148

8   Objectives and Targets Development and Action Plans 151
8.1   Objectives and Targets 151
8.2   Making Targets SMART 153
8.3   Objective and Target (O&T) Template and Developing Action
      Plans 154
      8.3.1   Explanation on How to Fill out the O&T Template 154
8.4   Establishing Objectives and Targets 157
8.5   Achieving Team Results Using Toyota Kata 164
8.6   Facilitator Exercises 168

9   Projects and Project Management 169
9.1   What Is a Project and Project Management? 169
9.2   Project Phases 171
9.3   Facilitator Exercises 174

10   Facilitators' Professional Behavior and Continuing Education ... 175
10.1   IAF Core Competencies 175
       10.1.1 IAF Facilitators' Core Competencies 175
10.2   Certification 176
10.3   Model Positive Professional Attitude 177
       10.3.1 IAF Facilitator Core Competencies 177
10.4   Self-Assessments 180
10.5   Facilitator Exercises 182

**11   Evaluation of IAF Facilitator Core Competencies for
       Certification 183**
11.1   The IAF Facilitator Core Competencies 183
11.2   Evaluation of the IAF Facilitator Core Competencies 187
11.3   INIFAC Core Competencies 187
       11.3.1 The Subcompetencies 188
11.4   IAF and INIFAC Core Competencies Comparison 190
11.5   Summary of Comparison 201
11.6   Results Facilitator Core Competencies 204
11.7   Critical Success Factors (CSFs) for a Facilitated Session 212
11.8   Facilitators' Core Competencies Recommendations 213
11.9   Facilitator Exercises 213

**12   Facilitator's Offshoots and Questions from New Facilitators
       (39 Different Areas) 215**
12.1   The 39 Areas 215

12.1.1 Subject Content...215
    12.1.1.1 Is It a Must That the Facilitator Know the
          Subject Content?...215
12.1.2 Responsibility for Results 216
    12.1.2.1 Is the Facilitator Held Responsible for the
          Results? 216
12.1.3 Team Composition 216
    12.1.3.1 Is the Facilitator a Team Member?...................216
    12.1.3.2 What Is the Optimum Size for a Team? 216
12.1.4 Team Momentum...217
    12.1.4.1 How Many Objectives and Targets (O&Ts)
          Are Necessary to Maintain a Team?....................217
12.1.5 Jumpstarting a Team...217
    12.1.5.1 How Can You Jumpstart a Team if Needed? 217
12.1.6 Facilitator's Skills..218
    12.1.6.1 Are All Facilitators Equal? 218
12.1.7 Seven Quality Control Tools 218
    12.1.7.1 Is Life over for the Seven QC Tools?.................218
12.1.8 Listening...218
    12.1.8.1 How Important Is the Ability to Listen for
          a Facilitator? 218
12.1.9 Training...219
    12.1.9.1 Who Provides the Training to New Team
          Members? 219
    12.1.9.2 Who Trains the Objective Champion
          or Strategic Council or Top Management in
          the EnMS?...219
12.1.10 Certification...219
    12.1.10.1 Should I Become Certified? 219
12.1.11 Communications...220
    12.1.11.1 How Can You Improve Communications?.......220
12.1.12 Feedback...220
    12.1.12.1 How Do You Ensure the Feedback You
          Give as a Facilitator Is Helpful?........................220
12.1.13 Group Stages 221
    12.1.13.1 Can You Actually See a Team Go through
          the Four or Five Stages of Group Dynamics?....221
12.1.14 Team Members 221

12.1.14.1 Has It Been Your Experience That the Team
Leader, Facilitator, and One or Two Team
Members Do Most of the Team Work?.............221
12.1.15 Team Members Replacement..221
12.1.15.1 On Permanent Teams, Do You Think
That Team Members Should Be Replaced
Periodically, for Example, Every Year? 221
12.1.16 Team Leader/Facilitator Coordination 222
12.1.16.1 Should the Team Leader and Facilitator
Meet before Each Meeting?..............................222
12.1.17 Meeting Length 222
12.1.17.1 How Long Should Our Meetings Last?.............222
12.1.18 Document Control Manager..223
12.1.18.1 Is It a Good Practice to Have the Team
Leader for an ISO Team Be the Document
Control Manager?...223
12.1.19 Award and Recognition..223
12.1.19.1 When a Company or Organization Has an
Awards Program, Does It Motivate Teams?......223
12.1.20 Energy Team 223
12.1.20.1 Does a Company Only Need to Have One
Energy Team or Are Others Recommended?...223
12.1.21 Lead Facilitator...223
12.1.21.1 How Do You Define a Lead Facilitator?...........223
12.1.22 Lean and Six Sigma 224
12.1.22.1 Do Lean and Six Sigma Efforts Need
Facilitators? 224
12.1.23 Objective and Target Responsibilities.............................224
12.1.23.1 Is It Good to Have Most, if Not All of
the Team Members, Be Responsible for
an Objective and Target on an ISO Team? 224
12.1.24 O&T Responsible Person 224
12.1.24.1 What Are the Responsibilities of an
Objective and Target Responsible Person?.......224
12.1.25 O&T Time to Completion 225
12.1.25.1 How Long Should an Objective and Target
Take to Finish or Complete? 225

12.1.26 Coaching Effectiveness...225
   12.1.26.1 How Do You Know Whether the Coaching
       You Have Been Doing Was Effective?.............225
12.1.27 kWh Intensity...225
   12.1.27.1 Why Is kWh/sq. Footage Used as an EPI
       When kWh Usage Tells You How Well
       You Did?...225
12.1.28 Team Types...226
   12.1.28.1 What Are the Different Kinds of Teams
       That Exist in Today's Organizations
       and Companies? 226
12.1.29 Facilitator Benefits..227
   12.1.29.1 What Are the Benefits of Having
       a Facilitator?...227
12.1.30 Neutrality..227
   12.1.30.1 Should a Facilitator Be Neutral and
       Not Participate in the Meeting Contents? 227
12.1.31 Team's Success..227
   12.1.31.1 When Is a Team Considered Successful? 227
12.1.32 In-House versus Outside Facilitator 228
   12.1.32.1 When Is it Best to Use an Outside
       Facilitator Instead of an In-House Facilitator?....228
12.1.33 LeBron James as NBA's Best Results Facilitator..............228
   12.1.33.1 Why Is LeBron James Called the
       Best Facilitator Ever in the NBA?.....................228
12.1.34 Results Facilitator Name Acceptability...........................228
   12.1.34.1 Will the Facilitator World, including
       the National Organizations, Accept
       the Term Results Facilitator?............................228
12.1.35 Things a Facilitator Can Do Badly.................................228
   12.1.35.1 What Are Some of the Things You
       Noticed That Facilitators Do Badly in
       Some Meetings?...228
12.1.36 Process Observers 229
   12.1.36.1 In My Last Organization, the Facilitator
       Used Process Observers to Help Monitor
       the Team Meetings. Do You Think They
       Are Useful?...229

12.1.37 Exit Interviews 229
    12.1.37.1 Should the Team Have Exit Interviews
           with Team Members Who Resigned or
           Ask to Be Excused from the Team? 229
12.1.38 Team Closure 229
    12.1.38.1 Should There Be Specific Activities
           Accomplished When a Team Is Closing? 229
12.1.39 Facilitators Phased out 230
    12.1.39.1 Don't Most ISO Standards Implementation
           Teams Phase out Facilitators When They
           Reach the Maintenance Stage? 230
12.2 Facilitator Exercises 230
13 Conclusions 231
Appendix 235
Bibliography 247
Index 253
About the Author 265

Preface

Facilitation is almost as important as leadership. Without facilitation, most organizations' visions, goals, and objectives would not be achieved. Improvement programs would falter and increased efficiencies and productivity would not be realized. Facilitation makes improvement easy and manageable. All facilitators need to possess certain skills, training, and education. These comprise core competencies, which have been established by the International Institute for Facilitators (INIFAC) and the International Association of Facilitators (IAFs). They use them to certify facilitators, who are now located throughout the world in many countries and, on a daily schedule, provide the necessary facilitation services. Both external facilitators and internal facilitators are essential today to worldwide organizations to help improve their meetings' and processes' effectiveness. To keep abreast of the fast-growing field, facilitators should follow the continuous learning process: Learn–Practice–Evaluate–Act. Most facilitators remain neutral in their sessions, not joining into the subject content, but merely keeping the meeting running on track and without interruptions and conflict. The International Standards Organization's (ISO's) implementation and other long-term, multiyear team involvement has challenged neutrality in all cases and has produced what is now the *results facilitator.*

Acknowledgments

I would like to thank Armando Olivera, former president and CEO of Florida Power & Light (FPL), who gave me my first opportunity to be a facilitator in 1980 and on several occasions thereafter, including FPL's successful pursuit of the Deming Prize.

I would like to thank Laura Winter at the DEA Environmental Section, who hired me to facilitate the Environmental Management Systems teams (8+ years) at several DEA labs, intelligence centers, division and districts offices, and an air operations center.

In addition, I thank my wife, Jackie, for her encouragement and patience and my oldest grandson, Chris Cline, who helped me with the tables, figures, and formats.

Special thanks to Prabu Naidu of Facilitation Network Singapore and Dr. Eileen Dowse, certified master facilitator (CMF) and chair of the International Institute for Facilitation for their contributions and suggestions to the author for improving the book's contents.

Chapter 1

Facilitation by Facilitators

1.1 Facilitator Definition

A *facilitator* is someone who helps a group of people understand their common objectives, and assists them in planning to achieve them, without the facilitator taking a particular position in the discussion (http://en.wikipedia. org/wiki/Facilitator). Examples include Kaizen* events, strategic planning meetings, and team meetings.

There are several definitions by authors of what a facilitator is and is not. The author's favorite is by Ingrid Bens (2000):

> One who contributes *structure and process* to interactions so groups are able to function effectively and make high-quality decisions. A helper and enabler whose goal is to support others as they achieve exceptional performance.

The key words are structure, process, groups, function effectively, decision making, a helper and enabler, supports others, and group achievement. Let's briefly explore these.

1.1.1 Structure

There are several definitions of structure, including being organized or following a plan or arranging several parts into a composite. They all fit well with a facilitator providing structure. The best tool or technique is to actively

---

* Kaizen, a Japanese term, means improvement.

listen to what the client hopes to achieve, and then working with the team leader to put together an agenda with purpose and items that, when completed, will accomplish the purpose or objective and the client's expectation. Establishing ground rules at the beginning of a meeting and spelling out the players' roles and responsibilities, such as the team leader, facilitator, note keeper, and others, provide structure.

1.1.2 Process

A process is a sequence of activities that when accomplished produces a product, a service, or information. A process diagram is shown in Figure 1.1.

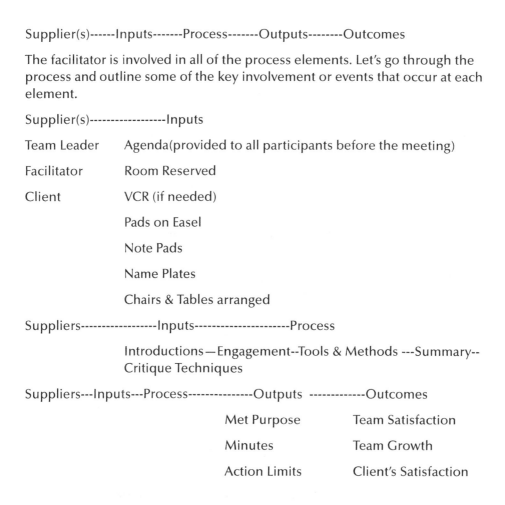

Supplier(s)------Inputs-------Process-------Outputs--------Outcomes

The facilitator is involved in all of the process elements. Let's go through the process and outline some of the key involvement or events that occur at each element.

Supplier(s)-----------------Inputs

Team Leader	Agenda(provided to all participants before the meeting)
Facilitator	Room Reserved
Client	VCR (if needed)
	Pads on Easel
	Note Pads
	Name Plates
	Chairs & Tables arranged

Suppliers------------------Inputs---------------------Process

Introductions—Engagement--Tools & Methods ---Summary--Critique Techniques

Suppliers---Inputs---Process--------------Outputs ------------Outcomes

Met Purpose	Team Satisfaction
Minutes	Team Growth
Action Limits	Client's Satisfaction

Figure 1.1 A process diagram.

Tool/Technique #1: Process Diagram

A process is where the facilitator molds the team or group into a decision-making, high-performance group or team. The facilitator opens the meeting on time, and every participant has an agenda. First, the facilitator introduces an icebreaker or goes around the room having each person give his/her name, where he/she works, and what expectations he/she has for the meeting. This is written on a pad on an easel and then placed on the wall. At the end of the meeting, the facilitator revisits these expectations and sees if they were all met.

The facilitator will need to use several tools or techniques to help the team's identification of problems, factors, scenarios, or generation of ideas, and then evaluation or analysis tools to identify root causes, process waste, opportunities, and other important issues or facts. A list of important tools and techniques will be outlined and discussed later. During the meeting, the facilitator should summarize where the group is at this point, what the members have done, and what remains for them to do. This summary is especially essential at the meeting's end. It helps to achieve group understanding and brings cohesiveness of purpose and buy-in to and between group members.

Lastly, critique what was accomplished in the meeting. This can be done by questioning the group or via a well-designed critique form issued to gather the pertinent information. The disadvantage of using critique forms is that the group has to wait until the next meeting to hear the results and often a facilitator may be tasked or contracted for a single meeting or event. The facilitator questions are simple:

Did we accomplish our meeting objective or purpose?
What did we do right?
What can we do to improve next time?

The answers to these three questions are essential for continuous improvement. Added to this list could be:

How did the facilitator do?
What can he/she do better?

Roger Schwartz (2002) defines process as:

> Process refers to how a group works together, including how group members talk to each other, how they identify and solve problems, and how they make decisions, and how they handle conflict. Structure refers to stable and recurring group processes, such as group membership and group roles.

Although this description does not fit the entire process diagram shown above, it does describe some of the important elements that go on during the meetings (which is the process part of the diagram).

1.1.3 Groups

The facilitator may engage groups of 30 to 100 or even more. These groups offer a real challenge to just keep order. The facilitator must plan the meeting, have an agenda, and keep the meeting interesting, focused and moving on time. In all group meetings, the facilitator will remain neutral.

1.1.4 Function Effectively

This is one of the primary roles of a facilitator. To help the team or group to function effectively starts with a good agenda, adequate ground rules, handling disruptions, and managing any conflict. These responsibilities are essential to keeping the group on subject and moving productively toward the meeting's purpose or objective. Due to their importance, the responsibilities will be discussed in detail later in the book.

1.1.5 Decision Making

In order to meet most meeting objectives or purpose, the group will have to make at least one decision, and, often, several. Whether the decision is one of consensus, where everyone agrees with the decision or majority rules, should be determined up front and even discussed when setting the ground rules. Making the right decision will largely depend on the data and facts gathered, the data's accuracy, turning the data into information, and the tool(s) selected to help arrive at a decision(s).

1.1.6 A Helper and Enabler

The success of the group could easily depend on the facilitator's ability to help the team and enable them to meet their objective. These tasks will vary by different kinds of group meetings and experience, education, and personalities of the group members. The facilitator needs to be able to help them understand the purpose and stay on track and enable them to succeed by using the appropriate tools and techniques. A facilitator is not one who is looking for credit. In contrast, enabling group members to succeed is a facilitator's primary mission. If the group is successful, then the facilitator has done his/her job.

1.1.7 Supports Others

This is very close to the key word described above, but extends to not only the meeting, but outside of the meeting as well. Helping others to get ready for a meeting; coaching a team leader on certain issues, tools, and other items that may happen in the meeting; providing team or group members training on certain tools or techniques; teaching your backup facilitator some aspects of facilitating; letting top management know exactly what is going to occur and how their opening comments could help; reviewing the meeting minutes with the note keeper to ensure accuracy and completeness are just a few examples of support for others. Yes, a facilitator does more than just facilitate the group meeting.

1.1.8 Group Achievement

Group achievement could be referred to as the report card of the facilitator and team leader. If the group is not successful, then the team leader and facilitator will be regarded as unsuccessful as well unless some factor occurred, such as management changing the scope or parameters of the meeting objective. The group or team should meet its meeting purpose or objective every time if proper meeting planning and facilitation were employed correctly.

1.2 Roles and Responsibilities of a Facilitator

First, the facilitator is not the team leader. He or she is a guide. A facilitator's job is to get others to assume responsibility of taking the lead and meeting the meeting objectives.

Second, the facilitator listens and focuses on how things are discussed and how the meeting is progressing, including:

- Methods
- Procedures
- Tools and techniques
- Style of interaction and disruptions of any kind
- Group norms and dynamics
- Group morale
- Group participation
- Tasks and opportunities
- Time and agenda
- Process
- Goals, objectives, and purpose

1.3 Core Practices for a Facilitator

A good facilitator, during a meeting, should practice the following:

- Listen actively (it is hard to listen when your mouth is opened and moving/talking)
- Ask probing questions
- Paraphrase and summarize at appropriate times
- Ensure common understanding of terms and definitions
- Synthesize and categorize ideas
- Track discussions and minimize interruptions and disturbances
- Use appropriate tools and techniques and language
- Plan and design meetings and activities
- Critique meetings

1.3.1 FNS 4D Facilitation Model and Core Practices

FNS (Facilitation Network Singapore) states that for meetings, the facilitator needs to start first by getting the clients and/or participants to agree on the meeting's objective, output, and outcome. Next the facilitator designs the approach to achieve the objective and delivers the output and implements the outcome to achieve organizational achievements. The objective and output refer to the session (meeting) and not business (company objective and outputs).

The FNS 4D Facilitation Model below shows that issues, challenges, and opportunities start with D1: Determine requirements, then D2: Design the session, D3: Deliver and debrief the session, and D4: Discovery of new learning (facilitator). Objectives are developed and divergence tools are used to establish criteria, then convergence tools used to produce outputs and outcomes.

FNS's core practices include: (1) Staying neutral, (2) listening actively, (3) asking questions, (4) paraphrasing, (5) collecting ideas, (6) synthesizing ideas, (7) surfacing assumptions, (8) staying on track, (9) giving and receiving feedback, and (10) concluding and follow-up. These 10 core practices symbolize what an excellent facilitator does to achieve the objectives, outputs, and outcomes of a meeting (Figure 1.2 to Figure 1.4).

INIFAC core competence for presence states:

> Master facilitators bring compassion and authority to the room. Through their verbal and nonverbal expression, they exude confidence, energy, and self-awareness while also conveying a high level of warmth and caring. They make adjustments in their style to better serve the group.

This is "right on." The excellent presence of a facilitator gets the foot in the door and gains respect immediately. INIFAC's and IAF's (International Association of Facilitators) core competencies will be shown throughout the book and will be compared in Chapter 11.

1.4 Neutral Is a Must

A facilitator is often brought into an organization for their facilitation skills, but also because they are neutral. They will make the meeting run smoothly and meet the objective, output, and outcome desired by the client. Being neutral, they do not comment or participate in the subject content, only the

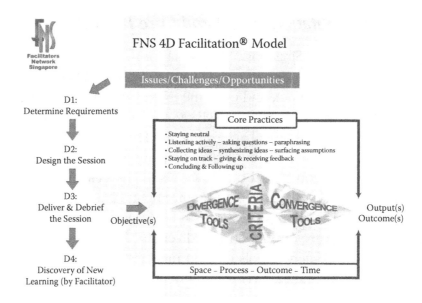

Figure 1.2 Printed with FNS's approval. They show an excellent formula for facilitation. The Space–Process–Outline–Time at the bottom of their first chart stands for SPOT, which is the thrust and representative of their facilitation efforts.

Figure 1.3 Printed with FNS's approval. They show an excellent formula for facilitation.

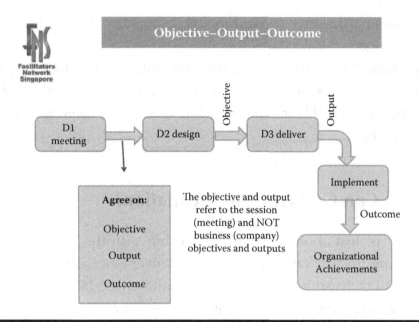

Figure 1.4   Printed with FNS's approval. They show an excellent formula for facilitation.

team leader and team discuss content. The facilitator helps minimize disruptions and conflict using tools and techniques that help meet the meeting objective. An internal facilitator who knows the subject content has to focus on facilitation principles and techniques and do his/her best not to discuss subject content. Neutrality has been a core competency for facilitators for years. Without neutrality, many successful facilitation sessions would not have taken place.

1.5 Benefits of a Neutral Facilitator

The apparent benefits include:

■ Bring to the surface different points of view by balancing the participation of introverts and extroverts while ensuring both participate.
■ Prevents the client or any one participant from monopolizing the discussion throughout the meeting.
■ Encourage participants to think creatively, solve problems, and make decisions.

- Increases participants' ownership and commitment by involving them in the solution.
- Saves time because the meeting runs smoothly. The facilitator keeps the discussion on track and focuses the participants on the meeting's objective.
- Facilitation is flexible and adaptable to all kinds of meetings and discussions.

1.6 What Can Go Wrong in Facilitation?

The answer is: Just about everything. Starting with the client and facilitator reaching unclear tasks, objectives, involvement, and other areas that will lead to frustration, inefficiencies, and chaos later on. Input can include a wrong sized room (a giant room that dwarfs the meeting or one too small to have enough chairs for all of the participants); a noisy room next to a mechanical room, boiler, HVAC, or laundry room; a VCR that did not show up; no pads for the easels; the agenda was not prepared in time; the wrong meeting room number was given out by a new staff member; and not all participants received word about the meeting. The list goes on and on. During the process, a fight could happen between two or more participants, a member continuously breaks in and filibusters over a subject he or she wanted to discuss, the agenda does not include all that needs to be done, cell phones are ringing, and people have to leave because their work calls. The possibilities are endless. For the output, no one kept notes so it will be hard to reconstruct the minutes, the meeting did not have a quorum so the group is not sure the meeting counts, and no one is cognizant of what was really decided. The wrong tools and process were followed leading to wrong decisions or no decision at all. As far as outcomes, the group is mad, management is disappointed, and the facilitator is confused as to what to do to straighten this out. How do we prevent these unwanted occurrences from happening? Read this book and learn the best practices, tools and techniques, engagement methods, and other facilitative skills and competencies that can keep these from happening and, thus, make you a successful facilitator.

1.7 A Hypothetical Company: Quality Value Systems (QVS)

QVS Inc., in Gun Barrel, Texas, has five buildings including a headquarters with a large data center, a distribution center, and three plants all in the same fenced-in area. QVS has established an energy reduction goal and chartered an energy team and appointed a management representative. They already have an environmental management team that is very active and successful. Some of the 40+ tools/techniques that we highlighted throughout will be used by the energy team or the environmental management team. Many will be explained for demonstrating the usefulness of the tool or technique and how to construct.

1.8 IAF and INIFAC Core Values/Competencies

INIFAC and IAF developed and published a set of core values for facilitators that are used for certification. They are comprehensive lists that the author uses in this book to help explain certain points. In Chapter 11, several additions to the lists are recommended to bring it up to date. The existing lists can be downloaded at: www.iaf.world.org.certification and www.inifac.org

1.9 Facilitator's Exercises

1. Facilitators do not have a chance to be certified. T __ F __
2. In a process, outputs and outcomes are the same. T __ F __
3. INIFAC means International Association of Facilitators. T __ F __
4. Open space technology is one of the 20 facilitation engagement processes. T __ F __
5. Effective critiques can be done in person at the end of meetings or by filling out a critique form and giving to facilitator when the participant leaves the meeting room. T __ F __
6. Ground rules should be established in the engagement part of the process. T __ F __
7. The process major activities include:
    a. __ Introductions–Icebreaker–Lessons–Outcomes–Critiques
    b. __ Introductions–Engagement–Tools and Techniques–Closing

    c. __ Introductions–Tools and Techniques–Engagement–Closing

    d. __ Introductions–Engagements–Tools and Techniques–Critiques

8. At the beginning of the meeting (if it has not already been done), the facilitator should get the participants to agree on:

    a. __ Decisions–Outputs–Outcomes

    b. __ Problem–Inputs–Outputs

    c. __ Objective–Target–Outputs

    d. __ Objective–Output–Outcome

(See Appendix 1 for answers.)

Chapter 2

Becoming and Sustaining Being an Excellent Facilitator

2.1 Becoming an Excellent Facilitator Takes Continuous Learning

The model for becoming an excellent facilitator is to practice continuous improvement. Facilitation requires a lot of skill, poise, confidence, and competence in handling different unplanned or unforeseen experiences.

Learn–Practice–Evaluate–Take Corrective Action

The above model mirrors the continuous improvement cycle of Plan–Do–Check–Act (PDCA) (Figure 2.1).

Plan: Set objectives and develop action plans	Learn: Study skills needed, Tools & Techniques, group dynamics
Do: Implement	Practice: Problem solving teams, group meetings, strategic teams
Check: Monitor, review, evaluate and analyze	Evaluate: Check periodically how you are doing, identify what you should change including training; a self-evaluation form will be presented later and a meeting evaluation form
Act: Take corrective actions	Act: Take corrective actions

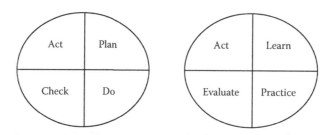

Figure 2.1 PDCA cycle and Learn–Practice–Evaluate–Act cycle.

Tool/Technique #2: PDCA Cycle

Learn all you can about facilitation before trying your skills. Read books, attend facilitation training, have discussions with experienced facilitators, and observe how they facilitate. Take notes and then *practice* what you have learned. Try your new skills, first in meetings where you know everyone. They will overlook any errors, but still give you feedback to help you improve. Take on larger facilitation opportunities as your skills and confidence increase. Plan how you are going to handle the facilitation effort prior to the event. After each facilitation effort, *evaluate* what you did. Ask what you did right? Then ask how could you improve? If you could do it over, what would you change? Use critique forms and then review them after the facilitation session. If critique forms are not used, go around the room at the end of the meeting or session and ask each person: "What did you like about the meeting?" "What could we have done better?" "Did we spend the appropriate time on each meeting subject areas?" "Did we achieve our objective?" As you gain experience, you will add other questions to these to learn more and then use them to improve your next facilitation effort. Apply what you learn by *taking appropriate or corrective action.* This process is continual. Use these after each facilitation effort and continuously improve your skills, tools and techniques use, coaching, presentation of new material, and creating a positive and dynamic climate that garners team synergy and produces superior results (Figure 2.2).

Tool/Technique #3: Indicator Graph

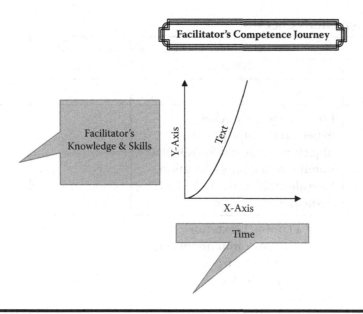

Figure 2.2 Facilitator's competence journey.

2.2 The Facilitator's Checklist

The author is often asked if there is a good checklist for facilitators to use to ensure that they don't forget to do something that should be done. The author researched the checklists on the Internet (see **Web Sites** in the back of the book) and did not find one that included all the essential items. Therefore, the author developed for facilitators and anyone designated to arrange and hold meetings, a comprehensive checklist. It is shown in Table 2.1. The checklist enables the facilitator to plan, conduct, and check on how well the meeting went. In other words, it covers the entire meeting life cycle.

Tool/Technique #4: Facilitator's Checklist

2.2.1 Prior to the Meeting

2.2.1.1 UNIFAC's Core Competency B Assessment

It states:

> Master facilitators know and ask the questions necessary to accurately assess a client's need. Based on their learning from past experiences, they create processes designed to address the client's specific requirements.

Table 2.1 Facilitator's Checklist

When	*What*	*Done (Yes/No)*	*Notes/Remarks*
Prior to			
	Know from client what is expected of you—purpose/objectives/deliverables/results/number of meetings, location, time allotted number of participants, charter.		
	Have a contract (exterior facilitator) or commitment (in house facilitator) from management to accomplish no. 1 above.		
	Select the topics that will be covered including the objectives. Coordinate with team leader or assigned point of contact.		
	Develop agenda using PAL (Purpose–Agenda–Limited) and get approved. Send to participants or team at least three days prior to the meeting.		
	Develop a "meeting needs list" to include handouts, PowerPoint® presentations, ice breaker, chairs and table arrangement, presentation needs, and critique forms (customize for this effort). If meeting has any training on the agenda, develop learning objectives and materials to accomplish them.		
	Develop some guiding questions that during the meeting would help information flow.		

(Continued)

Table 2.1 Facilitator's Checklist (Continued)

When	What	Done (Yes/No)	Notes/Remarks
Just before			
	Arrive early and ensure room is set up the way you desire for best communications results.		
	Ensure your technical requirements are met: Do you need a PC, a PowerPoint projector, a white board, an easel with a pad, an overhead projector?		
	Review the materials/handouts to ensure you understand all the information.		
	Is the room temperature and ventilation adequate?		
	Were the snacks provided, pitchers of water with glasses, and a pad and pen on the table?		
During meeting			
	Introduce yourself and let each participant introduce him/herself. Have them sign a meeting sign-in sheet.		
	Have icebreaker if planned and appropriate. Introduce ground rules.		
	Go over the agenda items. Say at least two sentences about each item to include what the outcome for each are expected and previously what has been accomplished (if anything).		

(Continued)

Table 2.1 Facilitator's Checklist (Continued)

When	What	Done (Yes/No)	Notes/Remarks
	Get volunteers for a timekeeper and a notetaker and scribe if needed.		
	Ask questions to quiet personnel and manage group dynamics and any conflicts that may happen.		
	Start on time even if everyone is not there. End on time.		
	Summarize what was accomplished at the meeting, decisions made, deliverables achieved or not achieved, and things that need to be addressed in the future. Give your critique of how the meeting went, what was good, and maybe how we can improve next time.		
	Set the time, place, and date for next meeting.		
	Administer the critique form.		
After meeting			
	Analyze critique forms and determine how well the meeting went and if there are areas you can improve for the next meeting.		
	Get with notetaker and develop minutes using PAPA (Purpose–Agenda–Points–Action Limits) and coordinate and send to all participants and interested personnel within three days of the meeting.		

(*Continued*)

Table 2.1   Facilitator's Checklist (Continued)

When	What	Done (Yes/No)	Notes/Remarks
	Brief client on deliverables, what went well and what did not, how the next meeting can be improved, next meeting date, any problems or support needed.		
	Use critiques, client feedback, issues and decisions from last meeting to develop the plan for next meeting to include agenda using PAL.		

Study your client's organization. The mission, vision, values, culture, and their facilitation needs. Determine the requirements for your services, exactly what deliverables are expected and when, whether any other facilitators are going to be involved, and the pay and how and when it will be received. Keep your client informed of status, issues, and achievements.

Place the facilitation requirements in a contract after they are determined and a consensus has been reached. Any time a requirement may not be reached on time due to any reasons, yours or the organization's, be sure the client knows ahead of time.

Someone once said that "battles are won before the fighting starts." That is certainly true with meetings. Before the meeting, the team leader and facilitator agree on an agenda, which should be sent to team members and guests a few days prior to the meeting so they can come prepared. The meeting room should be booked at least two weeks prior to the meeting to ensure availability. Meeting material and presentations, if needed, should be prepared and reviewed prior to the meeting. A sign-in sheet should be ready and printed. The sign-in sheet should state what kind of meeting, e.g., EnMS (Environmental Management System) team meeting, a management review, etc.; the date of meeting; persons' names that attended; and their title, telephone number, email address, and signature. In any ISO (International Standards Organization) meetings or training sessions, sign-in sheets are a "must." They provide auditors, who later inspect your system, with assurances that the meetings and/or training actually occurred.

2.2.1.2 Using OAR and/or PAL

What is OAR? What is PAL? What do they have to do with managing meetings? Can they be used for any kind of meeting? These questions and more will be answered in this section.

We have meetings for many different reasons: staff meetings, department meetings, process improvement team meetings, DMAIC (Define–Measure–Analyze–Improve–Control) meetings, board of directors meetings, Kaizen event meetings, safety meetings, environmental management systems meetings, strategic meetings, scheduling meetings, management reviews, headlight team meetings, quality improvement meetings, and project management meetings, to name a few. Meetings are how we communicate, coordinate, direct, plan, improve, and gain buy-in on a proposal or new way of doing something. It is hard to imagine a workplace without meetings. In a previous research study presented on a Dallas news station (date unknown), employees said the biggest reason for them feeling unproductive is the many ineffective and boring meetings they attend. In this section, we cannot directly address the boring issue, but we certainly can outline how to make each meeting effective. In doing so, hopefully, it will make the meetings more interesting and organized, thus mitigating the boring issue.

What does OAR and PAL bring to the meeting management arena? These are two different acronyms, but are basically the same approach. OAR was introduced in 2005 by the author. PAL has been with us for over 30 years. It was introduced by someone in the early Total Quality Improvement days prior to the Six Sigma era. They stand for:

OAR: Objective, Agenda, Restricted
PAL: Purpose, Agenda, Limited

Tools/Techniques #5 and #6: OAR and PAL

Both send the same message. Because PAL is more widely known and accepted, let's use it. The P in PAL simply states for every meeting there must be a *purpose*. Write it on the agenda along with the items that will be covered during the meeting. For each item to be covered, show how much time is allotted for each and who is the responsible person for each one. This action is the limited or restricted part. Also, place on the agenda a title for the meeting and place of the meeting, the date, and start time. Agendas do not have to be long to be effective. One page or less is acceptable and useful. Of course, long meetings with large participation could require several agenda pages. Whatever it takes in length to include purpose, all agenda items, and responsible persons is what is needed.

The limited part of PAL also means to hold the meeting for only the time needed. Most meetings can be completed in 30 minutes to an hour if they use PAL. Whenever meetings are not planned and no organization is accomplished, meetings can stretch in time and can become frustrating to the participants. Let's see how PAL looked for QVS's Corporate Energy Team's first meeting.

Meeting 1

QVS Energy Team Meeting Agenda: October 20, 2010
Date/Time: Oct 20, 2010/Time: 10–11 a.m.
Place: Quality Conference Room
Purpose: To review ISO 50001 EMS, draft an energy policy, analyze utility data, and determine team focus for energy policy deployment.
Agenda:
10–10:05 QVS Energy Team Charter   *Team Leader*
10:05–10:15 ISO 50001 EnMS Review   *Team Leader*
10:15–10:40 Review several draft energy policies, select one or rewrite   *Team Leader*
10:40–11 Analyze Data and Determine Our Focus   *Team Facilitator*

Of course, the team leader and facilitator had prepared some energy policy drafts prior to the meeting and brought them to the meeting to get team members' input.

The facilitator should make all the arrangements for the room and the equipment needed for the meeting. Visualize the meeting and develop some general questions that you may want to use to keep the meeting flowing toward achieving its purpose. Examples for this agenda would be:

What should a charter include?
Does your charter contain all the important elements?
How is ISO 50001 comparable to ISO 14001 EnMS?
What should the energy policy do? What should it contain?
What do the data tell us? Are they pertinent to our assignment?

2.2.2 Just Prior to the Meeting

Arrive early to the meeting room. Be sure all the items, such as handouts, copies of the agenda, VCRs, pads and easel, and any ordered refreshments, such as coffee or cold drinks, have arrived. Ensure chairs and tables are in the configuration you desire for the meeting. This builds your confidence and makes you available to greet the group members as they arrive.

2.2.3 During the Meeting

2.2.3.1 The Process

The items on the checklist are specific and need to be done. At this time, the facilitator is following the process outlined in Chapter 1.

Introductions–Engagement–Tools and Techniques–Summary–Critique

The introductions phase can include an icebreaker, introduction of guests and self instruction of group members and their expectations, housekeeping items (such as restroom locations), lunch options, breaks, transportation availability, tours, etc., and roles and responsibilities of certain group roles and setting ground rules. Engagement is to get the group actively pursuing the meeting objective. Certain tools and techniques will be used to help in ideas or issues generation, evaluation, selection, and decision making. The facilitator should summarize at times when a key point has been made or the next step is not clear. Always summarize at the end of a particular subject on what was accomplished and any items not achieved, and who will be responsible to do them. Next, critique by asking questions and/or administering a prepared critique questionnaire form.

The meeting should open with an introduction of guests, if any. Next, the purpose of the meeting should be explained, the agenda covered, status of action items, any major events or happenings since the last meeting, and then follow with the agenda. If it is an ISO meeting, have all team members and any visitors sign the sign-in sheet for ISO 50001 EnMS for documentation for later audits or self-inspections. Facilitators can benefit by using the sign-in sheets even if it is not an ISO meeting. The sheets provide excellent documentation and can be used later in follow-ups with any personnel who attended the meeting.

Later, how to handle difficult personalities and manage conflict will be discussed and examples provided.

2.2.3.2 Establishing the Ground Rules

It is important to set ground rules for meetings. There are several ways to do this. Some are informal, some are written. In the military, young officers learn quickly that the lead chair is where the commander sits. You will not see a sign saying that, but everyone knows that chair is taken. There are other unwritten rules, such as don't speak up unless you are asked or asking a question. Don't leave the room until the boss has left. Most nonmilitary meetings should set ground rules so everyone knows what is allowed and expected. In the military and government agencies, improvement meetings, such as Six Sigma, ground rules also need to be set.

There are so many things that can happen to derail a meeting. Cell phones ringing, people coming in late, someone wants to do all the talking, side talking, discussions breaking down, conflicts occurring, discussion getting off track onto current events or unrelated subjects, insufficient participation due to work requirements, lack of trust, someone has his/her own agenda, and many more inhibitors.

Often the team leader and facilitator get together and draft the ground rules. Sometimes the team leader or facilitator lets the team brainstorm possible ground rules and then use multivoting or ranking to determine the ones they feel should be selected. Turning off a cell phone has become a favorite one because a ringing cell phone is an irritating interruption. Another popular ground rule is that everyone should participate. Also, silence means approval. (If you do not approve, speak up.) Instill the 100-mile rule: Do not let anyone from your office interrupt you unless they would do this if you are a 100 miles away. Limit side discussions. Follow through on assignments or action plans. Another popular ground rule is: Your opinions are sought.

The ground rules are put on a flip chart (sometimes placed on the meeting room wall.) They are covered by the team leader or facilitator at the first meeting. Normally that is all that is needed. Often, in a later meeting, someone will bring them up when they think someone has broken a ground rule. Remember, ground rules help to improve meeting effectiveness through improved behavior, better participation, and paying better attention to the meeting details. They are accepted by the team and help keep the focus on achieving the meeting's purpose and deliverables.

An example of a good set of ground rules include:

1. Respect each other and refrain from making personal attacks.
2. It is okay to disagree.
3. Listen to others; don't interrupt unless it is absolutely needed to correct something.
4. Everyone participates.
5. Adhere to time limits: be on time, start on time, and end on time.
6. All ideas are potentially good ideas; don't rush to decisions; keep an open mind.
7. Use the agenda; stay on track.
8. Do your homework before the meeting and bring any needed material to the meeting.
9. Respect confidentiality; what is said in the meeting should not be quoted outside of the meeting if it is intended to remain for team members only.
10. Use the 100-mile rule; make arrangements not to be interrupted during the meeting.
11. **Turn off cell phones.**

Tool/Technique #7: Ground Rules

2.2.4 After the Meeting

Of course, the team leader and facilitator had prepared some energy policy drafts prior to the meeting and brought them to the meeting to get team members' input. After the meeting (recommend within three days), the notetaker or facilitator should transcribe the minutes and distribute them to the appropriate personnel including the objective champion/energy champion and any other interested personnel. This task is easy if you think and use the PAPA concept.

PAPA: Purpose, Agenda, Points, Action Items
Tool/Technique #8: PAPA

Using this concept, first go to your files and find the agenda. Change *agenda* to *minutes* and save it. Now, open the saved minutes to the agenda and change in the title line the words *agenda* to *minutes*. Next keep Date and Time, Place, and Purpose. Click on first agenda item, erase time and responsible person, leaving the title of the agenda item. Now write a summary of the main points that resulted from the discussion and conclusions or decision(s) on this item. If anyone has an assignment from this, note Action Item #__, and explain who has to do what, when, and where, if applicable. At the end, mention the time and date for the next meeting. Any PowerPoint® presentations or other material presented may or may not be attached to the minutes. Often a slide can be copied and used in the minutes to describe what happened. Prior to finalizing the minutes, send them to the team members and have them review to see if anything should be added, deleted, or changed. The minutes could look like this:

QVS Energy Team Meeting Minutes October 20, 2010
Date/Time: October 20, 2010/Time: 10–11 a.m.
Place: Quality Conference Room
Purpose: To review ISO 50001 EnMS, draft an energy policy, analyze utility data, and determine team focus for energy policy deployment.
Agenda:
QVS Energy Team Charter: Team leader stated the Strategic Council has approved a Strategic Objective "to reduce energy costs." The target, percent reduction from a selected baseline year, will be determined later. The director of Operations was selected as this objective's champion. He appointed the vice president of Strategic Planning as the Energy Team's team leader and the director of Quality and Continuous Improvement as the facilitator. Eight other team members were appointed to the team covering all major staff and plant functional areas. Our primary responsibilities are to plan and implement an energy reduction program for our company using ISO 50001 EnMS as a guide. (See Attachment # 1-QVS Energy Team Charter, dated Oct. 1, 2012).
ISO 50001 EnMS Review: The team leader explained the five phases of the ISO 50001 and the 23 elements that comprise the five phases (see Attachment 2). He stated that we would use these elements as a guide including the documentation requirement. The team leader said that he would be the documentation manager for the team and ISO 50001 EMS.
Action Item #1: The team leader is to set up a file on SharePoint for the energy reduction efforts and for ISO 50001 EnMS documentation by elements by December 1, 2010.
Review several draft energy policies: The energy team reviewed five draft energy policies that the team leader and facilitator had researched from other companies' energy policies, and used some of their words as appropriate, in developing these draft energy policies. The team selected the following draft energy policy after a few words were changed:

QVS Corp. is committed to purchasing and using energy in the most efficient, cost effective, and environmentally responsible manner possible. Therefore, QVS facilities shall:

■ Practice energy conservation at all its facilities.
■ Lower its peak demand at facilities.
■ Improve energy efficiency while maintaining a safe and comfortable work environment.
■ Lower our kilowatt hours per square foot to best in class levels.
■ Increase our percentage of renewable energy used.
■ Continuously improve our performance.

Action Item #2: Team leader is to present to objective champion/energy champion for his approval or disapproval next week.

Analyze Data and Determine Our Focus: The team analyzed the 2010 energy and water usage data costs. Electricity cost is 95.17% of the total utility cost and 97.77% of total energy cost. Therefore, the team decided to focus on electricity cost and kWh usage (see Attachment #3 Utility Costs).

Action Item # 3: Team leader will discuss the graphs and team focus with objective champion/energy champion by October 28, 2010, and ensure team is on the right course of action.

Next Meeting:

The next meeting will be held on November 15, 2010, in the Quality Conference room starting at 10 a.m. An agenda will be developed and distributed three days before the meeting.

Approved:

Team Leader, QVS Energy Team

Attach #1: QVS Energy Team Charter, dated October 1, 2010
Attach. #2: ISO 50001 EMS Five Phases and 23 Elements
Attach. #3: Utility Costs

Using PAPA makes writing meeting minutes easier while ensuring no important information or key points are omitted. Identifying action items in the minutes helps ensure they get done. These action items should be reviewed at the next meeting for status.

If possible, analyze the critique forms or answers in the meeting and include in the minutes. Brief the client on the output. If feasible, take the team leader with you in informing top management.

2.3 Self-Evaluation after Each Meeting

After each meeting, use the self-evaluation tool in Table 2.2:

Tool/Technique #9: Meeting Self-Evaluation

Table 2.2 Meeting Self-Evaluation Matrix

Item	*Timeliness*	*How Did I Do? Poor, Satisfactory, Good*	*Way to Improve*	*Comments*
1. Agenda prepared with PAL?	Sent to all team members at least three days prior to meeting			
2. Did meeting start on time?	Within five minutes + or – of start time			
3. Meeting forum obtained?	At least majority of team members attending			
4. Meeting finished on time?	Within five minutes + or – of finish time			
5. Was the purpose or objective of meeting obtained?	If not, explain why.			
6. Meeting minutes finished within three days after the meeting?	Within three days and using PAPA for efficiency in preparation			
7. Did meeting minutes include action items?	Responsible person accepted action; also, action item status covered in next meeting			
8. Did I have to interrupt meeting to handle any disruptive behavior?	If so, how many times and was it excessive?			

(Continued)

Table 2.2 Meeting Self-Evaluation Matrix (Continued)

Item	Timeliness	How Did I Do? Poor, Satisfactory, Good	Way to Improve	Comments
9. Were the correct facilitator tools and techniques used?	Tools and techniques used for generating ideas, prioritization, root cause identifications, and formulating solutions and others			
10. Were the subjects covered clearly, appropriately, and made interesting to the participants?	In other words, was the time spent on each subject appropriate and interesting?			

2.4 Using TOTs to Get Team Back on Track

TOTs (**T**eam **O**bjectives and **T**arget**s**) were developed by the author when facilitating government facilities Environmental Management Systems teams. TOTs can be easily changed to fit any team's situation. This technique is useful for a team that has multiple meetings and falls behind for some reason. The example shown below changes from an Environmental Management System to an Energy Management System (EMS). Even with ground rules, certain problems will occur every now and then. There is a tendency to go to the team's leaders (bosses) to obtain their help on issues, such as poor meeting attendance, poor execution of assigned work, and other meeting effectiveness inhibitors. These team problems need to be corrected; however, going to the team's bosses and asking for their assistance in solving these types of problems will normally reduce team cohesiveness and morale. It is best to have the team members solve these problems themselves with the assistance of the facilitator and use of TOTs.

PURPOSE: EMS teams develop objectives and targets to improve the organization's and/or facility's electricity usage reduction performance. The
team effort drives EMS improvements and continuous improvement.
However, seldom are these improvement initiatives aimed at improving
the team itself. They address organization or company issues, problems,
or opportunities. TOTs are designed to address team-only issues and
problems.

METHOD (Step 1): The TOTs instrument is administered to the team. The
EMS team selects one to three team objectives for improving the team's
performance and their synergy and capability. (Step 2) A target is added
to include a "timeframe" and a "how much" if possible. (Step 3) An
action plan is developed to accomplish each team objective selected.
The team leader or selected team member(s) are the responsible
person(s). (Step 4) Implementation begins. (Step 5) The TOTs objective
and target progress are checked at each EMS team meeting and corrective action is taken if needed. Once the problem is solved or the objective is achieved, then it no longer needs to be a meeting agenda item.
The author found that over 95% of the team objectives were solved in
three meetings or less.

PLAN–DO–CHECK–ACT: TOTs follows the PDCA concept in that a plan
is developed, implemented, and checked for progress, and action taken
where needed. The TOTs instrument administered to the team follows.
It can be altered to fit a particular team problem if not already included.

Introduction (TOTs): Please select three objectives and targets (O&T)
that you feel our EMS team needs to improve during this year, quarter,
six months, whichever is appropriate.

     __ 1. Improve team meeting attendance
     __ 2. Increase O&T completions on time
     __ 3. Improve meeting accountabilities
     __ 4. Increase O&Ts that address significant energy users or have
        estimated significant contributions
     __ 5. Increase team member participations as O&T responsible
        persons
     __ 6. Improve recognition of team's efforts
     __ 7. Improve team's communications to other organization's
        employees
     __ 8. Improve our teamwork and team synergy
     __ 9. Improve our documentation system
     __ 10. Add new objectives and targets

  __ 11. Add new team members

  __ 12. Receive more EnMS topic training to improve our technical skills

  __ 13. Improve top management commitment by involving them more

  __ 14. Other: __

Tool/Technique #10: TOTs

 The facilitator should have these filled out at one meeting, then summarize the results and present at the next meeting. In a few meetings, you will most probably see TOTs improve your team's efficiency and effectiveness. Why? Because you put it into meeting minutes, and supervisors and managers receive copies, and the team members know this. Therefore, participation, for example, may increase as the absent team members come back and start participating because they do not want any intervention by their supervisors. The problem arises because people can get very busy. Being on a team is not normally in their everyday duties, so it is easy to rationalize that they are too busy to attend the meetings. TOTs helps them get back to attending meetings again. Then it is up to the team leader and facilitator to keep them motivated and participating so they will want to attend all the meetings.

2.5 Tool to Use When the Team and/ or the System Needs Jumpstarting

If management is involved and provides excellent support, an excellent team with a competent team leader and facilitator, the team should not need jumpstarting. However, after awhile, many teams become complacent and members start missing meetings and lose enthusiasm for the system and team efforts. Then, much more than TOTs has to be implemented to get things back on track. Jumpstarting is the tool that will be needed. If we drew a picture of the momentum, we would start with planning (three months), development (three months), implementing (six months), and maintaining (three months) all going upward at about a 45-degree angle. All of the sudden, the trend line turns downward showing a significant momentum loss. This is a call for the facilitator and team leader to spring into action and stop this undesirable trend.

Jumpstarting, as defined by the author, consists of four distinct steps.

Step 1: Use a Why–What chart. The why is for: Why did we lose momentum? The what is: What happened that we need to fix? First, brainstorm the key areas that comprise the past support that provided the momentum, e.g., management support, resources provided, employees involved. If you know the critical success factors necessary for a successful implementation and maintenance of the system, use them. For example, the critical success factors for implementing ISO 14001 EMS include: (1) top management support, (2) resources provided, (3) objectives and targets, (4) employee involvement, (5) communications, (6) intergraded into daily work, and (7) management reviews held. The Why–What chart should show what broke down in the CSFs (Critical Success Factors) accomplishments.

Why?	What Happened?
Top management support	Management lost enthusiasm due to no recent successes.
Resources provided	No problem here, resources are available.
Objectives and targets	Team had moved from 4 to 7 O&Ts being addressed at any one time to now just one a year being worked.
Employee involvement	Other than recycling paper and cans, employees did not participate. They were unaware of where the system stood.
Communications	Communications between team and employees had shut down. With management, once a year.
Intergraded into daily work	Did not happen. Only team knows what is going on and what needs to be added?
Management reviews	Last management review was almost 20 months ago.

Step 2: Create a "jump start plan." The facilitator recommended that the jumpstart of the EMS be a team objective. The team agreed. OT-14-02 was born The objective is to gain momentum again in EMS actions and support. The target is to fix what has not gone right with the CSFs for EMS. The action plan is:

What	*Who*	*When (Completed By)*	*Status*	*Remarks*
1. Develop a presentation to management about past, present & future plans and present to them.	Team leader & facilitator	By October 31, 2014		This action will improve communications to management.
2. Identify at least two more O&Ts, develop, and implement.	EMS team	By November 15, 2014		This action should give the team more to focus on and get them back involved.
3. Increase communications with employees and gain their involvement by developing, communicating to all personnel an environmental awareness updates training and include an energy conservation part to the training.	Team leader & facilitator	By November 30, 2014		This will provide communications to the employees, supervision and contractors. Getting everyone involved in energy conservation will make EMS more of what happens daily. Also keep up emphasis on recycling and add a few more items to be recycled.
4. Team does a self inspection to determine what deficiencies they may have versus the standards and organization's procedures and legal requirement. Develop corrective actions to fix any nonconformities or deficiencies.	EMS team	By December 15, 2014		Should show areas where inactivity has caused deficiencies and show what is needed to get back on track technically to meet the environmental management system standards.

5. Plan and conduct a management review.	EMS team	By January 31, 2015		Should provide some good ideas and recommendations and continuous improvement.

The EMS team leader should get the management representative's approval on the objective and target.

Step 3: Once the plan is approved by the management representative, the EMS team responsible persons (WHO) should start implementing the actions on the plan.

Step 4: Track implementation, monitor results, and take corrective action. The EMS team can do this by holding one-hour monthly meetings. After all has been implemented, assess whether the EMS team feels the momentum has been regained.

2.6 Facilitator's Exercises

1. It is best to evaluate each meeting soon after it was held. T __ F __
2. TOTs are an excellent technique to keep children happy. T __ F __
3. A facilitator only has responsibility for conducting or orchestrating the meeting and no duties before or after the meeting. T __ F __
4. Either using PAL or OAR is okay. T __ F __
5. It is okay for the facilitator to help write the meeting minutes. T __ F __
6. Meeting minutes should be completed and distributed to the participants within three business days. T __ F __
7. The facilitator's continuous learning model is:
    a. __ Learning–Evaluation–Check–Act
    b. __ Learning–Doing–Check–Act
    c. __ Planning–Evaluating–Check–Act
    d. __ Learning–Practice–Evaluate–Act
    e. __ Planning–Practice–Evaluate–Act
8. Jumpstarting can help regain lost team/system momentum. True __ False __
9. It is best if the team solves their own problem(s). True __ False __

(See Appendix 1 for answers.)

Chapter 3

Different Types of Facilitators

3.1 Types of Facilitators

Normally, when someone mentions facilitator, we think of a meeting facilitator. Are there any other kind? To start with, there are internal and external facilitators. External facilitators are hired when neutrality is extremely important and the management feels the internal facilitators will not be considered neutral by the participants or not experienced enough to accomplish the meeting facilitation necessary to achieve the objective.

There are two types of facilitators: active facilitators and developmental facilitators (http://www.extraordinaryteam.com/faqs/are-there-different-types-of-facilitators).

The active facilitators are usually employed for a short-term need, such as when a decision needs to be made quickly and a problem needs to be solved. The facilitator meets with the team to prepare for the meeting and agree on the outcome. Then, the facilitator actively leads the team through the process to achieve the desired results. He or she allows the team leader to participate fully in the session.

During team implementation projects, they may initially use active facilitation, gently tapering off their involvement using the developmental facilitation strategy.

The developmental facilitators use a longer-term strategy where the team learns how to facilitate their own processes. In developmental facilitation, the facilitators spend more time coaching the members on the process, roles, tools, and techniques before and after the meeting. During the meeting, the facilitator observes team dynamics and only intervenes in a way that teaches the team members facilitation skills. The end goal of developmental facilitation is for the team to get to the point that they won't need an outside facilitator anymore. This strategy is used on long-term efforts, such as ISO implementation where teams maintain and sustain their system continuously. It is a journey, not a destination. Normally, the original facilitator is one from the headquarters or a contract facilitator. Even so, there may be a drop in meeting efficiency when the original facilitator is no longer available.

Both types of facilitators facilitate meetings, coach team members, train team members, and mentor some who show potential to be a facilitator. Facilitating, coaching, and training are considered separate in expertise and core competencies. Each is represented by international organizations that have certification programs. For coaches, there is the International Association for Coaching (IAC) that also has core competencies and a certification process (www.certifiedcoach.org). There are several international organizations for trainers. To find these, Google "international organization for training."

At en.wikipedia.org/wiki/facilitator, several types of facilitators are listed. They are listed below.

3.1.1 Business Facilitators

Business facilitators work in business and other formal organizations, but they also may work with a variety of other groups and communities. It is a principle of facilitation that facilitators will not lead the group toward the answer that they think is best even if they possess an opinion on the subject matter. The facilitator's role is to make it easier for the group to arrive at its own answer, decision, or deliverable.

3.1.2 Training Facilitators

Training facilitators are used in adult education. These facilitators are not always subject experts, and attempt to draw on the existing knowledge of the participant(s), and to then facilitate access to training where gaps in knowledge are identified and agreed upon. Training facilitators focus on the foundations of adult education: establish existing knowledge, build on it, and keep it relevant.

3.1.3 Conflict Resolution Facilitators

Conflict resolution facilitators are used in peace and reconciliation processes both during and after the conflict. Their role is to facilitate constructive and free discussion between groups with diverse and usually diametrically opposing positions. Conflict resolution facilitators must be impartial to the conflicting groups (or societies) and must adhere to the rules of democratic dialogue. They may not take part or express personal opinions. Their most usual role is to support groups in developing a shared vision for an ideal future, learn to listen to each other, and understand and appreciate the feelings, experiences, and positions of the "enemy."

3.1.4 Wraparound Facilitators

Wraparound facilitators are in the social services community. They originally supported disabled teens who were transitioning into adulthood. Now, they include facilitators serving children between birth and 3 years of age who are in need of services. Outside the meetings, the facilitator organizes meetings, engages team members, and conducts follow-through meetings. During meetings, the facilitator leads and manages the team by keeping the participants on track toward achieving the meeting's objective and encourages a strength-based discussion addressing the child's needs. The facilitator encourages equal participation among team members and helps this occur using facilitation skills.

3.1.5 Small Group Facilitation

Facilitators can be assigned to accommodate the engagement of participants of small- and medium-sized groups that aim to work though a particular agenda. In order to ensure the successful workings of the group, the facilitator is assigned in place of what would once have been a chairperson's role. Groups that have adopted this type of facilitation include prayer groups, men's groups, writing groups, and other community organizations.

Facilitation jobs in many locations are located on www.indeed.com. There you will find almost an endless number of facilitator titles. Some listed include:

- Risk Facilitator
- Access Facilitator
- Youth Facilitator

- Lead Facilitator
- Discharge Facilitator
- Tour Facilitator
- Learning Facilitator
- Safety Facilitator
- CQI (Continuous Quality Improvement) Facilitator
- Visitation Facilitator
- Agile Facilitator
- Maintenance Facilitator
- Service Facilitator
- Rehab Facilitator
- Lead Production Facilitator
- Discharge Facilitator
- Parts Facilitator
- Reservation Facilitator
- Enrollment Facilitator
- Innovative Process Facilitator
- CPI (Continuous Process Improvement) Facilitator
- Operational Excellence Facilitator
- Quality Projects Facilitator
- Team Building Facilitator
- Success Facilitator.

Hospitals and schools list the task that an individual will do and assigns a facilitator to follow it. In the past, they would probably have used a coordinator instead of facilitator. The title *facilitator* is a well-liked one that sends a message of one who helps others to get something accomplished.

Hospitals and other businesses use facilitator in their job titles instead of the usual coordinator. Some of the most notable types of facilitators in business today are listed in Table 3.1.

Dr. Eileen Dowse, CMF (certified master facilitator) organizational psychologist with Human Dynamics and chair of the International Institute for Facilitation (INIFAC) developed a "differences" matrix showing in six important areas how consultants, coaches, mentors, managers, leaders, educator trainers, and facilitators differ (Table 3.2).

Facilitation means to make something easier, such as managing a meeting or assisting in an improvement meeting. Facilitation is very helpful in group events; problem-solving teams; partnering sessions; issues teams; strategic teams; Kaizen events; planning, developing, and implementing ISO

Table 3.1 Types of Facilitators

Types of Facilitators	Primary Focus	Get Upfront Approval of Objective, Output, & Outcome	Multiple Meetings with Same Group or Team	Usually Does Coaching, Training, Action Planning, Objective and Target Setting, and Project Management
Meeting	Achieve meeting objectives	Yes	Not normally	Could do action planning and training
Process	Achieve process objectives	Yes	Yes	Training, objective setting, action planning
Content	Facilitates and participates in content discussion	Yes	Yes	Training, objective setting, action planning
Active	Facilitates a meeting and achieves meetings objectives	Yes	Depends	Action planning and training.
Development	Facilitator develops team members to do their own facilitation	Yes	Yes, and then works themselves out of the meetings	Coaching, training, objectives setting, and action planning
Results	A meeting, process, and content facilitator	Yes	Yes, multiple meetings in multiple years	Coaching, training, action planning, objective and target setting, and project management

standards; family issues resolutions; and numerous others. The meetings normally have a team leader and others that play a role, such as a facilitator, notetaker or a timekeeper, an operations manager, and/or a document control manager. Most experts believe that a true facilitator is a person who does facilitation and will not get involved in the meeting contents, but will

Table 3.2 Differences

	Consultant	Coach	Mentor	Manager	Leader	Educator Trainer	Facilitator
Approach	Discuss	Guide	Educate	Tell	Promote change	Educate	Guide
Works with	Clients	Clients	Mentee	Staff	Followers	Groups	Groups
Knows and understands	What others have done	How to ask the right questions	End result	Content	End result	Contents	Group process methods
Depends on	Past experience of self and others	Self awareness of client	Past experience of self and others	System	Personal abilities	Research, current information	Ability of group
Time frame	Short term	Long term	Long term	Short term	Long term	Program specific	Adaptable
Goal achieved through ….	Development	Growth of other person	Success and advancement within organization	Plans and maintenance of system	Strategic goals	Skill proficiency	Group's desired outcome

help the team to be focused on the purpose that the team is pursuing. The facilitator must understand the process and techniques or tools to be used during the meeting to achieve an objective or task. Normally the facilitator is considered the expert of the process, activity, tools, or techniques, and provides structure for accomplishing the team objective or purpose. The team leader and team members are responsible for the meeting contents and achieving the goal(s), objective(s), or result(s). In other words, the facilitator always should be neutral. Some experts say the facilitator should get things started and then be quiet and let the team discuss the issue or pursue the problem. Depending on the situation, the facilitator may lead the meeting or not. Being neutral is a core value of the International Facilitators Association (IAF) and INIFAC. They say this characteristic should never be violated. The facilitator must be neutral to the discussion. This frees the facilitator to concentrate on the group rather than the discussion content, enabling him/her to ask pertinent, stimulating, and probing questions.

Tool/Technique #11: Matrix

Dr. Dowse did an excellent job in defining the differences in each of these key people. The assumption is they are completely separate and their roles do not interact or commingle (Figure 3.1).

Tool/Technique #12: Venn diagram

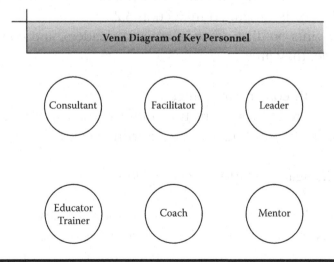

Figure 3.1 The Venn diagram.

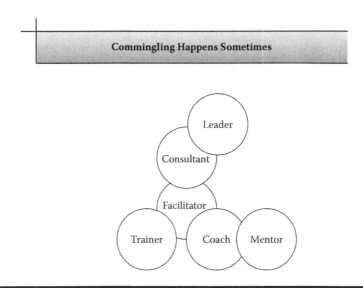

Figure 3.2 Roles commingle or intersect.

In business, sometimes facilitator roles can interact and the relationships could look like Figure 3.2.

The consultant briefs the leader who uses some of his concepts in his promotion speeches. The consultant uses some facilitation skills to help drive his or her agenda. The facilitator is asked to provide both training and coaching to management. The mentor uses coaching to his or her mentee.

Process or content, or both types of facilitators, are mentioned as two different types where one focuses on the process and the other on both the process and subject content. The latter description will be discussed when the results facilitator is explained in Section 3.2.

Dr. Dowse points out that when instructors, leaders, and consultants use a facilitative style, they are:

- experts in both content and process;
- tasked to ensure learners' direction and decisions are on target;
- responsible for motivating learners, creating positive learning environment; and
- guides to instigators, partners, and leaders.

Facilitators don't perform their roles and responsibilities in a vacuum, even though it is often explained like they do. Sometimes, needing to train the team and management on new concepts or tools, they need to coach a team leader, team member, or facilitator-in-training. When the objective is to

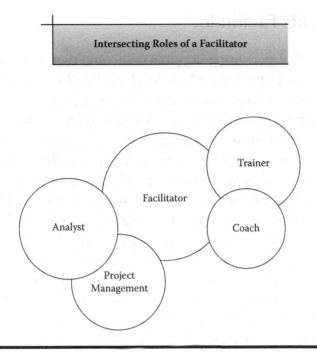

Figure 3.3   Interfaces with facilitation.

develop and implement projects, this endeavor will require some basic project management skills. Statistical analysis and regression analysis sometimes are requirements to achieve the objective. Now, some basic analyst skills are required to perform the needed tasks (Figure 3.3).

This interface looks simply like Figure 3.4.

Facilitators' roles can be simple meetings or process jobs and may not require all of the skills above. More complicated quality improvement or ISO planning, development, and implementation jobs will require all of the skills.

Figure 3.4   FACT-PM (Facilitator Analyst Coach Trainer–Project Manager).

3.2 The Results Facilitator

Good facilitators desire to bring about an outcome that is in the best inter-
ests of the group, not one he/she has developed and believe is the best
solution for the group or individual. However, in a long-term team, such as
an ISO implementation team, the facilitator may offer a plan or objective and
target to help the team move forward in its continuous improvement journey. As facilitators move from facility to facility doing the same thing at each,
they develop a "consultant view" of the journey and can suggest items or
objectives that have been tried and did not work or those that worked beau-
tifully. The consultant in a facilitator role using facilitation tools and techniques becomes results-focused and participates in both process and content
while managing disruptions and handling disruptive personalities. This new
facilitator, called the *results facilitator*, facilitates teams that don't adjourn
as Tuckman's fifth group stages, say, but continue on a path of continuous
improvement. The teams are on a journey that does not have a destination,
but a commitment by their management for their ongoing role and responsibility. They are a new kind of a facilitator; they are the "results facilitator."
Yes, they have to deal with group dynamics; be able to observe, listen, and
know when and how to intervene; know what facilitation tools and techniques to use; know how to run effective meetings, but, most of all they
possess the skills to achieve goals and results. They primarily use facilitative
tools, techniques, and processes to achieve the team's goals.

A normal facilitator and results facilitator differ in a few areas (Table 3.3).

Tool/Technique #13: A Comparison Table

This new trend will be explored in this book along with the changing
roles and responsibilities of the "results facilitator." We are now seeing "results
facilitators" in the NBA. Kobe Bryant (Los Angeles Lakers) and LeBron James
(Cleveland Cavaliers) are being called facilitators. They get the ball to their
players who are open and can make a basket. They are involved in the game
content and are not "neutral." Their facilitation efforts lead to results. Of the
two, LeBron is the true facilitator. His assist to teammates is the best ever
achieved in the NBA. He has a three-point strategy. If the defender backs
up, he shoots. If the defender gets up on him, he drives to the basket. If his
teammates are open, he passes to them. Miami Heat coach, Erik Spoelstra,
calls LeBron "arguably the best scorer who is a facilitator." LeBron is a "results
facilitator" who makes everyone he plays with better. He said, "I don't think I

Table 3.3   Normal versus Results Facilitator Comparison

Normal Facilitator	*Results Facilitator*
For obtaining results–neutral, team is responsible.	*For obtaining results–indirectly responsible.*
Responsible for keeping team on process and structure.	Responsible for keeping team on process and structure.
Responsible for teaching the tool or technique being used.	Responsible for teaching the tool or technique being used.
Don't need to be an expert on the content being discussed at the meeting. Do not participate in the content.	*An expert on the meeting content.*
Managing conflict.	Managing conflict.
Preplanning the meeting with team leader to include an agenda.	Preplanning meeting with team leader to include an agenda.
Not responsible for producing the minutes. The notetaker is and approved by team leader.	*Responsible for producing the minutes and the contents of the organization's filing system.*
Team leader leads the meeting and facilitator is quiet unless called upon.	*Shares running the meeting with team leader, especially when using a tool or technique.*
Not responsible for project management.	*Is responsible for managing projects.*

Note: Differences are highlighted in italics.

could see an open teammate and not pass it." LeBron is a player who wants to win every game if possible. He is a facilitator because he makes his teammates better through his play. He distributes the ball to the player with the best opportunity to score. He is part of the team game plan and strategy and scores himself when he can. He is a "results" facilitator (Figure 3.5).

Results facilitators are the most evident as facilitators for ISO planning, implementation, and maintenance, and in-house facilitators for problem solving or other improvement teams. The meeting facilitator, where a facilitator facilitates one or several meetings, is neutral. Even when the facilitator is a member of the group, an internal facilitator, neutrality must be maintained. Often an internal facilitator, to show his/her neutrality, will wear a facilitator's hat, a funny shirt, or do something that says he/she is not part of the group during the meeting. Does this work? Maybe.

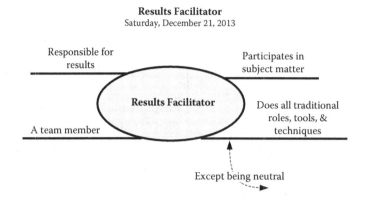

Figure 3.5   Results facilitator, facilitating a meeting.

Facilitation is almost as essential to any organization as leadership. Without effective facilitation, a leader's vision will never be achieved and organization and process improvement will seldom occur. To achieve a vision, projects or actions planning and identification of necessary goals and objectives must be identified. These projects or actions must be implemented, managed, and brought to fruition. Facilitation or use of facilitators is essential in this process to ensure good outcomes and achieving the vision or meeting purposes. Facilitation should become a core competency for a company if facilitators are used in their strategic planning, process improvement, problem solving, and ISO planning, development, implementing, maintaining, and sustaining efforts.

The purpose of this book is to present the skills a facilitator needs to possess to help organizations achieve their mission, improve their processes, productivity, quality, sales, and customers' satisfaction. Strategies for dealing with disruptive behaviors, conflict, and team compliancy will be discussed. In Chapter 12, there are examples of questions and answers that new facilitators have wanted to know in past training seminars. The 40+ tools and techniques needed to be understood by facilitators will be demonstrated. Anyone who has to plan and conducts a meeting will benefit from reading this book. Lean and Six Sigma green and black belts and their team leaders and subject experts will benefit in their facilitation efforts by learning the strategies outlined in this book, adding to their skills toolbox some of the skills sets required for the results facilitator. Remember, to become an experienced facilitator, one must follow the continuous improvement cycle of Learn–Practice–Evaluate–Take Corrective Action.

Figure 3.6   Hendecagon: A skill set of a results facilitator.

3.3 The Hendecagon Model: The Skill Set of an Experienced Facilitator

The facilitator must understand group dynamics to be effective in helping a group or team to reach their goal or objective. He or she must have an arsenal of tools and techniques for different applications, such as generation of ideas, prioritizing, evaluating and analysis, selling solutions, project management, measuring progress, and other tasks. This book will outline the skill set needed for an advanced facilitator to be successful in every facilitation effort in which he or she will be involved. The desired skill set needed for any facilitator including the "results facilitator" is shown in Figure 3.6.

Tool/Technique #14: Hendecagon Diagram

Why did the author select skill set instead of core competencies? Skills can be taught and obtained in a relatively short time. Core competencies take longer. The difference is that the core competencies consist of skills, knowledge, and strengths. A *core competency* is a concept in management theory originally explained by C. K. Prahalad, and Gary Hamel, two business book writers (1990).

In their view, a core competency is a specific factor that a business sees as being central to the way its employees work. It meets three key criteria:

1. It is not easy for competitors to imitate.
2. It can be reused widely for many products and markets.
3. It must contribute to the end consumer's experienced benefits.

Criteria 2 and 3 hold true today, but no. 1 is becoming easier for competitors to achieve.

The International Association of Facilitators (IAF), a worldwide professional body established to promote, support, and advance the art and practice of professional facilitation through methods exchange, professional growth, practical research, and collegial networking, developed a set of core competencies with support of IAF members and facilitators. They identified six major core competencies (IAF breaks down the six into several components). The six core competencies include:

1. Create collaborative client relationship
2. Plan appropriate group processes
3. Create and sustain a participatory environment
4. Guide group to appropriate and useful outcomes
5. Build and maintain professional knowledge
6. Model positive professional attitude

Under these six categories, there are many important subcategories. As the skill set above is described, the related IAF core competencies will be shown.

IAF headquarters is located in St. Paul, Minnesota. It offers a facilitator certification program that includes documentation of your experience and achievements, interviews and review of your experience and qualifications, and facilitating several groups. Certification is available only after you receive training and have gained at least three years or more experience with notable achievements. Certification also is offered at INIFAC (International Institute for Facilitation) located in Bellevue, Washington. INIFAC-certified facilitators are certified master facilitators (CMFs), which is the highest level in the industry. The two facilitation certifications programs will be explained further and compared in Chapter 13. This book will give you the skills to get you started or to enhance your present skill level so you can gain additional knowledge and experience. The skills set included in this book will enhance your ability to meet with clients, to plan group events, to select the right tools and techniques, to gain consensus in groups, to meet desired outcomes and deliverables, create a participatory environment, manage group or individual conflict, and add to your professional knowledge and confidence. Should you obtain certification later? The author highly recommends it, especially since it will increase your networking capability, make current practices information available to you, and for you to be recognized as a professional facilitator. The first thing you will need to do is to gain experience and achieve several facilitating successes. Facilitation is not easy; it is work. It can be physically tiring, and is always mentally demanding. Facilitators can be put into situations not experienced before and they must use their skills and core competences to find a satisfactory way out. The skill set outlined below (and in the Hendecagon [see Figure 3.6] and the coming chapters) will help you do so. Facilitators are made through training, experience, self-assessment, and continuous improvement, not born. Facilitation can be a rewarding and satisfying profession.

Skill #1 is to possess the ability to influence. A facilitator's most important skill is to be able to influence the client, the team leader, and the team. Influence tools and techniques are shown that result in influencing the way improvement meetings and management reviews are held. Some people's personality enables them to influence others easily. Some are not so good at influencing. The DiSC® personality test is recommended to determine your ability to influence or not. A high I (influence) means you do have that ability in your workplace to influence people. However, even if you do not possess a high I, but have high ratings in D (dominant), S (steadiness), and C (compliance), you can still be a facilitator; however, you will have to control certain personality traits at times, such as listening–not talking, showing empathy, and a caring attitude. Remember, good facilitators are made, not born. Learning is a life goal and your ability to influence can benefit from following the improvement model of Learning–Practice–Evaluate–Act. The facilitator must be able to deal with senior management to gain their buy-in and support. Gaining confidence in your ability and knowing your strengths will help you do that.

Skill #2—managing meetings—is to know how to achieve effective meetings. They just do not happen; planning is necessary. This skill set will teach the facilitator how to use OAR or PAL. OAR is developing an **O**bjective, an **A**genda, and makes **R**estrictive requiring time limits for the agenda line items. PAL is the same with P to identify the **P**urpose of the meeting, **A** is for developing an **A**genda for what is going to be covered by whom, and **L** is to **L**imit the line item to allot the correct amount of time to cover the item. Either OAR or PAL enables a facilitator, with the tool, to achieve effective meetings. There are several other effective practices for meetings that will be covered as well below.

Skill #3 is for the facilitator to be well versed in managing conflict, and understanding and assisting in group dynamics so that teams can move to a more productive state. (Bruce Tuckman's four stages (Forming, Storming, Norming, Performing) will be covered in Chapter 5 and a recommendation to add the fifth one will be made to accommodate the results facilitator.) How a team moves through the stages to become increasingly more productive will be discussed. Other group dynamics characteristics and best practices will be discussed in this book. Intervention methods will be outlined and explained when they are to be used. How to jump-start a team that is struggling also will be covered.

Skill #4 (team building) is a highly effective skill that all team facilitators need to know. Team building exercises, to be used by facilitators, will be demonstrated in building high-performance teams. Teamwork is essential to building a high-performance team.

Skill #5, knowing the technical area, is an important (probably the most important) skill. It is one that a facilitator should know first before facilitating an improvement meeting. The technical knowledge a facilitator will need for an improvement meeting will vary considerably depending on the meeting's purpose and tools/techniques needed. For example, partnering meetings (in construction) to develop agreements and processes will vary considerably from a Lean Six Sigma meeting in a manufacturing company. To be an excellent facilitator, you first must understand what the partnering process components are and the deliverables and the same with Six Sigma if that is the nature of your meeting.

In **Skill #6**, facilitator tools and techniques needed to produce the deliverables must be known and a facilitator trained to use them. The process and tools/techniques for the Lean Six Sigma meeting will be different than other purpose meetings, such as a strategic objective meeting. The facilitator should be the expert on the process and tools/techniques to use to achieve the meeting's purpose and deliverables. This shows why knowing the facilitator's tools and techniques, Skill #6, is so important. It is to know and be able to employ at the right time the over 40 tools/techniques and concepts to help achieve the meeting's purpose, objective, and deliverables.

Skill #7 is to be able to develop objectives and targets and include an action plan to accomplish the target. Objectives and targets should be SMART (specific, measurable, actionable/achievable, relevant, and time-framed or time-based) and how to do this will be fully explained.

The last major skill set, **Skill #8**, is to develop action plans and projects, and then manage the projects (project management) so they are completed on time, within cost, and with safety and quality. This includes both objectives and targets action plans and repair or construction projects.

The eight basic skill sets for becoming a successful facilitator are shown above. This book will help you make these a part of your toolkit and enable you to be a successful "normal and results facilitator." Facilitators today are essential in any organization, government, manufacturing, service, construction, maintenance, or industrial. Without facilitation, the organization's performance will be less and continuous improvement of operations and processes will be almost nonexistent (Table 3.4, Figure 3.7).

The facilitator's "musts" is self-explanatory. They increase the skill set because they include duties in developing and implementing an improvement action and learning more about the clients and reaching agreement with the clients on their requirements. The expansion brings them closer to IAF's core competencies for a facilitator. The facilitator may be a company employee or an outside consultant facilitator. Most of the time, more than

Table 3.4 Results Facilitator's Skill Set

Skill	Chapter Covering the Skill
1. Ability to influence	Chapter 4
2. Possess effective meeting knowledge	Chapter 2
3. Manage conflict	Chapters 4.4–4.10
4. Team building	Chapter 4
5. Know the technical knowledge	Chapter 6
6. Know the facilitator tools/techniques	Chapters 2–13
7. Objective and target development	Chapter 8
8. Project management	Chapter 9
9. Communicate	Chapter 3
10. Know client organization	Chapter 3
11. Agree on deliverables	Chapter 3

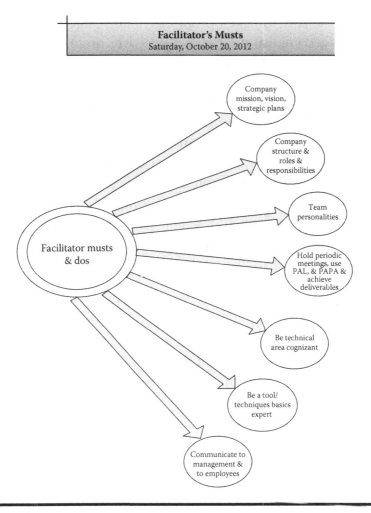

Figure 3.7 Facilitator's musts.

one facilitator is needed to deploy strategic initiatives throughout the company. They can be a mixture of company and consultant facilitators or all company facilitators or all consultant facilitators.

Skill #9 is to communicate. Communications with the team meetings and to outside personnel are vital to success. Open communications enable a team to identify solutions that solve problems and to do so with consensus. It also allows for the facilitator to keep the client aware of progress, issues, barriers, and successes.

Skill #10 is to possess client knowledge. The facilitator must understand the organization's mission, vision, strategies, and objectives.

Skill #11 is to identify the client's requirements and reach a satisfactory agreement. The facilitator must have a clear understanding of his or her responsibilities and deliverables. Responsibilities, pay, and other factors should be discussed and agreement reached, and a contract developed and signed by both parties (client and facilitator). If the facilitator is internal, then his or her role must be defined, sessions to be facilitated, and deliverables desired need to be spelled out.

Tool/Technique #15: A Relationship Diagram

The facilitator(s) should know the company strategies, the roles and responsibilities of the key players, the team personalities, hold periodic meetings using PAL and PAPA (explained in Chapter 2), be an expert on the technical area being pursued, plus use the right facilitator's tools and techniques, and communicate with management and employees on an ongoing basis to keep them informed and maintain their support. In Skill #11, the facilitator must be able to work with the client to determine exactly what is expected from them, the deliverables, and at what time period, etc. (Figure 3.7).

3.4 Facilitator's Exercises

1. The result facilitator is a new kind developing over the last 10 years. True __ False __
2. Most of the skills of a normal facilitator also are applicable to the results facilitator. True __ False __
3. IAF is the only organization that certifies facilitators. True __ False __
4. What is the facilitator's model for continuous improvement? __
5. Which one of the possible skills is not appropriate for a facilitator?
   a. Ability to Influence __
   b. Stubborn __
   c. Objective development __
   d. Excellent knowledge of conducting meetings __
6. What is the difference between a skill and a core competency? __

7. What is the single largest difference between a results facilitator and a normal facilitator? __

8. What is the best process for a facilitator to continuously improve? __

(*See Appendix 1 for answers.*)

Chapter 4

Ability to Influence

4.1 Be Able to Influence

Almost all of the writers on facilitation would agree that the following attributes need to be possessed by facilitators.

Personal skills and characteristics of an excellent facilitator include:

- Confidence
  Must be able to motivate and instill confidence in the group by appearing knowledgeable, purposeful, and in control, therefore, minimizing any group insecurities or fears.
- Flexibility
  The ability to fulfill different group or team roles, such as leader, supporter, questioner, in order to keep the team or group process flowing and focused on the meeting's purpose or objective.
- Integrity
  To be an example to the team and/or group of how to conduct oneself at work and with honesty in everything the facilitator does. Integrity should always be first on a facilitator's mind and demonstrated in personal actions.
- Patience/Perseverance
  Must give others a chance to offer their opinions and suggestions. Sometimes this is difficult with a slow-talking, shy, or nonfocused team member. Facilitator must appreciate the difficulties of team and group dynamics and workings and have the determination to see an activity or task finished.

- Perception

  Facilitator must have the capability to identify undertones or potential problems in the team and/or group and then use the positive ones to the team's and group's advantage while countering the negative ones to minimize them.

- Ability to Influence

  Must be able to influence clients, team leader, and team or a group. Obtain a desired and acceptable contract with the client. With team leader influence, he/her should use the necessary process and to preplan every meeting or event. With team or group members, influence them to get involved, follow the agenda, do homework when required, and help meet the group's or team's objective.

You should start with integrity and improve the others through the Learning–Practice–Evaluate–Act cycle as your competency increases over time. In this chapter, the author will explore further the ability to influence.

Facilitators need to be able to influence their clients, their team leaders, and their teams or groups. This influence should come from your confidence and competence as a facilitator. For teams and individuals, influence can come from coaching, in addition to facilitation.

First, it starts with knowing yourself. How do you react in an emergency? What areas do you excel in and what do you need to improve? How do you manage time? Once you know this about yourself, you can better understand others and how best to relate with them to achieve the team's or group's charter or mission.

4.2 Knowing You

To be a natural born leader, such as General George Patton, one normally would possess a leader's profile that would have a lot of dominance (D). A natural born facilitator's personality would be high in people skills or high in the ability to Influence people. General Dwight Eisenhower possessed a high "I" or Influence. Which one would you rather have leading the troops into battle and which one was more suitable coordinating all free nations in an invasion of Europe? The United States had the right general in the right job. General Eisenhower would find facilitating something he could perform after easily learning the skills. However, General Patton would have a difficult time. With his type of personality, he would want to dominate the teams or events.

Which personnel profile are you? You could be high in steadiness (S) and/or conscientiousness (C). Each of these traits is different than having a high D or I. There is a personnel profile that can fit everyone into one of these areas called DiSC®. The author has administered this personality profile to thousands of people and never found anyone that the correct profile did not fit. Once, while teaching a process improvement course, he had one participant say that his profile did not represent his personality. We reviewed the profile and his objections in front of all in the seminar. At his table were four individuals who worked with him on a daily basis. They all laughed and stated his profile described him perfectly.

The *DiSC profile* is a self-scored behavioral assessment commonly referred to as a profile. Personality styles are grouped in four categories: **D**ominance (D), Influence (I), **S**teadiness (S), and **C**onscientiousness (C). Full interpretation of the results is included in the profile booklet. DiSC personality profiles provide feedback for building on strengths and increasing personal effectiveness. If you are a high I, then you have a natural personality to be a facilitator. If you are a high D, you love to lead or be in charge, and you would have to suppress your desire to talk in order to be a good facilitator. You would have to work on improving your listening skills. On the other hand, you could be a natural team leader. DiSC profiles are available for teams to improve their behavior and working relationships, and for the individuals (team members) for improving their leadership and management effectiveness. Anyone can be a good facilitator, but knowing your strengths and weaknesses, how you would react in an emergency, and where you can best improve to be more effective would help you be a better facilitator, leader, salesperson, doctor, nurse, or any position. You can purchase a DiSC booklet for $25.95 at Corexcel (Learn@corexcel.com) or by calling 1-888-658-6641. If you are interested in knowing yourself, your strengths, how you react in an emergency, and areas where you can improve, the author suggests you purchase a DiSC profile or a similar personality test. There are other good personality assessments, such as the Myers-Briggs Type Indicator and the Herrmann Brain Dominance Instrument, to understand behavior, personalities, and thinking styles of team members. However, the DiSC has been the one the author has used successfully on many occasions.

4.3 Know Your Client

4.3.1 IAF Core Competencies in this Area

a. Create collaborative client relationship
b. Plan appropriate group processes
c. Create and sustain a participatory environment
d. Guide group to appropriate useful outcomes
e. Build and maintain professional knowledge
f. Model positive professional attitude

4.3.1.1 Create Collaborative Client Relationships

1. Develop working partnerships
   - Clarify mutual commitment
   - Develop consensus on tasks, deliverables, roles, and responsibilities
   - Demonstrate collaborative values and processes, such as in co-facilitation
2. Design and customize applications to meet client needs
   - Analyze organizational environment
   - Diagnose client needs
   - Create appropriate designs to achieve intended outcomes
   - Predefine a quality product and outcomes with client
3. Manage multisession events effectively
   - Contract with client for scope and deliverables
   - Develop event plan
   - Deliver event successfully
   - Assess/evaluate client satisfaction at all stages of the event or project

These core facilitator competencies are good to follow whether you are outside the organization (a contractor or consultant) or an assigned organization facilitator.

1. Develop working relationships:
   A facilitator needs to know exactly what the requirements are, what management's expectations are, what products or deliverables are required, what outcomes are desired, understand the culture, and the purpose or objective that management has established. The facilitator and management should enter either into a written or unwritten

contract and both know what the total requirement for facilitation is, what the roles and responsibilities are, and what are the tasks and deliverables required and by what date for each deliverable. Consensus should be reached on these commitments and placed in a contract or Letter of Commitment, signed by management (either the contracting officer or a manager) and the facilitator or his/her organization or company. For outside facilitators, what groups are you facilitating and at what levels of the organization should be discussed? What is the purpose of each group you will facilitate, who are the members, will there be any co-facilitation? If so, will you be the lead facilitator? What is your role and responsibility to the other facilitators and their teams? You will probably be assigned a point of contact (POC) and it is extremely important to get to know him/her quickly because he/she will probably be your biggest ally and supporter. The POC can assist you in overcoming barriers and rescheduling events and rounding up team members if needed.

It is very important to keep your POC informed, as well as the management personnel with whom you entered into the contract.

2. Design and customize applications to meet client needs:
The new facilitator should analyze the organization's environment to assess what is the present organizational climate; what are the organization's vision, values, mission, and strategic objectives; and how do the facilitation roles and responsibilities support the corporate strategic plan. What is the client asking to be accomplished? How are you going to accomplish each task, method, as well as who, when, and where? Write down the expected outcomes. Predefine a quality product or outcome with each major task identified in your charter, Letter of Commitment, or contract and run it by your POCs to see if they agree that that is what is expected. If it is facilitating for a specific top manager, such as the environmental champion or energy champion, or for a quality department, coordinate with them and reach a consensus. Write minutes of the meeting and ensure both parties have a copy and agree on its contents.

3. Manage multisession events effectively:
Ensure the contract with the client for both internal and external facilitators has both the scope of duties to perform and the deliverables. Estimate the number of meetings and tasks required and the facilitation or consulting days that are needed to perform them. If you are an external facilitator, reach agreement on the amount per day or

hour you will get paid, plus include in the contract expenses, such as videos, pads (if you have to furnish, plus costs for any offsite conferences), and any travel expenses including transportation, such as airplane tickets, car mileage, and taxi cabs as well as hotel and meal expenses. If there are any events, such as a Kaizen event, an offsite conference on any subject, a benchmarking trip, a visit to one of the plants, or any other special happenings, make a separate cost estimate, purpose, length, special arrangements, and associated costs, etc., for each event. Then summarize them into an event plan for use by management and other participants. As discussed above, figure what outcome is desired of each event and how you are going to achieve the outcome. Develop critique forms to be administered at the end of the events. Summarize the critiques and discuss with management, contracting officer, or POCs, whichever is appropriate. Determine for each event the participants and the management's level of satisfaction. Be sure to document how well the outcomes were obtained and any areas of improvement along with lessons learned. Publish a small satisfaction assessment after each event originating from the critiques and/or discussions with the participants.

4.4 Facilitator and Team Leader Interface: Keys to Their Success

No team will be successful if the team leader and facilitator do not work together to achieve the meeting's objectives and help the team function as a whole. They need to respect each other, share responsibility, and work together in the meeting to resolve any conflict, keep the team focus, ensure there is teamwork and synergy, and continued focus to achieving the desired objective.

4.4.1 Share Responsibility

Plan the meeting together and produce an agenda with a purpose, agenda items with time limits, and minutes of the meeting with actions that need to be done.

4.4.2 Work Together

This does not mean to do each other's jobs, but to ensure that the meeting's flow is focused on the objective or problem and, by the time the meeting is ended, the meeting's purpose is achieved. Help each other diffuse any conflict; assist each other in keeping the meeting moving toward the purpose. When the meeting is over, ensure good minutes are taken and necessary future actions are highlighted.

4.4.3 Keeping Focused

This is the primary duty of the facilitator, i.e., to keep the meeting on the process. The process can be a problem-solving process, such as Toyota kata, DMAIC (define–measure–analyze–improve–control) from Six Sigma, or an objective development process or any structured process such as 5 Whys or 5 Ss (sort, set in order, shine, standardize, sustain). Sometimes, the team leader, who is the primary subject matter expert, can help the team get back on track through summing up the progress made or other helpful techniques.

4.5 Know Your Team Members

By knowing the profile of your team members, you can work more effectively with them and help them over their weakness and to build on their strengths. The DiSC profile provides information on which profiles work best together and which do not. For example, a D, an I, an S, and a C (four-person team) would work good together. A four-person team of D, D, D, and D would not. Each D would try to be in charge and there would be a lot of talking and not much done toward meeting the team's deliverables. The author was teaching an advanced facilitation course at Oklahoma State University in Oklahoma City a few years ago when the DiSC was used to identify the participants' personalities. The course members were primarily from the Federal Aviation Administration (FAA), the U.S. Air Force, and local businesses. Knowing their profiles, the author assigned them to six teams of five members each. The assignments were made so that five teams met the desired compatibility recommendations, except one team of five people possessed all "D" personalities. The author gave each team an assignment to complete in 20 minutes. Five teams did so in 20 minutes or less; however, the five "D" team members did not even get started. Each of them thought they should be in control, so they argued and discussed who should lead and what the assignment was until the time was up. This demonstrated the importance of knowing your team and having the right mixture of personalities. Use this design in formulating teams or subteams if possible.

The normal and results facilitator must be able to deal and influence people at all levels. They must be able to deal with the workers on the floor, the administrative employees, the supervisors and middle management, and the senior managers. It is important to let the senior managers know what to expect, their involvement and support, and keep them informed of progress and any major problems. Sometimes, the facilitator corrects a problem, teaches a new skill, or helps a team member accomplish something that he or she does not have sufficient skills to do on his/her own. That is when the tool or technique, called coaching, comes in handy. Let's look at the coaching process. It is one positive, excellent way to influence others.

4.6 Coaching

4.6.1 Introduction

Sometimes coaching is needed. This is a skill that a master or results facilitator needs to possess. When is it done? There are several reasons to coach. They include:

1. When an individual is struggling with a challenging assignment and needs help
2. When someone wants help with something or needs feedback on his/her ideas
3. When a person is performing a task and you believe there is a more effective manner or way to accomplish it
4. When anyone needs feedback or assistance to improve their skills, and desires the assistance
5. When someone needs to know how to use a tool or technique by him/herself without a facilitator present to assist

Is there a process to follow? Yes, there is a five-step process. Also, there are a few guidelines to follow or adhere to in coaching.

4.6.2 *Guidelines and Coaching Process*

First, the coach and the player must be focused on achieving the same result (goal). Secondly, the player must want to receive coaching. Third, the player must have confidence in the coach's abilities, believe the coach shares the same goals he or she does, and he or she must be open to receiving the coach's suggestions. When these conditions are evident, then the five steps process can be employed.

1. **Establish the performance area for development and why it is important.** Begin by establishing what is of interest or concern to the person being coached or by describing the area the coach recommends for improvement.
2. **Determine the type of coaching that will occur.** For example, observe the person in action. Then critique performance and recommend areas for improvement. Sit down and brainstorm together the other ways for a person to improve.
3. **Engage the player in a self-assessment of the situation and a discussion about his/her current ideas or abilities to manage it.** For example: "What is your view of this situation?" "How do you plan to improve?" Let the player be candid in the discussion of needs, wants, ideas, and his/her abilities. Keep the discussion open and focus on improving the player's abilities.
4. **Give feedback on the player's ideas and add new ones.** This step puts several ideas up for consideration. A candid discussion allows both the player and coach to zero in on the best ideas and the coach to provide feedback on areas for improvement.
5. **Summarize key points, next steps, agreements, and commitments**. The coach should express confidence and support. Next, the coach summarizes the points made. Together, they discuss the next steps they should take. The player agrees to try the suggestions that they both had agreed on and the player commits to continuing the improvements until the goal is achieved. The coach should offer to be available if the player has any questions or needs clarification on any points.

Example: The team leader of an energy team, Bill, was asked by the objective champion or energy champion to present (10 minutes) at the next Strategic Council on what is the difference between Lean and Six

Sigma and should the company pursue both. Also, will the team members use either on their opportunity? Bill asked the facilitator if she would coach him. She accepted. This is an excellent way to influence the team leader and top management as well as teaching them two excellent improvement techniques.

Step 1: Establish the performance area for development and why it is important. The performance area is Lean and Six Sigma. The importance is Bill has been tasked to explain the difference to the company's top management at the next Strategic Council meeting.

Step 2: Determine the type of coaching that will occur. The facilitator and Bill discussed the type of coaching needed. The facilitator asked Bill a few questions about Lean and Six Sigma. Bill could not answer any of the questions. The facilitator suggested that Bill read a few references on this subject that the facilitator provided and they would meet again at the same time the next day and discuss.

Step 3: Engage the player in a self-assessment of the situation and a discussion about his/her current ideas or abilities to manage it. The facilitator and Bill met as planned. The facilitator asked him to give a short talk on the difference between Lean and Six Sigma. He stated that they both focus on improving processes. The difference, he said, is that they use different tools and techniques. The facilitator said that that is true. However, maybe a different example would be clearer for the Strategic Council members.

Coaching Point #1: Lean focuses on the flow of the process whereas Six Sigma focuses on reducing the variability of the process. Bill said he liked that difference statement. Can you add more to those statements?

Coaching Point # 2: Lean is to improve the speed of the process. Take all the waste out and make the process less complex. Six Sigma is to reduce the variability of the process by decreasing the number of defects it produces. By doing so, we increase the quality level of the process.

Coaching Point # 3: Six Sigma is when a process produces 3.4 defects per million opportunities. Most U.S. processes are producing around 60,000 defects per million opportunities.

Step 4: Give feedback on the player's ideas and add new ones. Bill said he liked these ideas. He believed he should show some of the tools that are used. The facilitator agreed. Bill said for Lean, he planned to cover two techniques: 5 Ss and process flowcharts.

Coaching Point #4: The facilitator said this was excellent. When you show the flowcharts, use a hierarchy with the SIPOC (suppliers, inputs, process, outputs, and customers) first. Next is a simple flowchart with only the major activities. Then finish with an activity chart where more detail is shown. Using the latter flowchart will enable taking nonvalue-added activities or subactivities out of the process. Bill said, "Okay." For Six Sigma, he planned to show the DMAIC approach and the typical tools used for each segment. The facilitator agreed. Which ones was he going to show? For the D, he was going to show the charter, the objective statement including the target or goal. For M, he was going to show the measures of importance, the baseline, the process map. For A, he planned to show a fishbone diagram, a histogram with control limits, Paretos, cause and effect matrix. For the I, he planned to show a countermeasures matrix, a force field analysis to help sell the proposed solutions, and an implementation plan (action plan). For the C, he planned to cover the control chart; a comparison of what we have now to that of what we had previously and future plans.

Step 5: Summarize key points, next steps, agreements, and commitments. Together, Bill and the facilitator summarized the key points. They are shown in the presentation they put together. Each of the above subjects are on a PowerPoint® slide (converted to MSWord® for the below representation), so they can be quickly shown to the Strategic Council.

Lean and Six Sigma

This presentation explains the difference between Lean and Six Sigma.

- The objective of Lean is to improve the process flow.
- The objective of Six Sigma is to decrease the variability of the process.
- The tools/techniques are different, but easy to train.
- If you do both, QVS (Quality Value Systems Inc.) will receive significant savings.

LEAN

- Lean's focus is on reducing delays.
- The two primary tools are 5 Ss and flowcharts.

■ 5 Ss is a technique originated in Japan but used widely now in the United States. The first S is to **S**ort. It is based on "a place for everything and everything in its place." For our manufacturing plants (and offices, if you desire), sort everything into meaningful items. The next S to accomplish is to **S**traighten. Everything has a place. The third S is to **S**crub. Clean and make everything shine. The fourth S is **S**tandardize. Standardize and have signs and information so everything is easy to find and everything is in its place. The fifth S is **S**ustain. That is, keep it going and improve continuously; put into a procedure. Inspect or check periodically to ensure five Ss are working fine.

■ Flowcharts are used to identify the process and to help find out where waste, such as delays, is occurring. There are three types of flowcharts used: SIPOC, regular flowchart of the process, and an activity process that is more detailed. The SIPOC shows the suppliers, their inputs, the process itself (high level), the outputs, and the customers receiving the outputs. The second level flowchart shows the major activities whereas the activity flowchart breaks the major activities into more detailed subactivities and subprocesses.

■ Typical Lean analysis line chart
Pareto(s)
SIPOC flowchart
Activity flowchart
Fishbone diagram
Verification of root causes

Six Sigma

■ Six Sigma's focus is on reducing variability in the process.

■ In doing so, you increase the quality level defined by the standard deviation of the process. Six Sigma is achieved when 3.4 defects per million opportunities are achieved. Normally, most of our processes are at 3 standard deviations or more than 60,000 defects per million opportunities.

■ The tools and techniques used in Six Sigma are many.

■ Line graphs, histograms, frequency diagrams, fishbone diagrams, turtle charts, Pugh matrix, other matrices, Pareto charts, check sheets, and FMEAs (failure mode and effects analysis) are probably the most used.

- Six Sigma uses a problem-solving process called DMAIC (design, measure, analyze, improve, and control).
- The D is for design. Included is the charter and management sign off.
- The M is for measure. It includes the measurement system analysis that is the current line chart for defects and the baseline.
- The A is for analysis. Fishbone diagram, cause and effects matrix, and other tools.
- The I is for improve. It would show savings and proposed solutions.
- The C is for control. It would consist of a control chart that is maintained and checked periodically to see if the quality level is being maintained.
- A typical analysis would look like:
  Line graph showing defects
  Histogram showing UCL (Upper Control Limit) and LCL (Lower Control Limit)
  Fishbone diagram
  Cause and effect matrix
  FMEA (Failure Modes Effects Analysis)
  Countermeasure matrix

OUR TEAM

- Our team is using Six Sigma now and will probably use Lean in the near future.
- Recommend that Lean–Six Sigma be adopted at our company.

The Strategic Council liked the presentation and adopted Lean–Six Sigma for its company to use in improving its processes. The facilitator was asked to put together a plan with cost for training the key personnel in Lean–Six Sigma. Bill was appointed the Six Sigma training guru and the company made it possible for him to start Six Sigma training, up to becoming a black belt. Through coaching, both the facilitator and Bill profited. It was a win–win situation that also proved to be a win–win situation for the company. The above five step process will work. Let's look at another five step process by CRM Films (Carlsbad, California) in its video "Coaching." There are barriers to coaching, such as fear of the unknown, fear of looking incompetent, learner becomes defensive when boss is the coach, and others. Teaching is providing knowledge. Teaching is different from coaching in that coaching improves performance. The process can be described as simply

Develop–Practice–Nurture. The first step is **Prepare Learner**. Put him or her at ease. The second step is **Demonstrate**. Teach the how and the why. Begin with what is familiar and then move to the new material. The third step is to **Create a Positive Atmosphere**. Make it easy for the learner to ask questions and give reinforcements to what the person has learned. The fourth step is to **Have the Learner Perform the Operation.** Practice and practice until the operation becomes routine. Remember, after the first session, the learner will remember only about one half of what was presented. Also, remember, we learn best by doing. The last and fifth step is to **Follow Up**. Ensure the learners understand what they need to know. Let them know what additional help is available, if needed. Discuss possible future problems that could arise and how to deal with them.

A lot of team members have never given or participated in giving a presentation to management. For management reviews, it is desirable to get as many team members involved as practicable. If asked, several would like to know how not to be nervous, how do you stand so you do not pass out, should you move or stand around, should you look at both sides or just straight ahead? They desire to know the Dos and the Don'ts of giving a presentation. A facilitator can use the five steps of coaching, just talk and show the team members what to do, let them do it, critique them, and keep on until the team members have learned the desired information or behavior. If there are several team members needing the coaching, then a PowerPoint slide presentation to help show them would be helpful. Another method is to (1) define the purpose, (2) establish the method of coaching, (3) present the ideas or coaching points, and (4) practice and critique the performance.

4.6.2.1 Coaching Method

- **Purpose:** To offer performance tips in the areas you had questions.
- **Method:**
  Present the technique–person practices–observe, and give
  recommendations
  Do a self-assessment and provide feedback
  Summarize key points

4.6.2.1.1 Presentations

- We have identified two areas for focus: physical and the PowerPoint slides.
- Physical tips:

Dress comfortably.

Hold a pen in your hand.

Bend your knees while presenting.

Move around.

Develop a good posture and head movement to keep your audience listening.

Memorize the first three sentences you are going to say.

Use the topic words on your slides to guide the rest of your speech. Tell them what you are going to say, say it, and then in summary tell them what you said.

4.6.2.1.2 Presentation Tips: **Dos** and Don'ts

1. Have a white board or an easel with pad so, if needed, you can write to explain something.
2. Have a pen for writing.
3. Make the slide presentation visible to all.
4. Use walls if pad sheets are too numerous from an idea generation exercise.
5. Ask questions and give the audience a chance to ask questions.
6. At the end, have the participants fill out a critique and use to continuously improve.

4.6.2.1.3 Other Presentation Tips: Dos and **Don'ts**

1. Don't use too many slides. One (1) per minute is a reasonable guide.
2. Don't put too much information or data on the slide.
3. Be consistent in using capitals.
4. Number the pages, but don't have numbers too large.
5. When using a template, be sure every slide is readable.
6. Be sure presentation transitions flow smoothly.

Tool/Technique #15: PowerPoint presentation and Six Sigma terminology
Tool/Technique #16: Team coaching process

The facilitator had each participant stand up and use the pen, bend his/her knees, practice moving while presenting, and maintaining eye contact. The participants were critiqued and they continued to practice until they felt they had mastered the techniques. The different slides and their errors were then shown and discussed. The main points were summarized at the end. Each participant felt he/she had benefited from this coaching exercise.

4.6.3 Coaching: Toyota Kata

Toyota kata originated as part of the Toyota Production System. It is beginning to catch on in the United States. The book by Mike Rother (2009) is helping kata to become a part of all the Lean and Six Sigma conference programs. At present, it is a part of Lean. Rother defines Toyota kata as a systematic pursuit of desired conditions by utilizing people's capabilities in a certain manner. There are two types of kata: coaching and improvement. In this example, we are going to use the coaching kata. Kata is not a new tool or technique. It is a learning/improving mindset similar to how we train in sports. We coach drills to develop skills and some are different at each coaching session. We don't go out and immediately coach how to win, but how to develop skills including a mindset on how to play. If they use the skills learned in a game, it will help them win. It is not the solutions themselves that provide a sustained competitive advantage. It is the people's ability to develop solutions. Today, in most of our organizations, we have black belts, green belts, strategic teams, and problem-solving teams, with the top management setting the goals and the people figuring out how to achieve them. We use normal, traditional tools to help solve our problems. A kata is a routine or pattern that one takes to go from where he/she is to a targeted and desired condition. In coaching kata, we use the strategy shown in Figure 4.1.

We have a starting point and know where we want to go, but don't know the way or steps we need to take to get to the target condition. We have to experiment and take small steps and then evaluate how well we have done and then modify our approach, if needed. We are doing this as an individual, not part of a problem-solving team. We keep doing this experimenting, taking an iterative approach until we finally achieve the targeted condition. We did not make it in a giant leap, but in small steps along the path. This is shown in a simple flowchart (Figure 4.2).

Tool/Technique #16: Simple Flowchart

The diagram in Figure 4.2 shows that kata is a routine you practice until it becomes a habit. Once a habit, then you will do it right even

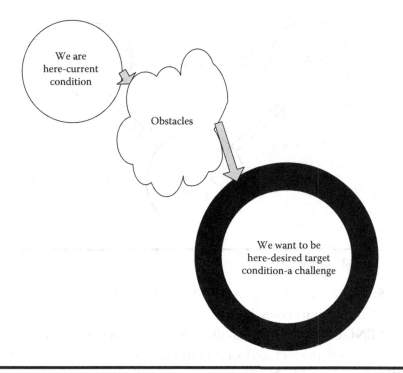

Figure 4.1   Kata.

without thinking about it. In other words, the practicing is done so one develops a mindset and the skill. This is shown in the coaching diagram in Figure 4.3.

Tool/Technique #17: Simple Relationship Chart

The significant change recommended in this approach is that it is not about what organizations do, but in how they do it. Their aim is to develop people who can deal with the dynamic and uncertain conditions in the workplace. Let's try this approach.

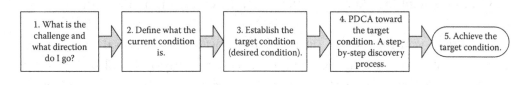

Figure 4.2   Kata flow.

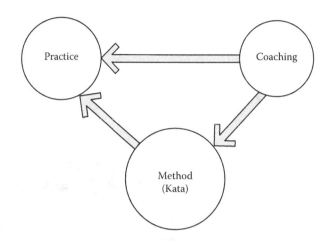

Figure 4.3   Kata relationships.

1. **FOCUS:** What is the focus process? Our boss has asked us to be able to write with both hands legible.
2. **CHALLENGE:** What is the challenge? Be able to copy the sentence: "Practice makes perfect and builds organizational excellence," legibly.
3. **TARGET CONDITION:** What is desired? Be able to copy the sentence: "Practice makes perfect and builds organizational excellence," legibly in 15 seconds.
4. **CURRENT CONDITION:** I have tried writing with my left hand (I am right handed) and practiced for several minutes and none of the sentences were legible.
5. **OBSTACLES:** In trying to write legibly, what are the obstacles or barriers that I encounter? Identify a few.
6. **PDCA CYCLE:** Each time that I practice is a Plan-Do-Check-Act (PDCA) cycle. I try to practice and overcome one obstacle at a time. I brainstorm to identify what the obstacles are. For example, I need a larger pen. I get a larger pen and practice. That is one PDCA cycle. I check and asked how did I do. I did better than before. The larger pen helped. Next PDCA cycle, I select another obstacle that is a larger writing pad. I keep the larger pen and try writing on the larger pad and finally my writing is legible. I keep practicing until I can do it in 15 seconds.

In practice, you may work on the same obstacle for several PDCA cycles with the cycle being defined as when you stopped and had to start again. For larger projects, you should develop a PDCA cycle sheet to record each cycle.

Process Metric
Date:
Process:
Step: What do you expect? **Result** (observe closely). **What did we learn?**
  Step 1
  Step 2
  Step 3

For our example, this sheet would look like this:

Process Metric: Time to write a sentence.
Date: March 15, 2013
Process: Writing legibly with left hand. **Targeted condition**: Write legibly with left hand in 15 seconds.
Current Condition: Cannot write legibly with left hand in 15 seconds.
Step: What do you expect? **Result** (observe closely). **What did we learn?**
  Step 1: Used larger pen, more legible. Clarity improved, larger pen helped.
  Step 2: Used larger pad to increase clarity. Increased clarity, larger pad helped.
  Step 3: Use larger pen and larger pad. Time reduced to 30 seconds. Practice increases ability to do it faster.
  Step 4: Practice to be faster—Meet target—Legible and done—Met target condition

Improvement, some innovation, and increased effectiveness occurred. This technique is systematic, scientific, and activates and motivates our creativity and solution development capabilities.

What does the coach do in this process? He or she asks the learner or the one doing the steps to get to the targeted condition; five questions at the appropriate time. The five questions used in the process with no new ones added:

1. What is the target condition?
2. What is the actual condition now?
3. What obstacles do you think are preventing you from reaching the target condition?
4. What is your next step? (Next PDCA cycle) What do you expect?
5. Then we go and see what we accomplished or learned from taking that step.

You repeat it at the appropriate time in the process.

1. What was your last step?
2. What did you expect?
3. What actually happened?
4. What did you learn?

This coaching method is simple since your questions as a coach are already defined for the iterative process and, by repeating them at the appropriate time, you help the learner achieve the target condition.

Process Metric: Time to write a sentence.
Date: March 15, 2013
Process: Writing legibly with left hand. **Targeted condition**: Question 1: Write legibly with left hand in 15 seconds.
Current Condition: Question 2: Cannot write legibly with left hand in 15 seconds.
Step: What do you expect? **Result** (observe closely). **What did we learn?**
Step 1: **Questions 3 and 4:** Use larger pen, more legible. **Question 5:** Clarity improved. Larger pen helped.
Step 2: **Question 1:** Use larger pad. **Question 2:** Increased clarity. **Question 3:** Increased clarity. **Question 4:** Larger pad helped.
Step 3: **Question 1:** Use larger pen and larger pad. **Question 3:** Time reduced to 30 seconds. **Question 4:** Practice increases ability to do faster. Time to write on pad reduced to 30 seconds.
Step 4: **Question 1:** Practice to be faster. **Question 2:** Meet target. **Question 3:** Legible and done in 13 seconds. **Question 4:** Met target condition.

Additional kata for team problem solving will be demonstrated in Chapter 9.

Tool/Technique #9: Toyota kata coaching

4.7 Facilitator's Exercises

1. Toyota kata can be done by an individual or a team. T __ F __
2. Facilitators are born since they have the desired influence personality. T __ F __

3. Toyota kata has a scientific base. T __ F __
4. A person who is dominant should not be a facilitator. T __ F __
5. Five Ss are a Lean tool/technique. T __ F __
6. The first S stands for Shine. T __ F __
7. Lean's primary focus is to eliminate waste. T __ F __
8. For presentations, when using the guide for a 30-minute presentation, you should not have more than 30 slides. T __ F __
9. Six Sigma's focus is on reducing variation of a process. T __ F __
10. Coaching should be provided to a team or team member only when everything else has not worked. T __ F __

(See Appendix 1 for the answers.)

Chapter 5

Understanding Group Dynamics, Handling Difficult Behaviors, and Managing Conflict

5.1 Teams and Groups

There are many kinds of team and group meetings that take place today: strategic improvement teams, headlight teams, process improvement teams, measurement teams, functional teams, cross-functional teams, tiger teams, DMAIC teams, Kaizen events, Town Hall meetings, self-directed work teams, natural functional teams, to name a few. What do they have in common? They all should have an agenda and a facilitator to keep the team, group, or event on track toward delivering or achieving its desired or required purpose and deliverables. If not, you will find attendees feeling unproductive and bored, and management will be disappointed as well because deliverables will be only partially delivered or not delivered at all. Most of these teams will go through four stages in their development.

5.2 Tuckman's Four Stages of Group Development

In 1965, Bruce Tuckman identified four stages a group must go through to be productive. They are Form, Storm, Norm, and Perform. Let's look at each of these stages.

5.2.1 Form

A group forms to solve one or more problems, to go after an opportunity, and to accomplish some objective or some kind of task. Hopefully, the group's purpose is spelled out in a charter or at least in a letter designating the team. The group can either be appointed or group members can volunteer. There are a number of different groups that are formulated to meet one specific purpose. A strategic group, a headlight group, a process improvement group, a problem-solving group, a customer's satisfaction group, a tiger group, a task group, a functional group, a cross-functional group, an energy group, an environmental management system group, a safety group, and many others. Now, when a group is formed, the next step it must go through is Storm.

5.2.2 Storm

Once the group meets, often group members ask themselves, "Why am I here? Why are they here? What is the role I need to play? What can I do that someone else couldn't do? Is this going to take away from my regular job? Who is going to do my duties when I am not there?" Often you hear a lot of questions and the noise level can be high with everyone talking at the same time. Hopefully, with good facilitation and group leadership, this stage will not last long. The author has seen examples of where some groups never got out of this stage. Were they productive and effective? Absolutely, not.

5.2.3 Norm

After awhile, the group begins to cooperate. The meeting becomes peaceful and the group is focusing and on track. Things begin to normalize. However, some groups may never leave this stage.

5.2.4 Perform

The group synergy is reached. Group members become super productive. We are a group and we can solve any problems. These are now called "high performance groups."

There is no magic way to get a group to go through these stages to get to the perform stage rapidly. Facilitation and group leader leadership are the two most prominent positive influences. Some groups, such as environmental management groups, may never get to that stage, primarily due to the long duration between group meetings and group members who change due to promotions, transfers, rotation, etc. Being associated with a government agency for the past seven years that had over 25 environmental management system groups, only five ever reached the perform level or high performance level. All but one of these was facilitated by the author.

Groups can suffice in the norm stage. Without excellent group leadership and facilitation, most groups would never move to the perform level. There is no magic time line to achieve each stage. The group members accept their responsibilities and get along together very well. In fact, if you are lucky, in some groups you may never see the storm stage. If you are unlucky, the storm stage may persist for a long time. When it does, the group may be disbanded by itself or the sponsor and a new group with different members may be appointed. The facilitator, knowing the group members' personality profiles, can help maneuver the group into the norm stage and, hopefully, into the perform stage. Success stories, recognition, pride, and trust can help achieve high performance. Group building is a tool that will be discussed later in chapters that can help a group work together.

Other useful tools that help considerably to facilitate meetings from storm to norm into perform are these simple ones:

- **Questions:** Develop questions that will help move the group forward in their progress. It is helpful to review the technical area or process first prior to the meeting and formulate some general questions to use if needed. Be able to determine, in the dynamics of a meeting, questions that help the group to better understand the problem or technique or data being studied and ask and discuss the answers with the group.
- **Summarize:** When a group reaches a lull, often the ability to summarize what has happened up to that point can help a group move forward.

- **Teach:** Know the tools and techniques well enough to explain them from theory to a practical example. Then the group will be able to effectively use them on the problem or opportunity it is addressing.
- **Show:** Use diagrams, processes, and sketches to show the groups how something works or is supposed to be accomplish.
- **Observe:** Yogi Berra once said, "You can see a lot by observing." A tool for observing will be provided later in this chapter.
- **Evaluate:** Critique the meeting. Evaluate how things went and determine ways to improve the next time. A self-evaluation tool will be provided later.
- **Act:** Observe, evaluate, and take appropriate action is always an excellent approach to improving group effectiveness and the facilitator's methods. Once improvements are identified, implement them.

Having a good problem where solutions are needed now or an objective that is meaningful to pursue are the best motivators for productive team work.

In 1977, Tuckman, jointly with another author, Mary Ann Jensen, added a fifth stage to the four stages: **Adjourning**. The fifth stage involves completing the task and breaking up the group. However, ISO and some other ongoing continuous improvement groups do not adjourn, but continue on their journey. Hopefully, they will continue in the perform stage and not progress backwards after performing for several years or more. Yes, groups can progress backwards when change in group leaders, facilitator, key group members, management, work situation, and other events occur.

5.2.5 New Stage Needed for the "Never-Ending, on a Journey" Group

Tuckman needs to add a new stage now for the "never-ending, on a journey" group, such as an ISO 50001 EnMS group or an ISO 14001 EMS group. That fifth stage is **Sustain**. The group needs to continue implementing their EnMS (Environmental Management System) or EMS (Energy Management System) and produce improving results. Often the level of activity lessens as time goes on, members change, leadership changes, procedures and policies change, work environment can change, new missions added or present mission modified, and other changes occur. How do the organization's management and group facilitator keep it going or, in other words, sustain the

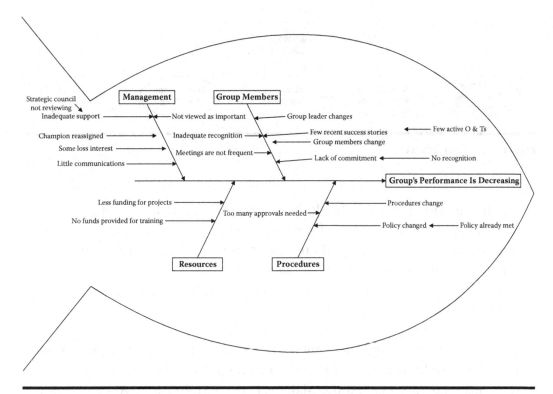

Figure 5.1   Fishbone diagram.

group's involvement and improvements? The fishbone diagram in Figure 5.1 gives us possible root causes.

Tools/Techniques #18: Cause and Effect Diagram—The Fishbone Diagram

How do we keep the momentum to ensure sustainment? There are a few "musts" that should be evident. They include:

1. Top management commitment and engagement must be a reality and seen by the energy or the environmental groups.
2. Adequate resources must be provided by management on good ROI (return on investment) objectives and targets and projects.
3. Communications to all employees and contractors must be ongoing, letting them know what is going on and why and how they can help.
4. Energy Performance Indicators (EnPIs) or Energy Management System (EnMS) key indicators must be maintained and visible for all to see; the progress targets and results.

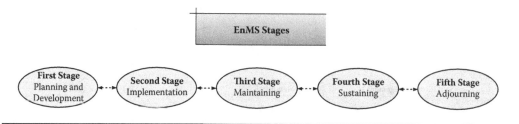

Figure 5.2   Five phases.

5. A recognition program should be put in place so that at least the group members have a chance to be recognized.
6. Any new group members should be trained, and group roles and responsibilities must remain in place.
7. A replication of good ideas should be accomplished throughout the organization.

If the above is accomplished, then the group will sustain its progress and results. Because both EMS and EnMS go through the following steps, the Sustain stage could be called the Maintain and Sustain stage. Also, planning and development is often combined into just one stage (Figure 5.2).

5.3 IAF Facilitator Core Competencies

5.3.1 Create and Sustain a Participatory Environment

1. Demonstrate effective participatory and interpersonal communication skills
   - Apply a variety of participatory processes
   - Demonstrate effective verbal communication skills
   - Develop rapport with participants
   - Practice active listening
   - Demonstrate ability to observe and provide feedback to participants
2. Honor and recognize diversity, ensuring inclusiveness
   - Encourage positive regard for the experience and perception of all participants
   - Create a climate of safety and trust
   - Create opportunities for participants to benefit from the diversity of the group

5.3.2 *Cultivate Cultural Awareness and Sensitivity*

Through all stages, the facilitator should develop rapport with the group members. The facilitator should create a climate of safety and trust. What happens in meetings other than the meeting minutes stays in the meeting room. The facilitator can create the desired climate through gaining the trust of members in how they deal with their supervisors, reports to management, practicing good listening skills, using several processes and/or methods to gain participation (such as going around the room and asking everyone to explain their background), what they can bring to the table to help the group, having members research an item and report to the group, etc. The facilitator should be a good listener thereby observing the group's needs, such as who is understanding and who is not. At the end of the meeting, it is helpful to critique the meeting, participants going first and then summarizing by the facilitator. The critiques are simply what did we do well and what can we do better. The group and facilitator should always look for ways to improve. Continuous improvement should always be a group goal.

Allow people with different cultural backgrounds or diversity to provide inputs to include some of where they are from and how differently their culture would handle a problem like the group is addressing. In time, all, regardless of their culture and backgrounds, should become a group; a group of people dedicated to solving the problem or achieving the objective and target.

5.4 Group Members' Behavior

Someone once said meetings would be perfect if they did not involve people. What they are referring to is that often some people's behavior is detrimental to having a good group meeting.

All of us have been in meetings where a few try to dominate the meeting, sometimes even to prevent the desired outcomes. The author has discovered in his facilitations that there are 10 behaviors that all facilitators have to deal with sometimes. (These difficult behaviors were substantiated by others: facilitoru.com/blog/meetings/dealings-with-difficult behaviors *and* www.masterfacilitatorjournal.facilatoru.com/archives/skill223.html.) Each needs to be addressed differently. If not, then ineffective meetings and disgruntled group members will prevail.

1. **Person is very argumentative:** Facilitator needs to maintain a calm appearance and also keep the group calm. Find a good point the person made, compliment him/her, and then move on to the subject you need to cover. If this does not work, at a break, talk with the person and try to win him/her over to your and the group's side.

2. **Person knows it all:** Normally this person is trying to build up his/her self-esteem. Often he/she does have some good points from past experiences. Find one and let him/her know that is a good point that we can use. Refer to him/her often for opinions. This treats his/her ego and provides the group with some good information. Don't make an enemy of this person because often, if you gain the support and cooperation of this person, he/she will significantly contribute to the group's purpose. In fact, he/she does know a lot due to vast past experiences.

3. **Person is overly talkative:** A very common behavior. Sometimes it is best to let the person vent for awhile and when he/she catches a breath, move the group toward its purpose. If you get all the group members participating, they will help you handle this individual by making comments, such as, "You have had your turn, it is my turn now." Or, "You have had your say, now it is our turn."

4. **Persons have side conversations:** Try not to embarrass them. Move closer to them so they know you are observing and when you get the chance, ask one of them an easy question or their opinion on what someone else had offered. If more than one sidebar occurs, then direct a statement to the group saying, "We should try to hold down these side conversations because they are disrupting the group in achieving our purpose today." This works well because it is not considered to be directed to any one person. No one's feelings are hurt.

5. **Personality clashes occur:** Inevitably, some personalities will clash and disrupt the meeting until this is resolved. The best procedure is to summarize what each has said, and ask the group what they think. Try to give each one involved in the clash some credit for a good point and to smooth over the situation as much as possible. Sometimes conflict can lead to positive results, but when it occurs, the facilitator must deal with it immediately so it does not get totally out of hand. Sometimes, this conflict may identify that, what the group is pursuing, is not the right approach and another path is better. A change such as this does not happen without some minor conflict.

6. **Person gets off the subject:** This will occur almost once in every meeting from any group member, especially concerning sporting events

the previous night or a big game happening this weekend, which are popular discussions. If they last for more than a minute, then the facilitator should try and get the group back on track by asking one or two subject questions. If it is one person over and over getting the group off track, then this is a more difficult problem to deal with, but deal with it you must to have productive meetings.

7. **Person rambles on:** Occasionally, you will find an individual that just rambles on and on and talks about everything but the subject at hand. When the facilitator gets an opening, thank the rambler for his or her comments and then ask a question to another group member on the subject. Try to get the person off his/her soap box or stage and get others participating.

8. **Complainer:** Normally the complainer complains about company policies or social policies, about too many meetings, or that the company does not care. Some group members may share their opinion. It is important to let the complainer know that the group cannot solve the policy issues or the social ones, and we need to get back on delivering what we need to at this meeting. When a company or organization is downsizing, complainers can take over meetings and render them totally unproductive.

9. **Person has negative personality:** This individual is negative about everything. He or she thinks the meeting is a waste of time. We would be better off doing something else. Like the complainer, the facilitator should acknowledge his or her negative comments, and turn the table by asking the other group members to identify any positive things about the subject. You are not going to change his/her negative personality, but hopefully you can help him/her refocus onto the purpose at hand. Often you will hear, "It will not work here." The group or facilitator may say, "Maybe not, but let's try it. It may help our organization. We need your support to make this happen."

10. **Person does not talk:** An individual does not participate in the meeting. The facilitator should ask him/her a few simple questions or after someone else has made a comment, ask the nontalker what his/her opinion is. Draw the individual into the discussion by asking him/her a few questions.

5.5 Intervention Approaches

There are defined intervention methods that can be used to augment the actions outlined above. They will be discussed later. Let's see if we can figure out why some people act the way they do.

1. For the no talker or quiet participant, why do you think they are this way?
   a. Shy and insecure.
   b. Don't care about the topics being discussed or are bored.
   c. Feel superior to the other group members.
   d. Distracted by work or outside issues.
   e. Could be any of the above.
2. How would you deal with this behavior?
   a. Make eye contact with the participant and ask a simple question.
   b. Ask during a break or in private why the participant is so quiet.
   c. Suggest that everyone takes a turn in sharing their opinion.

Answers: All of the above are viable options. Normally #2a is the first option a facilitator should use. Most of the time, this option will get them participating with the rest of the group.

3. A group member talks too much, rambles on and on, and is generally dominant. This may be caused by:
   a. A natural need for attention and loves being the center of attention.
   b. Being either overly prepared or unprepared for the meeting.
   c. Wanting to show he/she possesses a large vocabulary or extensive knowledge so as to impress other group members.
   d. Having the most authority outside of the meeting.
   e. Just loves to talk.
4. What solution would you try first?
   a. Glance or stare at your watch while the participant is speaking.
   b. Summarize and emphasize relevant points and time limits.
   c. Ask the participant to explain how her/his comments adds value to the topic or subject being discussed.
   d. Remind everyone of the time limit for this item.

Answer: Any option above may work. Although option 4c may be the most direct, it can lead to making the person a nonparticipant. Option 4b or 4d may prove best.

5. A group member is disrupting the meeting by being involved in too many side conversations. This may be because the participant:
   a. Feels the need or desire to introduce an item not on the agenda.
   b. Is bored with the meeting's contents and discussions.
   c. Has a point or points to raise that he/she feels makes other items on the agenda less important.
   d. Is discussing a related topic or subject, but is not being heard.
   e. Desires to be the center of attention.
6. How would you handle this situation if you were the facilitator?
   a. Ask the participant to share their idea(s) with the group.
   b. Casually walk around near the participants having the side conversation and look toward them.
   c. Call the participant(s) by name and ask if they want to add the topic or subject of their discussion to today's agenda.
   d. Restate or summarize a recently made point and ask for their opinion.

Answer: All four may work, but 6a is the most used to handle this situation. Option 6c is also a good approach to eliminate this situation.

7. A group member is highly argumentative. This may be because they:
   a. Have a combative personality or a hangover.
   b. Become upset by others' opinions or a specific meeting issue or comment.
   c. Is a show-off or dominant personality.
   d. Is a know-it-all.
   e. Feel that they are being ignored and becomes irritated.
8. Possible solutions: Which solution would you use?
   a. Paraphrase the argumentative participant's comments, and after his/her response, recap his/her position in objective terms.
   b. Look for some merit in his or her suggestions, express agreement, then move on.
   c. Respond to his or her comments, not attack what he/she initially did.
   d. Open the discussion of his/her comments to the group for their opinions.
   e. State that, due to time constraints, his/her comments can be put on the agenda for the next meeting.

Answer: Options 8a and 8b normally work. If not try 8d and 8e.

5.6 Managing Conflict

5.6.1 IAF Facilitators' Core Competencies

5.6.1.1 Create and Sustain a Participatory Environment

1. Manage group conflict:
   - Help individuals identify and review underlying assumptions
   - Recognize conflict and its role within group learning/maturity
   - Provide a safe environment for conflict to surface
   - Manage disruptive group behavior
   - Support the group through resolution of conflict

Conflict or arguments occur in meetings, especially in the Storm stage or when groups are under pressure to deliver a solution and nothing has been achieved. Proper intervention may solve the situation. Let us look at a few possible conflicts and you determine the best course of action.

The group, after reviewing a Pareto chart, was ready to decide what it is going to work on first. Two group members began to argue over whether the first or second bar should be the first thing the group addressed. Both agreed the first bar would provide the most savings, but the second bar would be easier to complete. The discussion gets heated, thus making the other team members uncomfortable. As the facilitator, what would you do?

1. "The discussion has gotten out of hand. Group, what should we do?"
2. Wait and hope the group leader will settle them down.
3. Say, "Both of you could be right. Why don't we list the advantages and disadvantages of each possibility and then select the best option."
4. "Does anyone else have a suggestion on why one of these should be selected over the other one?"

It is possible all four options could solve the argument. Possibilities 1 and 4 try to get help from the group members right away. Option 2 depends on someone else to take action. Option 3 addresses the two in conflict and attempts to get their agreement on doing something that will shed more information on which bar should be selected before one is actually selected. If you answered 3, you have selected the possibility that, if they agree, would bring the group more quickly back to focus. Their feelings will be directed to the next action and a selection would be eventually using a technique that the two who were arguing agreed upon. Conflict resolved.

Normally, major conflict is not the problem. If it occurred, the group leader probably would dismiss the group and he/she would try to handle the conflict outside of the meeting. Problem behavior is very common. Why don't we address one of the most common problem behaviors.

The group has two people who love to talk and on any subject. The other group members think that they love to hear their own voices. Both of the talkers are good group members when you keep them on track. When they are not quiet and focused, they do not allow any other person to talk or discuss any issues. You are the facilitator. What course of action would you choose?

1. Suggest that the group review the ground rules that includes no excessive talking.
2. "Joe and Nancy (the two talkers), let's give the other group member a chance to participate."
3. "Let's go around the room and get everyone's opinion, then summarize."
4. "Nancy and Joe, you two have taken over the meeting. Please let someone else talk."
5. Do nothing, let the group leader handle the situation.

Numbers 2 and 4 are direct approaches and may work, although it could hurt their feelings. If so, you will lose their participation in the rest of the meeting. Numbers 1 and 3 are indirect intervention and will probably work. Number 3 would be most effective since 1 directly points the finger at Joe and Nancy. Number 5 may take too long, thus the meeting efficiency would be lessened.

As facilitators, we need to recognize that conflict is inevitable and sometimes can be constructive. Often we have choices on how we intervene or attempt to manage the conflict. When conflict exists, acknowledge to the group that it does exist. Break down the conflict so you and the group can deal with it. Determine if the conflict is about goals and facts (factual conflict) or about methods or values (judgmental conflicts). Brainstorm to find alternatives to resolve the conflict. Determine areas of agreement. Develop a plan to act on those areas of agreed alternatives and do it.

A third situation has come up. Jim and John don't feel the meeting is important. They both said they should be spending their time doing their job, not going to meetings. What would you do as their facilitator?

1. Do nothing. This is a group leader problem.
2. Ask the other group members if they feel the meeting is important?
3. Tell them the meeting is important because the group is working on a company strategic objective. "The group needs your expertise and involvement. Please bear with us. The meeting will get more interesting as we get farther into the meeting and opportunity."
4. Ask them to leave and try to get new members to replace them.

This is both a group leader and facilitator problem. Look at the group leader and if he or she doesn't say anything, then this is your problem. Doing nothing is not a satisfactory solution. Asking the other members about the meeting is somewhat risky. What if they agree with Jim and John. Now you have a bigger problem. If you selected possibility 4, then you have unnecessarily created a problem that will delay the group in meeting its commitment. Possibility 3 is the best choice. The chances are you will satisfy them for this meeting. In future meetings, plan on getting them more involved.

What skills do facilitators need to manage conflict? First, you must be able to listen, accurately hearing the total message, including words and feelings. You should be listening to what the other person wants to say, not for what you want to hear. Secondly, be able to ask questions to get information or to discover additional problems. Dealing with another or your anger is a need. Focus objectively on the relevant facts in a situation. Don't let the situation escalate. Stay calm and let the others calm down slowly.

5.7 Observing Group Dynamics

A facilitator has very special responsibilities. You are entrusted with a large portion of the future success of an organization's groups' program. Whether your company or organization achieves its vision and strategic goals and objectives will depend on its facilitators to help groups work as a group and achieve value-added results. Teamwork is vital for a group's success. The best way to achieve teamwork is to have the team work together to achieve a result. Some exercises can help while the group is in the Form and Storm stages and even in the Norm stage.

The facilitator should make observations after the meeting, he/she can critique the group's performance, can interact with the group leader after the meeting, and, off line, coach individuals so group effectiveness can be improved. It is up to the facilitator to communicate to the group leader what was done in the meeting and what should have occurred. This helps as a reference for future meetings. One of the author's favorite exercises is:

Purpose: To provide additional practice with others to achieve consensus observing behavior and giving/receiving feedback.

Procedure: The group is divided into teams by the instructor. Each team is assigned an observer and is given 25 index cards and a roll of tape.

Task(s):

1. The teams are to develop the best possible product from the materials distributed to them. (It is important that the product is part of a team effort.) Develop products that are useful.
2. Observers will record group interaction on the form in Table 5.1.
3. Everyone must stand.
4. Teams may begin as soon as they have the materials.

Time Limits:
10 minutes for Plan (do not touch the cards.)
8 minutes: Do
10 minutes: Check
5 minutes: Act with observers and team
Total: 33 minutes

Table 5.1 Teamwork Observation Check Sheet

First Names	PLAN		DO	Remarks
	Speaking	Disagreement	Doing (+) (−)	

For observers using the Teamwork Observation Check Sheet (Table 5.1):

1. List the team members' names in the matrix. During the first five minutes of the PLAN stage, simply make a mark beside the name when each speaks.
2. During the next five minutes of the PLAN stage, note where there are any disagreements in the group (place a D by names.)
3. During the eight minutes of the DO stage, note who is physically involved in the task (touching the index cards and scotch tape) and who is not, by placing a plus (+) or a minus (–) by their name in the DO column.
4. During the 10 minutes of the CHECK stage, the observers critique the team on what they saw. (Use the matrix and general observations.)
5. During the five minutes of the ACT stage, discuss with the team how they could do it better the next time.

Tools/Techniques #19: Observation Check Sheet

Ask how well you did? Who do you think contributed the most and why? Do you feel like you contributed and why? If you did this exercise again, do you think your team would improve? Was there appropriate interaction between team members? What was the highest number of products made that were useful? The team record is 20 useful products from 25 index cards and a roll of tape. However, please don't expect this many applications. Five or six is still acceptable.

An alternative is to use a survey after certain team activities or work sessions. Have the team fill out the survey, then discuss the results. Let the team identify ways they can improve (Figure 5.3).

How well did you work together?

Tools/Techniques #20: Team Survey

A recap of the team's answers and corrective actions if needed should be done.

An example of the team's answers was:

1. How much did you participate in the problem solving part your team accomplished?									
Not at all									Completely
1	2	3	4	5	6	7	8	9	10
2. To what extent did you feel you had some control over the work of your team?									
Not at all									Completely
1	2	3	4	5	6	7	8	9	10
3. How satisfied are you with the amount of your involvement in your team's work?									
Not at all									Completely
1	2	3	4	5	6	7	8	9	10
4. To what extent do you feel ownership for the product that your team devised?									
Not at all									Completely
1	2	3	4	5	6	7	8	9	10
5. Considering both the information given and time limitations, how good was the product you developed?									
Not Good									Very Good
1	2	3	4	5	6	7	8	9	10

Figure 5.3   Team survey.

1. How much did you participate in the problem solving part your team accomplished?

Not at all   1   2   3   4   5   6   7   8   9   10   Completely

The average answer was 4.3 (all team members' score summed and divide by the total number of team members). This answer shows the need for the team leader and the facilitator to work on getting everyone involved in the next and future meetings.

2. To what extent did you feel you had some control over the work of your team?

Not at all   1   2   3   4   5   6   7   8   9   10   Completely

The average answer was 8.4. This shows that the team members feel that they are important to the team and they can influence the decisions and products and deliverables of the team.

3. How satisfied are you with the amount of your involvement in your team's work?

Not at all   1   2   3   4   5   6   7   8   9   10   Completely

The average answer was 5. This low answer relates to the responses on question 1. At the next meeting, this should be a question for the facilitator to ask the team: "How can you be more involved in the team's work?" Get their responses and evaluate for some possible solutions.

4. To what extent do you feel ownership for the product that your team devised?

Not at all   1   2   3   4   5   6   7   8   9   10   Completely

The average answer was 5.1. The team leader and facilitator should strive for consensus more in the future meetings. Also use multivoting as much as possible and summarize what the team did and produced at the end of each meeting.

5. Considering both the information given and time limitations, how good was the product you developed?

Not at all   1   2   3   4   5   6   7   8   9   10   Completely

The average answer was 9. This shows the products or deliverables are perceived to be good. No corrective action needed.

You do not want to give a survey to the team after every meeting. Distribute it when you detect a problem or at least twice a year. Communications can be very helpful to the team, especially when the team members' input is considered, evaluated, and discussed with all team members.

5.8 Group Guidance and Self-Awareness

5.8.1 Guide Group to Appropriate and Useful Outcomes

5.8.1.1 Facilitate Group Self-Awareness about Its Task

- Vary the pace of activities according to needs of group.
- Identify information the group needs, and draw out data and insight from the group.
- Help the group synthesize patterns, trends, root causes, frameworks for action.
- Assist the group in reflection on its experience.

The meeting pace will be different depending on the agenda and the different tools or techniques being used. The facilitator should vary the pace depending on the team's or group's needs and the agenda changes. Prior to the session, the facilitator in planning for the meeting should identify the information needed to be obtained and then guide the group so data and/or information are obtained. When needed, the facilitator should help the team if it gets bogged down in interpreting trends or patterns of data, performing a root cause analysis, or determining framework for solving problems or generating ideas. At the end of the session, it is helpful for the facilitator to assist the group or team members in reflecting on the experience they had in the session including both positive and negative experiences. The focus should be on what they did, what they achieved, what barriers they encountered, and what they learned.

5.8.2 Model Positive Professional Attitude

5.8.2.1 Trust Group Potential and Model Neutrality

- Honor the wisdom of the group.
- Encourage trust in the capacity and experience of others.
- Be vigilant to minimize influence on group outcomes.
- Maintain an objective, nondefensive, nonjudgmental stance.

The normal facilitator stays neutral and does not participate in the subject expert areas. The facilitator does summarize what has been said and also guides the group toward achieving outcomes. The facilitator trusts that the participants' experiences together have the ability to solve the problem or take advantage of an opportunity. The results facilitator has knowledge of the subject area and also is accountable along with the group for results, therefore, he/she can participate in the subject discussions and not remain neutral.

5.9 Facilitation Engagement Processes

Dr. Eileen Dowse, CMF organizational psychologist with Human Dynamics International (Calabasas, California) and chair of the International Institute for Facilitators (INIFAC) lists 20 examples of facilitation engagement processes. They are shown in Figure 5.4.

All of these can be found by using the Google search engine. Some are self-explanatory. Therefore, only the ones that the author has found very helpful and useful in unusual situations will be discussed.

1. Polling
2. Interviewing Partners
3. Debate
4. Rating
5. Group projects
6. Performance – showing how it might play out
7. Role playing
8. Games
9. Questionnaires/quizzes
10. Critical incidents
11. Flashcards
12. Stories
13. Cartoons
14. Tag
15. Movement
16. Posting Polarized Views
17. Open Space Technology
18. Gap Analysis
19. SWAT
20. World Café

Figure 5.4 List of facilitation engagement processes.

1. **Polling:** Like the political polls, the facilitator goes around the room polling participants and writing results on a whiteboard or pad that is placed on an easel.
2. **Interviewing partners:** Using interviews to gather information is an excellent tool. Learning how to ask open-ended questions and follow-up questions is very helpful to both a facilitator and group members.
3. **Debate:** Select one or more participants to debate one or more participants. The facilitator either gives the problem or opportunities to each side or lets them select one unless both want the same topic to debate. Set the debate for at least 10 minutes with each side getting equal time to present its views and then let the audience pick the winner.
4. **Rating:** An excellent technique to use to determine best counter-measures or most probable root causes. Give each the opportunity to rate an alternative from 1 to 5 with 1 meaning low and 5 meaning high.
5. **Group projects:** Assign projects to be done either in meetings or completed prior to the meeting of subgroups and have each subgroup present its conclusions at the meeting.
6. **Performance:** Simulate how the objective or purpose will turn out by making a few assumptions and using the tools that probably will be selected.
7. **Role playing:** Assigning roles to individuals and having them play in a group or team meeting is an excellent facilitative training technique. This gives facilitators experience in handling disruptive people, managing conflict, and handling other situations, such as engagements, summaries, and keeping a team or group on track. In developing a video for INIFAC certification, the facilitator doesn't know what the roles of the group members are since they are secretly given to the five members of his/her group.
8. **Games:** Very good for opening up a meeting and getting everyone involved. The game is not as important as its ability to be easy to understand and everyone can play.
9. **Questionnaires/quizzes:** Development of a questionnaire or quiz on the subject content or other areas, such as tools and techniques, can be interesting and engaging.
10. **Critical Incident:** A critical incident is something that happened to the facilitator that he or she uses as a teaching point.
11. **Flash cards:** Called process flash cards or sometimes "cheat sheets" that contain facilitation processes with tips on when to use them.

12. **Stories:** Appropriate and related stories can engage the group well at the beginning. Something that is interesting or funny to the group. The author likes to tell stories about when he first met Elvis and other times he saw him or his mother around Memphis, Tennessee.

13. **Cartoons:** The facilitator brings in appropriate cartoons and has the group participants discuss them. Dilbert cartoons that have management philosophies are always good candidates to spur discussion. Another way, although time consuming, is to have subgroups draw cartoons about their pursuit.

14. **Tag:** Similar to the game we played as kids, we cover a tool or technique or make a suggestion and then pass it onto to another person who is then tagged to do the same.

15. **Movement:** The best use of movement facilitative technique is breakout sessions. These are especially useful in strategic planning. The facilitator breaks up the group into smaller groups that go into a normally smaller conference room to work on the issue and then, after the allotted time, come back together and each group presents its findings.

16. **Posting polarized views:** These are posted in the group room so everyone can see. Have a few participants take one view and discuss it with the group and then another do a different one. Leave them on the wall so everyone can visit them throughout the meeting breaks. Also, they can be used to start the meeting by discussing and contrasting them with accepted views or positions.

17. **Open space technology:** Open space technology (OST) is an approach for hosting meetings, conferences, corporate-style retreats, symposiums, and community summit events that are focused on a specific and important purpose, task, or objective. It is highly changeable, flexible, and adaptable. OST has been used in meetings of 5 to 2,100 people, therefore, size is not a limiting factor. The approach is characterized by the basic characteristics below:

    a. A broad, open invitation that explains the purpose of the meeting is sent to the invited participants.

    b. All the participant chairs arranged in a circle.

    c. A "bulletin board" of issues and opportunities posted by participants (normally pads on easels are used).

d. A "marketplace" with many breakout spaces that participants move freely between, learning and contributing as they "shop" for information, data, and ideas.

e. A "breathing" or "pulsation" pattern of flow, between group and small group breakout sessions.

The approach is most distinctive for its initial lack of an agenda, which sets the stage for the meeting's participants to create the agenda for themselves, in the first 30 to 90 minutes of the meeting or event. Typically, an "open space" meeting will begin with short introductions by the sponsor (the official or acknowledged leader of the group) and usually a single facilitator. The sponsor introduces the purpose; the facilitator explains the "self-organizing" process called "open space." Then the group creates the working agenda, as individuals post their issues in bulletin board style. Each individual "convener" of a breakout session takes responsibility for naming the issue, posting it on the bulletin board, assigning it a space and time to meet, and then later showing up at that space and time, kicking off the conversation, and taking notes. These notes are usually compiled into a proceedings document that is distributed physically or electronically to all participants. Sometimes one or more additional approaches are used to sort through the notes, assign priorities, and identify what actions should be taken next. Throughout the process, the ideal facilitator is described as being "fully present and totally invisible," "holding a space" for participants to self-organize, rather than managing or directing the conversations.
Harrison Owen (2012)

18. **Gap Analysis:** Gap analysis identifies gaps between the optimized allocation and integration of the inputs (resources), and the current allocation level. This reveals areas that can be improved. Gap analysis involves determining, documenting, and approving the difference between business requirements and current capabilities. Gap analysis naturally flows from benchmarking and other assessments. Once the general expectation of performance in the industry is understood, it is possible to compare that expectation with the company's current level of performance. This comparison becomes the gap analysis. Such analysis can be performed at the strategic or operational level of an organization (www.mindtools.com by Caroline Smith).

19. **SWAT** Special Workshop Analysis Technique for SWOT (strengths, weaknesses, opportunities, and threats): The group does a SWOT analysis for the group. The participants identify what a group does well and what they do not do well, opportunities outside of the group that they may feel would help the group, such as an event, and threats are anything that could negatively impact the group, such as a competitor. For each SWOT, brainstorm and select no more than 12 for any one of them. Place in a matrix with opportunities and threats at the top and strengths and weaknesses coming down the rows. Each participant has nine points and assigns them to each S-O, S-T, W-O, or W-T depending on the impact on each other. Strategies are developed with the ones with the highest score. This exercise takes about two hours.

20. **World Café method:** Drawing on seven integrated design principles, the World Café methodology is a simple, effective, and flexible technique for hosting large group dialogue. World Café can be changed to meet a wide variety of needs. Specifics of context, numbers, purpose, location, and other circumstances are factored into each event's unique invitation, design, and question choice, but the following five components comprise the basic model:

    1. *Setting:* Create a "special" environment, most often modeled after a café, i.e., small round tables covered with a checkered tablecloth, butcher block paper, colored pens, a vase of flowers, and optional "talking stick" items. There should be four chairs at each table.

    2. *Welcome and introduction:* The host begins with a warm welcome and an introduction to the World Café process, setting the context, sharing the café etiquette, and putting participants at ease.

    3. *Small group rounds:* The process begins with the first of three or more 20 minute rounds of conversation for the small group seated around a table. At the end of the 20 minutes, each member of the group moves to a different new table. They may or may not choose to leave one person as the "table host" for the next round, who welcomes the next group and briefly fills them in on what happened in the previous round.

    4. *Questions:* Each round is prefaced with a **question** designed for the specific context and desired purpose of the session. The same questions can be used for more than one round, or they can be built up on each other to focus the conversation or guide its direction.

5. *Harvest:* After the small groups (and/or in between rounds, as desired) individuals are invited to share insights or other results from their conversations with the rest of the large group. These results are reflected visually in a variety of ways, most often using graphic recorders in the front of the room.

5.10 Group Building, Teamwork, and High-Performing Groups

5.10.1 Groups

What is a team? A team is several people joined together to accomplish a specific task or mission. Team size can vary from 2 to 20, but around 5 to 7 seems to work together better. Teams can be functional. They are strictly addressing tasks in the functional area. This team is normally called a natural work group. Some teams should be cross-functional (people from several functional areas) when representing the entire company, division, directorate, or agency, and could be much larger to have all major functional areas represented. When processes go across several functional areas, a team formed to address this problem should be cross-functional. There can be strategic highlight teams that search for possible strategic objectives or strategic objectives teams to develop an objectives action plan and implement to achieve the desired results. Today, Lean teams focusing on eliminating waste from processes or implementing the 5 Ss to achieve cleanliness and order in their workplace are common. Teams and groups are essential in today's organizations to solve problems, increase organizational efficiencies, productivity and quality, and especially to achieve excellent customers' satisfaction. Therefore, it is important that team members work together to accomplish their missions. This activity is called teamwork. Teams must have a mission or task. It is good when management charters a team in a memo spelling out their purpose and mission. Once formed, teams must have specific goals or objectives. A team in today's environment normally has around 5 to 10 members. A group may have from 11 to 50 people depending on the purpose and objective. A Kaizen event can have even more people depending on the process to be improved and the number of people associated with the process. Team building can work with each, but the methods could be different because of its scope.

5.10.2 Group Building

What is team building? Team building is a concerted effort to get teams to work effectively together to solve a problem or to achieve an objective. Team building is a large business today. There are companies that design and provide team building scenarios, games, retreats, and exercises that organizations can participate in and hopefully improve their teamwork. There are several goals normally pursued in these events or happenings. They include (1) building trust, (2) improving communications, (3) learning more about what is expected of the team members and the team, and (4) improving their ability to work together better to achieve a task or activity. Other purposes/objectives will often be claimed, such as improved courage to take on new ideas and adventures, increased creativity and innovation, coloration, coordination, improved efficiency and productivity, improved awareness of roles and responsibilities, and others. In many cases, these purposes or objectives are met in some form or another. For example, several team-building consultants assign two people together to walk around for a time period of, say, 15 minutes, one is blindfolded, the other is to guide his/her journey through the building and the grounds. The purpose is to build trust. Another consultant has people walk over hot coals in their bare feet. He wants them to believe (mind over matter) they are ready to do anything in the world. They have no fear. The difficulty is to relate the exercise, event, etc., back into the organization and also on the team or group because no one leads others blindfolded nor is it common to walk on hot coals to prove something. Also, if the participants do not feel like management supported the effort or thought through what they endured or assigned to help achieve, the team building could even have an adverse effect on the participants. If not properly planned, team building can become just an icebreaker or part of the entertainment for a group meeting.

5.10.3 Teamwork and High-Performance Results

During its quest for the Deming prize in the 1980s for Quality, Florida Power, & Light (FPL) had many quality improvement teams. Most of them were facilitated. Many teams had success in solving their problems. Most teams were disbanded after they solved their problem or met their goal. This was not a requirement because they could select another problem and obtain approval to pursue. There were a few tasks teams that just did not want to disband. They wanted to continue their team. If they were a functional team, there was no problem. However, if they were cross-functional and members had to travel a considerable distance to get to the meeting, or if someone on the team was promoted, there could be a problem. Observing this behavior caused the author to attempt to identify what characteristics caused this team to want to continue and stay together. First, the team consisted of both men and women. Secondly, they had solved an important problem. Third, they were located in various offices, but in the similar career fields. Fourth, they received some type of award and recognition. Fifth, the members were proud to be on the team and were very happy. It is amazing that if you find a high-performance work team, you are going to find happy people. Of course, these teams had excellent team leaders and facilitators who worked together well to produce positive results. The author found these same or almost the same characteristics in high-performance teams in the U.S. Air Force and the U.S. Drug Enforcement Administration (DEA).

Both facilitating teams and groups require the facilitator to plan and prepare for the meeting(s). The tools and techniques recommended in Chapter 2 will help the facilitator to prepare.

Facilitators can help teams improve by observing, critiquing, and providing feedback. At times, when the team leader is running the meeting, the facilitator should observe behaviors including contributions, attitudes, quality of information and data, and team momentum. At the end of the meeting, the facilitator should go around the room and ask each member: "How did the meeting go? What did we do right? Also, what can we do to improve our meetings and team performance?" The facilitator should then summarize what team members said and emphasize the most pertinent comments and recommendations. This is positive information for the team. Be careful on the criticism portion. Pitch in a constructive, understanding manner. Team feedback is information that can significantly help to improve team performance.

Team training is important whether it is team building, roles of a team, characteristics of high performing teams, tools and techniques, benchmarking or documentation needed, and what systems the company has and what they provide. Training can help a team jell quicker into a high-performance team.

Teams should be recognized for their achievements. The recognition should fit their contribution and be provided in a timely manner. The presenter should be sincere, knowledgeable of what team accomplished, and appreciative of the team's contribution.

The simple model for a team includes:

Establish a Team
Do Team Building
Have Teamwork
Achieve High-Performance Results

There are so many factors that impact this simple formula. For example, someone in the 1980s showed that the more people on a team, the more difficult communications and interactions became. Let's look at some of these factors that come into play (Figure 5.5).

Tools/Techniques #21: Impacts Diagram

Next, team building has its impacting factors as well. Figure 5.6 shows some of the most relevant.

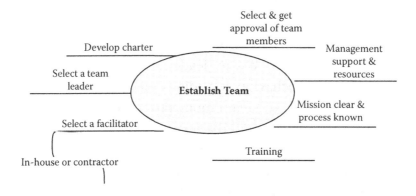

Figure 5.5   Establish team.

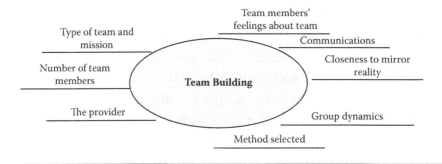

Figure 5.6   Team building.

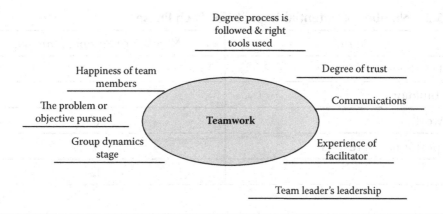

Figure 5.7 Teamwork.

All of these factors impact the team-building effort (read top down). If after the team building, the team worked a problem, exercise, or event to a successful conclusion and all team members are happy to be on the team, then team building was successful. Most of time, more than one team-building effort is required. In some high-performance teams, team building continues even after high-performance results have been achieved and maintained. Figure 5.8 shows the most relevant factors impacting teamwork.

All of these factors have a potential of impacting either favorably or being a barrier to good teamwork. Figure 5.6 shows the most common factors that can impact the results.

There were 32 factors identified that can impact the simple formula (Table 5.2). These are the most relevant, but many other potential barriers or impacts can happen to keep a team from becoming a high-performance team. Changes in organization leadership, change in vision or mission, team leader change, facilitator change, team members changed or rotated, the

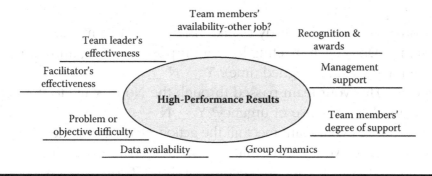

Figure 5.8 High-performance teams.

Table 5.2 Number of Potential Impacts for Each Phase

Phase	Number of Potential Impacts
Establish the team	7
Team building	8
Teamwork	8
High-performance results	9
Total	32

problems or opportunities difficult to solve, amount of support received, lack of feedback, bosses of team members acceptance of the team, finances, and other factors can have a negative impact on achieving high-performance results and then being called a high-performance team.

5.10.4 Quick Check on Whether a Group Is High-Performance or Not?

How do you know if the team is becoming a "high-performance team?" If the answer is "yes" to these questions, your team is certainly on its way to achieving this goal.

Question 1. Are all team members committed, cooperative, and participatory? Y __ N __

Question 2. Do team members accept responsibility for tasks or objectives and deliver? Y __ N __

Question 3. Are all team members focused on the team mission and goals or objectives necessary to accomplish the mission? Y __ N __

Question 4. Do team members seem to enjoy working with each other? Y __ N __

Question 5. Is your team ready to take risks to meet its mission? Y __ N __

Question 6. Does each meeting have a Purpose, Agenda, and Time Limit (each topic has an assigned time)? Y __ N __

Question 7. Has your team passed through the Norm stage to the Perform stage and have a sense of urgency? Y __ N __

Question 8 Does your team meet all the action plan's milestones? Y __ N __

Question 9. Does your team evaluate how things are going and adjust? Y __ N __ Do they critique meetings and use TOTS when needed? Y__ N __

Question 10. Does the team leader possess excellent leadership skills and is the facilitator one who knows the technical area, gets everyone involved, and ensures a logic approach to every problem or opportunity, and possesses the skill set of an advanced facilitator that facilitates for results? Y __ N __

5.11 Facilitator Exercises

1. Tuckman's four stages of group involvement are:
   a. Form, Norm, Storm, & Perform _____
   b. Storm, Form, Norm, & Perform _____
   c. Charter, Form, Storm, & Perform _____
   d. Form, Storm, Norm, & Perform _____
2. Name two of the most difficult behaviors that a facilitator must be able to deal with at meetings:
   (1) _____
   (2) _____
3. The skilled facilitator approach stems from the same purpose as the mutual learning model. True __ False __
4. The same teaching approach for adults does not vary much from that for middle school children. True __ False __
5. What are two ground rules set for meetings that should always be included?
   (1) _____
   (2) _____
6. What new stage does the author recommend to be added to the present four? _____
7. Flash cards are sometimes called "Cheat Cards". True __ False __
8. The engagement process called "tag" is similar to the game we played as kids. True __ False __
9. Why don't you hear the word GroupBuilding? _____
10. The main thrust of group building is to get the group to work and complete something together. True __ False __
11. Is it possible to have a "Group of one"? True __ False __
12. Which is more difficult to facilitate, a group or a team? Group __ Team __
13. If a group is performing in a manner that a facilitator says they have teamwork, would teamwork be visible if you observe the meeting? Yes __ No __

(See Appendix 1 for answers.)

Chapter 6

Know the Technical Area or Process (Four Key Examples)

6.1 Introduction

In "Facilitating for Results," the facilitator should be the process expert. This differs from being the functional (marketing, human resources, operations and production, stores and materials, accounting, etc.) experts, which is represented by the team leader and team members. If you are facilitating an organization that is developing a strategic plan, the facilitator must know the different components that comprise the strategic plan and what actions, information, and data need to be considered and used in each development step. For example, for the customer's voice, what data and information does the company have? Do they have a Customer Satisfaction Survey? Has it been administered annually? What has been the trend? Are we improving and if not, why? Does the company have a Customer Profile database? What is the mission? Has this been approved by the board of directors or has any mission statement been officially approved? If not, what should a good mission statement include? What is our vision? Do we have one and what period of time does it cover, and is it what the leaders want the company to become? Is it long-reaching and compelling? What are our values and guiding principles? What should our goals be for the next five years? What should the strategic plan developers consider in establishing the goals? How do goals and objectives differ? Which comes first? Has a SWOT (strengths, weaknesses, opportunities, and threats) analysis been accomplished? If not, then do one with appropriate participants and use in the strategic planning process.

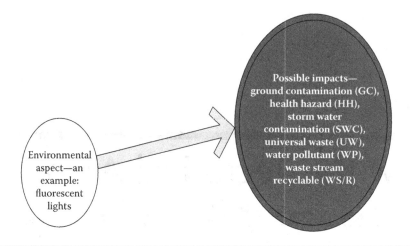

Figure 6.1   Aspects and their impacts.

The facilitator must know each component, which should be done first. Then next, which needs are to be considered when developing a component, what the results should look like from the beginning of the plan to the metrics that show how well the company is doing, and the strategic implementation plans. If not, the process of developing a strategic plan will bog down and may never be finished (Figure 6.1).

6.2 Example 1: ISO 50001 Energy Management System (EMS)

As shown previously, ISO 50001 EMS has five major phases: policy, planning, implementation, checking, and management reviews. Included in these five phases are 23 specific elements, each requiring some type of action. The facilitator should plan the meetings around these elements, starting with "policy" and proceeding to "management reviews," developing the requirement or deliverable for each and documenting them per the documentation required element. The facilitator, not necessarily the team, needs to be the expert on the ISO standard. He/she ensures the team follows or meets the standard requirements. The team gains knowledge as the deliverables are planned and achieved.

To facilitate an ISO standard planning, developing, implementing, maintaining, and sustaining effort, the facilitator must be a results facilitator. The standard effort is a continuous one and occurs continually, year after year. It is important to know the elements, what they require, and when they should be accomplished. A facilitator gets things done by ensuring that different processes are implemented correctly and produce the desired results. A results facilitator not only knows each element, but understands how implementing the standard works—any ISO standard. The team that developed the standard (after ISO 9001 Quality Management System) used an existing ISO standard as a guide. ISO 14001 EMS used ISO 9001 QMS as a guide. ISO 50001 EnMS (Environmental Management System) used ISO 14001 EMS as a guide or benchmark. Then, for the subject selected, ISO does the following, which the author developed and calls the "ISO Development Blueprint." This should help a newcomer to ISO to understand its processes better.

1. **First, know the essential focus with which you are dealing**. For example, ISO 14001 EMS, the environmental aspects and their impacts. For ISO 50001 EnMS, the energy profile and significant energy uses (SEUs) are what is needed. The purpose is to reduce energy. The boundary where the reduction is to occur should be established.

2. **Create the elements that can impact the organization's culture**. Leadership or management responsibility, communications, business processes, policy, measurement, and action plans. When these are done well and show positive results, then the culture for this topic will be impacted in a positive way.

3. **Provide an improvement focus**. Objectives and targets and action plans do this. Of course, prior to development, the team must consider legal and other requirements, such as resources and the organizational climate. The establishment of an ongoing, cross-functional team enables this focus to occur and obtain success.

4. **Control what is important**. Operational controls are created and put in place to lessen the aspects' or SEUs' impacts. Audits every three years as well as annual self-inspections ensure these controls are working or can work if needed.

5. **Measure and monitor progress and results**. Environmental indicators and energy performance indicators show progress made against targets or goals and whether the organization ever met its strategic goals or not. After an objective and target has been put into place, some things still need to be monitored, such as for EMS recycling paper, paper products, metal, aluminum, batteries, ink cartridges, and electronics, such as end-of-life computers, monitors, and laptops. SEUs are examples in EnMS that need to be monitored.

6. **Document what you did**. Document control and control of records enables the team to achieve this. Without documentation, no organization could have a successful audit internal or external. Also, documentation enables the team to show problems, progress, and results to their management and all organization personnel.

7. **Reflect and continuously improve**. The management reviews held at least once a year allow a team and management to reflect back on what was done well and what the team and organization can improve on in the coming year. Often the teams will do an annual assessment (normally in November) and present to the environmental or energy champion. Understanding the Plan–Do–Check–Act wheel and following it helps the team and organization continuously improve. Using corrective action reports helps eliminate problems and improve the organization's environmental and energy performance.

The 17 elements of the EMS standard and the 23 of the EnMS standard, when followed, enable the team to accomplish the seven major processes described above. OHSMS (Occupational Health and Safety Management System) 18001 also used this process.

6.3 Example 2: ISO 14001 Environmental Management System

ISO 14001 EMS has five phases and 17 elements. ISO 50001 EnMS is very similar because it is designed with ISO 14001 as a guide. In ISO 14001, identifying the environmental aspects and their impacts and reducing the risk or controlling the impacts are the main thrusts of ISO 14001 EMS (Figure 6.1). The phases are shown in Figure 6.2.

The facilitator must be not only familiar with these phases and all 17 elements that comprise these 5 phases, but be an expert in exactly what needs to be done and how to do it in order to be in compliance with the standard and reduce risks in the workplace.

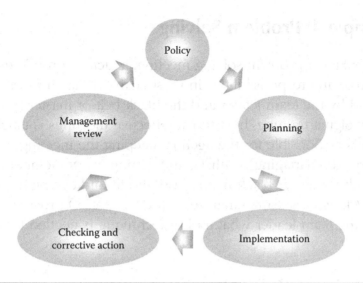

Figure 6.2 The phases.

Tool/Technique #22: A Phases Diagram

6.4 Example 3: Construction Partnering

In the past, many construction projects ended in litigation. It took months to resolve the issues in court. Partnering was introduced by the U.S. Army Corps of Engineers to help resolve this problem. Stakeholders on construction projects would meet to develop a construction partnership agreement, which included basic objectives and a problem resolution process. Partnering's main ingredient is trust or building trust among all stakeholders so problems can be resolved by the stakeholders and not in a court of law. Realistic objectives are developed along with measures that would show the success of the partnering agreement at the end. A facilitator is necessary to bring all parties together, to develop trust and establish objectives, performance measures, and design a problem resolution process (attempt to solve the problem at the lowest level with empowered personnel and escalates to the next level only if the lower level cannot solve or resolve). The partnering agreement is signed by all participating partners. Sometimes it is enlarged, placed on a sign board, and made visible for all to see. Partnering has saved millions in litigation fees, brought more projects in on time, saved money and resources, and improved customer satisfaction.

6.5 Example 4: Problem Solving

In a Lean Six Sigma problem-solving meeting, a facilitation role exists. The facilitator's role and responsibilities in most Lean Six Sigma meetings are jointly shared by the team leader and the black belt or master black belt. In the Lean Six Sigma training, how to run effective meetings is taught. The team leader is responsible for the agenda, keeping the meeting on track to meet its purpose, managing conflicts, and getting every member involved. The black belt or master black belt is responsible for keeping the team on the DMAIC (design–measure–analyze–improve–control) process and recommending to the team leader what tool or technique is needed for each step (Figure 6.3).

Tool/Technique #23: DMAIC

Figure 6.3 shows development of the problem or opportunity statement or an objective statement is what is needed for the D in DMAIC. Someone once said, "When you complete this step, you have half the problem or opportunity solved." Notice that the statement is specific and has the target (10%). The M in DMAIC is to measure. In this opportunity or problem statement, kilowatt hours (kWh) is our primary measure with kWh/gross square feet used also to make comparisons. These are calculated monthly and cumulated at the year's end and compared to last year's number to determine percent reduction achieved. Kilowatt hours is normalized with gross square feet so the results can be compared to other facilities. The number of

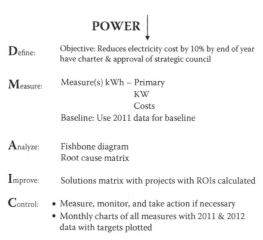

Figure 6.3   DMAIC.

people or computers used also could be used to normalize, but kWh/gross square feet is a traditional measure called *energy intensity* or, in this case, *electricity intensity*. The other measure is cost of electricity compared to last year. Measures often have to be developed to measure the impact or progress of the problem or opportunity statement. In this case, traditional measures are available so a new one does not have to be developed.

Analyze or the A in DMAIC is shown as a fishbone diagram. When analyzing any problem, normally the fishbone is a good place to start. From the fishbone, proceed to a root cause matrix and summarize here while determining the root cause. It is a simple technique that can be used often. Other techniques used to analyze are histograms, frequency diagrams, Pareto charts, statistical analysis, scatter diagram, regression analysis, flowcharts, five whys, to name the ones frequently used. The facilitator needs to know when to use what tool or technique for the specific problem or opportunity.

For organizations that use a problem-solving process originating from PDCA cycle:

1. Identify the problem or opportunity
2. Show the current situation
3. Gather essential data and information
4. Perform analysis and develop countermeasures
5. Sell the countermeasures and implementation
6. Check the progress and results
7. Take actions and standardize
8. Develop future plans

A facilitator needs to know this process and the tools and techniques most often needed to solve the problem. These include developing a problem or opportunity statement, using a check sheet to gather data, developing an indicator and target, using a Pareto chart or histogram, developing a process flowchart, performing a root cause analysis, using a root cause evaluation matrix, developing countermeasures for the root causes, doing a force field analysis or barriers or aids analysis, standardization techniques, and matrix diagrams. These are mostly tools and techniques used for over the past 35 years. Occasionally, one of the other Six Sigma tools will be used, such as a cause and effect diagram, failure analysis, Pugh matrix, and statistical analysis will be needed. Master black belt or a black belt should not be needed in this problem-solving process. The organization's team leader and

1. Check Sheet—To collect data
2. An Indicator—To measure the current situation and then later show the results achieved after the countermeasures have been put in place
3. Pareto—Prioritizes and shows what should be addressed
4. Histogram—Shows the frequency of the data and dispersion around the mean
5. Cause and Effect Diagram—Helps identify root causes
6. Control Chart—Shows where process is under statistical control or not
7. Scatter Diagram—Shows whether there is a correlation between two variables

Some have added flow charts as the seventh QC Tool. For description of the seven QC tools, see Mears, Peter, PH.D., "Quality Improvement Tools & Techniques", McGraw-Hill, New York, 1995.

Figure 6.4   The seven quality control (QC) tools.

facilitator should know the process and tools and techniques to solve the problems (Figure 6.4).

Some have added flow charts as the seventh quality control (QC) tool. For a description of the seven QC tools, see Mears (1995).

Tool/Technique #24: Seven QC Tools

The I in DMAIC is to improve. Normally, a countermeasure chart or a summary chart of proposed projects or solutions is developed. A force field analysis to help sell the projects or solutions would be helpful.

A force field analysis or barriers and aids analysis identify what forces are pushing for the solution and what are pushing against (Figure 6.5).

Tool/Technique #25: Barriers and Aids Analysis

The C in DMAIC is to control the process. Management or project reviews checking the measures' trend and actual versus target is the best control mechanism. If the project, objective, or action plan is not on track, then corrective action, such as providing additional resources, funds, or other items should be taken. Often a control chart measuring product output is used in controlling manufacturing processes and products' variability.

Forces Pushing For	Forces Pushing Against
Strategic council established a goal that this objective will positively impact	Many other critical items competing for funding
Energy champion is in favor	Costs money which is in short supply
Can be completed in less than six months	Must be approved and contracted quickly to achieve results in this time period
Contribution estimated to reduce kWh by 2% during the following year	Need more contribution to meet corporate goal
Payback period is 2 years and below	Strategic council has been approving projects with payback periods of 3 years and less

Figure 6.5   Barriers and aids analysis.

6.6 What Is CAPDO (Check–Act–Plan–Do)?

Most people have heard of the Deming wheel or cycle. It is described as PDCA or Plan–Do–Check–Act. The wheel is shown in a circle. You start with developing a plan. Next, you implement (the do). Once you implement, you do not run to the next plan do, but instead you check for progress. Is the implementation plan being implemented properly and are the results expected being achieved? If not, you take corrective action (Figure 6.6).

Tool/Technique #26: CAPDO

This wheel or cycle is the basis for strategic planning, business planning, problem-solving process, ISO 9000 and 14001, and others. Where did it originate? In the early 1940s, Dr. Edwards W. Deming was in a conference/

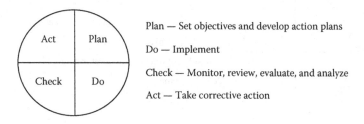

Plan — Set objectives and develop action plans

Do — Implement

Check — Monitor, review, evaluate, and analyze

Act — Take corrective action

Figure 6.6   Plan–Do–Check–Act wheel.

meeting where the statistical giant, Dr. Walter Sheward of Bell Labs, was giving a speech. He outlined a cycle on the way we should think. We should develop a plan, then implement it (he called it DO), but don't walk away and start planning and doing other things as we Americans tend to do, but instead study it and take corrective action, if needed. This became known as the Sheward Cycle. Dr. Deming, along with Dr. Sheward (the inventor of statistical process control (SPC)), was a great supporter of using SPC in the workplace. When he went to Japan in the early 1950s, he introduced them to SPC and the PDSA concept. Japan loved the new concept, but asked him to change the Study to Check because it is more representative of how they thought. Therefore, PDCA became known as the Deming wheel or cycle. The idea is to go through the cycle or wheel and don't stop, but start over and continue to do so, and make incremental continuous improvements as "you spin the Deming wheel." It is an ongoing effort, not a one-time event. This wheel is the best way to demonstrate continuous improvement. Once you have gone through the cycle, you start over with a plan to further improve.

What about improving an existing process? You will need to develop a plan. But, first, you need to check. How is the process performing? Is it meeting expectations or is there room or need for improvement? If it needs improvement, then what action do I need to take? Form a team, bring in a consultant, use process improvement, or reengineer the process? Once this is decided, then an action plan is needed and then implemented. Now we are back to checking for progress. How is the plan being implemented? What are the results? Do we have a gap between our target and actual performance? If so, what are we going to do to close the gap (act) (Figure 6.7)?

Where did the phrase CAPDO come from? In the early 1980s, Dr. Noriake Kano, JUSE (Japanese Union of Scientific Engineers) counselor, in a counseling session with Florida Power & Light (FPL) on its successful pursuit of the

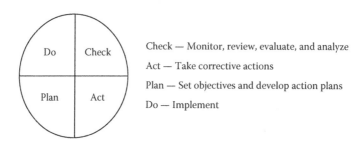

Figure 6.7   CAPDO (Check–Act–Plan–Do).

Deming prize, mentioned that to improve an existing process you employ CAPDO. The author of this book was in the audience and attended numerous sessions taught by Dr. Kano.

6.7 Tools and Techniques Needed for PDCA and CAPDO

The tools and techniques employed will vary by the type of problem or objective addressed. However, there are some that are the basics of each element and are almost always used (Table 6.1).

Table 6.1   Element Tools and Techniques Table

Element	Basic	Often Used to Develop Basic Tools	Areas Where Commonly Used
Plan	Action Plan	Environmental scan, SWOT analysis, affinity diagram, nominal group technique, objective development techniques including SMART, vision & mission statement, force field analysis, cost benefits analysis, root cause analysis	Strategic planning, business planning Problem solving ISO 9000, ISO 50001 & 14001, & others
Do	Implementation plan Project management	Gantt chart, action plan	"Do" means to make it happen, i.e., implementing or executes the plan
Check	Performance measure(s), dashboards, score cards	Measurement systems	Most of the time, more than one measure is needed to adequately tell what is happening
Act	Gap analysis, root cause analysis, countermeasures development	Structure analysis, Fishbone diagrams Feasibility study Cost analysis	"Act" is to take corrective action to get things back on track

6.8 Facilitator Exercise

1. Using DMAIC, where would the problem definition be? (Please check correct one.)

    __ D __ M __ A __ I __ C

2. When using DMAIC, where would the control chart be included? (Please check correct one.)

    __ D __ M __ A __ I __ C

3. When using DMAIC, where would the metric be located? (Please check correct one.)

    __ D __ M __ A __ I __ C

4. When using DMAIC, where would a cause and effect diagram most probably be included? (Please check correct one.)

    __ D __ M __ A __ I __ C

5. What are the seven QC tools?

    (1) ____

    (2) ____

    (3) ____

    (4) ____

    (5) ____

    (6) ____

    (7) ____

6. Which tool of the seven QC tools is used to prioritize what should be worked on next?

    ____

7. Which tool of the seven QC tools is used to show whether a process is in or out of control?

    ____

8. Which tool of the seven QC tools is used to show if there is any correlation between two variables?

    ____

9. When would you use CAPDO instead of Plan–Do–Check–Act?

    ____

(See answers in Appendix 1.)

Chapter 7

Facilitation Tools and Techniques

7.1 Introduction

A results facilitator and/or an experienced facilitator must be a master of tools and techniques that enable a team to generate ideas, evaluate and analyze them, and to sell them to management. He or she must be able to help a team accomplish numerous tasks, such as determining a name for the program, identifying factors that are critical to success, generating ideas or data, evaluating options or alternatives, finding the root causes of a problem, determining a good metric for measuring progress or success, graphing the data to show trends, determining the relationship between factors or data, to name a few. The key tools and techniques for generating ideas, gathering data, evaluating ideas, analyzing data, and selling your solutions are presented in this chapter.

There are additional tools and techniques that a facilitator should know how to use and when to use them. They are covered in the other chapters where appropriate.

7.2 Facilitator's Toolkit

Facilitator's toolkits vary depending on their training, experience, and education. At first, some may use divergence tools, such as brainstorming, brainwriting, and then switch to convergence tools at the end of the session. Examples of convergence tools are dot voting, weighted voting, and criteria-based decision grids.

Using tools and techniques by "use category" is a straightforward approach that works. These categories are shown below with the minimum tools and techniques needed for a "results facilitator" to function. In addition, coaching, training, and ISO standards knowledge and capability will be necessary to successfully fulfill their mission as results facilitators, and be beneficial to all types of facilitators. The normal progress includes:

Objective and problem definition
Generation and/or collection of ideas and data
Evaluation of ideas/data
Analysis of data
Countermeasures
Implementation

7.2.1 Objective and Problem Definition

Problem: The problem and the gain. Write the specific problem and gain
    if fixed.
Objective: Specific and made SMART (specific, measureable, actionable,
    relevant, time-framed). Make the objective specific, showing what you
    want to achieve and then apply the SMART technique.

7.2.2 Generation of Ideas and Collection of Data

The techniques that are excellent for generating ideas include:

■ Brainstorming
■ Nominal group technique
■ Green lighting
■ Brainwriting
■ Gap analysis
■ Gallery walk and gallery run
■ Visioning
■ Affinity diagram

Check sheets

SOAR (Strengths–Opportunities–Aspirations–Results)
Surveys
Interviews

Performance Indicators

SWOT (Strengths–Weaknesses–Opportunities–Threats)
Environmental scan

7.2.3 Evaluation of Ideas/Data

The most notable techniques for evaluating ideas and data include:

■ Multivoting
■ Weighted voting
■ Ranking
■ Criteria-based decisions matrix

Pareto analysis

7.2.4 Analysis of Data

The techniques useful for analyzing the data include:

Fishbone diagram

■ Structure tree
■ Root cause evaluation
■ Five whys
■ Checklist

Scatter diagram

■ Flowchart
■ Regression analysis

Histogram
Control charts

Note: The tools in italics are the seven quality control (QC) tools.

7.2.5 Countermeasures

The techniques for helping sell countermeasures or solutions include:

- Solutions matrix
- Force field analysis
- Barriers and aids analysis

7.2.6 Implementation

When implementing a solution or countermeasure, these tools are helpful:

- Action plan/implementation plan
- Gantt chart
- Project management

All of these tools and techniques have been in the facilitation body of knowledge for years. If the reader is not familiar with any one of them or needs more information than shown for some of the key ones below, then it would be beneficial to do a Google search or use the *ask* search engine.

First, a facilitator needs to know how to generate ideas and information. An efficient approach is to use brainstorming or nominal group techniques to generate ideas or possibilities, then multivote to the three or four best, and choose the best one by using the criteria in a comparison table. This will be demonstrated, starting with Figure 7.1. In Section 7.3, strategic tools, such as an environmental scan, a SWOT analysis, and an affinity diagram, will be explained. In Section 7.4, gathering data techniques, such as check sheets, observations form, and surveys will be covered. Section 7.5 will show tools for evaluating, followed by 7.6 that provides analyzing tools. In Section 7.7, tools that are helpful in selling solutions will be demonstrated.

__ 1. Energy Busters
__ 2. Energy Down
__ 3. Energy Aware
__ 4. Energy Emphasis
__ 5. Conserve
__ 6. Man Elect (Manage Electricity)
__ 7. Power Down
__ 8. ERAS (Energy Reduction Awareness System)
__ 9. ERASE (Energy Reduction Awareness System Effectiveness)
__ 10. ERAS (Electricity Reduction Awareness System)
__ 11. ERASE (Electricity Reduction Awareness System Effectiveness)
__ 12. Power Off
__ 13. DPEP (Down Power Electricity Program)
__ 14. DPEP (Down Power Energy Program)
__ 15. EAR (Electricity Awareness Reduction)
__ 16. SAVER (System Awareness Volunteer Electricity Reduction)
__ 17. PACE (Program Awareness Conserve Electricity)
__ 18. PARE (Program Awareness Reduction Electricity)
__ 19. PACER (Program Awareness Conserve Electricity Reduction)
__ 20. ESAP (Electricity Savings Awareness Program)
__ 21. RCRP (Resource Conservation & Reduction Program)
__ 22. REAP (Resource Electricity Awareness Program)
__ 23. REAP (Reduction Electricity Awareness Program)
__ 24. EPRA (Electricity Program Reduction & Awareness)
__ 25. ERAP (Electricity Reduction Awareness Program)
__ 26. EOREP (EO Reduction Electricity Program)
__ 27. SAVES (System Awareness Volunteer Electricity Savings)

Figure 7.1   Possible names for an electricity reduction program. (Continued)

__ 28. PARE (Program Awareness & Reduction Electricity)
__ 29. FORE (Focus On Electricity Reduction)
__ 30. ERAP (Electricity Reduction Awareness Program)
__ 31. RED (Reduce Electricity Deployment)
__ 32. ARED (A Reduce Electricity Deployment)
__ 33. PARES (Program Awareness & Reduction Electricity System)
__ 34. ERP (Electricity Reduction Program)
__ 35. EARTH (Electricity Awareness, Reduction, Training, & Handle)
__ 36. EARTH (Electricity Awareness, Reduction, Training, & Heads-up)
__ 37. EARTH (Electricity Awareness, Reduction, Training, & Headway)
__ 38. SEAR (Saving Electricity Awareness & Reduction)
__ 39. SEARS (Saving Electricity Awareness & Reduction System)
__ 40. SEARP (Saving Electricity Awareness & Reduction Program)
__ 41. READ (Reduction Electricity Awareness Deployment)
__ 42. REAP (Reduction Electricity & Awareness Program)
__ 43. ERASE (Energy Reduction Awareness Save Electricity)
__ 44. SEE (Save Electricity Emphasis)
__ 45. SEEP (Save Electricity Emphasis Program)

Figure 7.1 Possible names for an electricity reduction program.

7.3 Generating Ideas

7.3.1 *Brainstorming and Nominal Group Technique*

There are several techniques that stand out here and are often used. Brainstorming, including green lighting, are probably the most used techniques by a team. These techniques have already been covered earlier, so they will not be covered here again. The second most used technique is the nominal group technique (NGT). It consists of four steps or stages.

When to use NGT:

■ When you want to generate a lot of ideas and want to ensure all members participate freely without any influence from other participants.
■ When you want to identify priorities or select a few alternatives for further examination.

Guidelines: First, the facilitator writes the problem, opportunity, or purpose for generating ideas on the whiteboard or somewhere visible to the team or group. Paper or cards (3 × 5) are given to participants. Next, **Step 1: Silent Generation** is accomplished. The team or group members are asked to write four or five ideas on a blank paper in an allotted time (5 to 10 minutes, normally). No one is allowed to talk during this time. Of course, that is why it is named silent generation. In **Step 2: Round Robin**, a scribe or the facilitator starts on one end of the room or conference table and goes sequentially around the room listing one item at a time from each individual on the whiteboard or on a pad on an easel and when the page is full, he/she tapes it to the wall or some other adequate fixture. This going around the room sequentially gives this step its name. The facilitator or scribe keeps going around until people start passing. Then he/she opens it up for anyone who has an idea to provide. All of the ideas are listed so that each team or group member can see. **Step 3: Discussion/Clarification**—Each item is discussed and clarified. Often the person who suggested the item is asked what he or she meant. Discussion continues until the participants all understand each item. **Step 4: Prioritization/Ranking**—Participants are asked to rank their list for their top 10 choices (often 5 is used, depending on the size of the list.) Sometimes cards are given out and the participants write the number of items on them and place the rank in the bottom right of the card. Then the cards are collected and the ranking averages are calculated. The rankings received are placed by each item on the list and then averaged. The highest rankings are circled and only those are ranked again. The highest ranked items are selected. The author prefers using multivoting to prioritize the items instead of ranking. It is similar to ranking and participants feel they have reached a consensus. Not so, when ranking is used.

Tools/Techniques #27: Brainstorming, and #28: Nominal Group Technique

Example: The QVS Energy Team used the NGT to come up with possible names for the electricity reduction program. The energy objective champion had requested the team to find a name or an acronym that everyone could relate to and that sends a powerful message to all QVS employees and contractors. The team used silent generation. Each team member (nine, including the team leader, but not facilitator) was asked to generate six possible names to describe QVS's electricity reduction program. They were given 10 minutes to do so. The facilitator used round robin and added each participant's possible names. The team members identified 54 possible names, but 9 were duplicates. After the discussion and clarification, only 45 remained. The list is shown in Figure 7.1.

In multivoting, you vote for one half of the items each time. The first vote was 23 votes. The second vote was 11, and only on the ones left with the highest number from the first vote. The facilitator had the team multivote (reduced to 22 on first vote and to 5 on second vote). The five that had the highest votes were:

1. Energy Busters
2. Energy Down
7. Power Down
15. EAR (Electricity Awareness Reduction)
42. REAP (Reduction Electricity & Awareness Program)

Tools/Techniques #29: Multivoting

The facilitator mentioned that now they were down to five. "Let's define the criteria we should measure these against so that we select the best one for us." The team leader said, "How about 'easy to understand and to remember' as a criteria. The facilitator said these are two good ones. A team member offered: "Sends the right message." The facilitator thought this was an excellent idea. No other criteria were added. Using the criteria, the team then selected **Power Down** to represent the electricity reduction strategic initiative (Table 7.1).

Tools/Techniques #30: Evaluation Using Criterion Matrix

Table 7.1 Possible Names Evaluation

Possible Names	Easy to Understand (1–5 with 5 being the best)	Easy to Remember (1–5 with 5 being the best)	Sends the Right Message (1–5 with 5 being the best)
1. Energy Busters	3	4	4
2. Energy Down	4	4	5
3. Power Down	5	5	5
4. EAR	3	5	2
5. REAP	3	3	2

7.4 Strategic Planning

7.4.1 Headlight Teams

We discussed headlight teams earlier. Normally they are high-level, cross-functional management teams looking for possible breakthrough improvements. There are several tools or techniques used to gather ideas by these teams. The four most frequently used are brainstorming (already covered), environmental scans, SWOT (strengths, weaknesses, opportunities, threats) analysis, and affinity diagrams. These four tools can be used by any type of team, depending on their needs.

7.4.2 Environmental Scan

This technique is used to scan the environment. It is normally accomplished by a team. The team will brainstorm what it believes will be changes in political and government regulations, what the economy will look like in 10 to 20 years, educational changes and availability, demographics, geographies, and technology. The energy scan is collecting important data for now and the future. It helps develop a SWOT analysis and goals.

Tools/Techniques #31: Environmental Scan

7.4.3 SWOT Analysis

A team is chartered by many organizations to perform a SWOT analysis. It is extremely helpful in strategic planning because it identifies the internal needs and assets and then the external environment. First, the team identifies the strengths of the organization and writes the key points on a sheet titled "strengths." Next, they identified the "weaknesses" of the organization, such as little cash flow, a lot of inexperienced employees, location not close to a railroad, etc.

Next, the team identifies through research, benchmarking, and other techniques to determine the possible opportunities available and write them under "opportunities." Finally, the team identifies the "threats" facing the organization now and in the future. Threats could be increased regulations, slow economy, or price wars to drive up the cost. The SWOT now has each of these four areas listed on one sheet with the key points included under each. The value added by the SWOT analysis is to now focus on strengths and opportunities. What strengths do we possess that can help us get any of the opportunities listed? Then what strengths can help us overcome any weaknesses or minimize any of the threats? This information can be used by the strategic planning team in formulating company goals and objectives and in formulating the organization's vision. SWOT analysis may be used in any organization in a decision-making situation when a desired end-state objective has been established. For example, QVS strategic objective: Reduce electricity usage in 2015 by 10% compared to 2010 usage (Table 7.2).

Tools/Techniques #32: SWOT Analysis

Strengths were used to overcome the weaknesses and grasp the opportunities. The threats will need to be addressed by the QVS utility representative with the utilities and, as problems arise, notify top company management.

7.4.4 Affinity Diagrams

Affinity diagrams are very helpful to teams, such as headlight teams and others, dealing with an abstract subject that is fuzzy at the beginning. The facilitator writes down the subject or topic area where it is visible to the team. Then he/she will give each team member several index cards. The facilitator will ask the team to write any idea on the card that will support or improve the subject or topic area. One idea per index card is the rule. Each

Table 7.2   SWOT Analysis Example: Electricity Reduction

STRENGTHS	WEAKNESSES

• QVS Corp has a strategic objective to reduce electricity usage
 	
• QVS has appointed a Strategic Objective Champion
 	
• A cross-functional energy team has been chartered and put in place
 	
• The team represents most functional areas
   • A team leader has been selected
   • A facilitator has been assigned
 	
• Electricity usage data is readily available
 	
• ISO 50001 EnMS has been selected to be used as a guide in planning, developing and implementing an electricity reduction program
 	
• A name, Power Down, has been selected to represent the program and people can relate
	• Employees are not participating in any energy conservation efforts
	
	• Employees not trained in how to conserve electricity
	
	• The temperature in most facilities has been maintained at a low 72°F and the employees expect it and are used to it
	
	• No analysis has been done as to how to reduce electricity economically
	
	• No policies in place on what an employee can have in his/her workplace and a lot of electrical appliances, such as radios, heaters, fans, microwaves, refrigerators have appeared
	
	• No program signs are in place throughout the buildings
	
	• Some areas have lights and AC on during off shift hours with no mechanism to control them
	
	• There is no building automation system in place

OPPORTUNITIES	THREATS
• Get employees involved in conserving electricity • Develop objectives and targets that will help reduce electricity usage • Identify projects that will help reduce electricity usage that have acceptable payback periods • Can benchmark companies or other organizations that have successfully reduced electricity usage to get ideas • Electric companies can often help with ideas and possibly resources • Can implement IT power management for computers, monitors, laptops • Can get UESC (Utility Energy Services Contracts) to help finance and manage projects	• Cost of electricity may go up • Government regulations may require QVS to purchase more renewable energy • Cost of producing products could increase and be passed on to the customers • Availability of electricity could be lessened if the grid is endangered • Power quality including reliability could be lessened if utility's systems are not maintained properly • Fuel shortages could threaten electricity availability

team member is asked to write as many as he/she can think of that apply somehow to this subject or topic.

The topic area written on the whiteboard by the facilitator was "Reduce Electricity Use Through Conservation Efforts." The responses were placed on a table so the team could go around and place the ones related or similar into an organized pile. Once several were associated with each other, a theme is written on a card in capital letters and placed by the pile. This makes the continuation of placing cards in the most appropriate place much easier. The themes and the ideas under the theme are written and studied by the team. From the themes and selected ideas, an electricity conservation program can be developed. The themes and ideas were as follows:

Theme 1: Employee Turn Off the Lights and Personal Electronics
1. Get employees to turn off lights when they are not in their areas or leaving a room, such as a conference room, break room, etc.
2. Place stickers on light switches reminding employees to turn off lights when not needed.
3. Have employees unplug their personal electronics when they leave at night, on weekends, and on going on a vacation or holiday.
4. Change lights to more efficient ones.

Theme 2: IT Power Management
1. Enable the Energy Star "Sleep Feature" on the monitors to turn off or go to sleep when they have been inactive for a specific time, such as 10 to 15 minutes.
2. Enable the Hibernate or System Stand-By feature on CPUs and laptops so they will reduce power after being inactive for 20 minutes.
3. Use a policy or software to check and ensure the sleep and/or hibernate feature is enabled.
4. Computers, monitors, and laptops turned off at night, weekends, and holidays and when the employee is on vacation.

Theme 3: Inactive Areas
1. Install occupancy sensors in break rooms.
2. Install occupancy sensors in mechanical rooms.
3. Install occupancy sensors in restrooms.
4. Install occupancy sensors in hallways.
5. Install occupancy sensors in copier rooms or spaces.

Theme 4: Advance Meter and Others
1. Install advanced electricity meter and submeters.
2. Hook up Building Automation System to electric system to turn off lights when not in use.
3. Make hot and cold aisles in data center.
4. Balance air flow in all the rooms.

Theme 5: Reduce Office Paper Use
1. Use duplex printing.
2. Use more electronic files and emailing.
3. Utilize used paper for memos.
4. Use network printers more.

Theme 6: Recycle
1. Recycle paper and paper products.
2. Recycle aluminum cans and glass bottles and plastics.
3. Recycle end-of-life electronics and imaging equipment.

Tools/Techniques #33: Affinity Diagram

The energy team used the information from the affinity diagram to develop the electricity conservation program PowerPoint® presentation that was sent to all QVS employees and contractors.

7.5 Gathering Data

7.5.1 Check Sheets

A check sheet should be used when there is a need for data, which do not have to be collected in a large amount and do not have to be random in nature, for example, if a parking lot was going to be restriped, with the objective of increasing the number of parking spaces. Presently, all of the spaces are for full-sized vehicles. A check sheet would allow the team to capture by day, for a week, the number of small cars that park in the parking lot. Then by analyzing this data, the team can have the parking lot restriped to allow a sufficient number of small spaces, thus, increasing the overall number of parking spaces. The design depends on the data to be collected. Normally, the collection method

Table 7.3 Teamwork Observation Check Sheet

First Names	PLAN		DO	Remarks
	Speaking	Disagreement	Doing (+) (−)	

is done manually. The check sheet would have the categories listed for days of the week and a check mark would be made whenever the measured event happened. For example, earlier, we used this check sheet in Table 7.3 to collect data.

Tools/Techniques #34: Check Sheet

7.5.2 Company's Information Systems

QVS, like all big companies, has numerous computer IT systems. From Human Resources Systems to Preventative Maintenance Systems to Accounting Systems, QVS has systems in the most functional areas and some in cross-functional areas. Reports can be retrieved easily. The data can be useful in the team's problem-solving or opportunity-searching sessions.

7.5.3 Research Internet

The Internet with search engines like Google, Ask, and others is an invaluable research tool for obtaining data for problem solving, comparisons, and benchmarking. It is a best practice to keep a record of useful web sites for certain data so teams can easily access them. Today, you can find almost any subject on the Internet.

7.5.4 *Surveys*

Surveys are valuable tools to obtain information when there is no data available. Areas, such as customers' satisfaction, employee satisfaction, or leadership effectiveness, can be easily measured by this tool. To get a metrics, periodic surveys would be necessary and the results posted on a graph for each survey. Targets for the above could be established as to what level you desire to obtain. The scales of surveys are outlined below.

Sometimes a satisfaction scale of 1 to 10 is used, with 1 being *Not at All* and 10 being *Completely*. The other numbers are not defined, but they are imagined by the participants as increasing degrees of satisfaction.

It is a best practice to add an importance scale with the different scales above when importance to the surveyor is very useful. This is especially important in measuring customs or employee satisfaction.

Likert Type Format

The scale can range from 5 to 7 with 5 being the absolute minimum. Under a 5 scale means a loss of significant reliability. The seven scale has a little more reliability than the five.

To Extend Scale	Not At All	To A Very Little Extent	To A Little Extent	To A Moderate Extent	To A Fairly Large Extent	To A Great Extent	To A Very Great Extent
	1	2	3	4	5	6	7
Frequency Scale	Never	Sometimes	Usually	Almost Always	Always		
	1	2	3	4	5		
Agreement Scale	Strongly Disagree	Moderately Disagree	Slightly Disagree	Neither Agree Or Disagree	Slightly Agree	Moderately Agree	Strongly Agree
	1	2	3	4	5	6	7
Satisfaction Scale	Extremely Dissatisfied	Moderately Dissatisfied	Slightly Dissatisfied	Neutral	Slightly Satisfied	Moderately Satisfied	Extremely Satissfied
	1	2	3	4	5	6	7
Reverse Answers	Very Satisfied	Moderately Satisfied	Slightly Satisfied	Neither Satisfied or Dissatisfied	Slightly Dissatisfied	Moderately Satisfied	Very Satisfied
	1	2	3	4	5	6	7
A Different Twist	Very Poor	Poor	Neutral	Good	Very Good		
	1	2	3	4	5		

Sometimes a 6 scale is added such as not observed, not-applicable, out-standing, etc.

The above scales are good for feedback on attributes such as timeliness, competency, courteous, etc.

The importance scale may look like this:

Importance Scale	Not Important	Somewhat Important	Important	Very Important			
	1	2	3	4			

This loses some realiability but may be a little clearer than going to five.

	Very Important	Unimportant	Half and Half	Important	Very Important		
	1	2	3	4	5		

Often scales such as below are used in importance performance.

Extremely Important	10	9	8	7	6	5	4	3	2	1

Tools/Techniques #35: Surveys

7.5.5 Focus Groups

Focus groups have several usages that make them a valuable tool for companies. When a company needs perceptions about a new concept, products, or services, a focus group is an excellent way to get current and quick data and information. Perceptions about an existing product or service can be obtained and, in this case, perceptions are actually reality. Normally, a focus group consists of five to eight people (the number varies depending on the groups, categories, or elements that will be covered) who have some knowledge of the company or similar products and services. They are invited (usually by letter) to attend a meeting (approximately four hours in length) at the location that has a conference room with a two-way mirror. The two-way mirror allows management, marketing, sales, administrative, and production people to observe the meeting without bothering the focus group members. The focus group has both an assigned moderator and a reporter. The moderator is like a team leader/facilitator and runs the meeting. He/she prepares the agenda prior to the meeting and reviews with the company's organization (the individual who requested the focus group) to assure agreement of the approach and content of meeting. The moderator can be from the company, but often is not. Thus, any bias is eliminated and the questions aren't self-answered in their statements. The reporter (more of a notetaker) is normally silent while taking minutes, but can help in writing things on a poster, whiteboard, or on an easel. Minutes should be published within five days after the meeting while the information is still on everyone's mind.

The focus group members are often paid a small amount for their time, which includes transportation costs. If not paid, something should be given to them as a remembrance, such as a pen, bracelet, plaque, or company emblems.

As mentioned earlier, focus groups can be used for other usages. If you have developed a hypothesis and desire to pretest it, a focus group would be an excellent method to do so. This application is the basis of much of the market research accomplished. Focus groups also can provide a good assessment of advertising or promotional concepts, programs, or ideas. It can be used to get interim or immediate feedback on how things are going, thus, providing the important check phase for continuous improvement.

Tools/Techniques #36: Focus Groups

7.6 Evaluating Ideas

7.6.1 Multivoting

Multivoting allows you to prioritize a large list of items down to three to five. Then it is best to establish criteria to measure these remaining items again to determine the first choice. This technique was demonstrated when Power Down was selected by the QVS energy team above. Multivoting has a unique characteristic in that it is fast and also the participants feel that the team or group reached consensus, even though technically they did not.

7.6.2 Pareto Analysis

The Pareto chart is named after Vilfredo Pareto, a nineteenth-century economist who stated that a large share of wealth is owned by a small percentage of the population (80% owned by 20% of the people: the 80–20 rule). He used this principle in explaining and obtaining taxes. This basic principle translates well into all kinds of problems. A Pareto chart is a series of bars whose heights reflect the frequency or impact of problems. The bars are arranged in descending order of height from left to right. This means the categories represented by the tall bars on the left are relatively more significant than those on the right. This bar chart is used to separate the "vital few" from the "trivial many." These charts are based on the Pareto principle, which states that 80% of the problems come from 20% of the causes.

When is a Pareto chart used?

A Pareto chart breaks a big problem down into smaller pieces, identifies the most significant factors that show where to focus one's efforts, and facilitates better utilization of limited resources. The chart can answer the following questions:

What are the largest issues or problems facing our team or business? (Dr. Kano, a JUSE (Japanese Union of Scientific Engineers) counselor calls the large or largest bar: The Fat Rabbit. Fat Rabbit, the largest bar, is the one that presents the most opportunity.

What 20% of sources, issues, or problems are causing 80% of the problems?

Where should we focus our efforts, to decrease the fat rabbit, and then come back and decrease the next fattest rabbit to achieve the greatest improvements and obtain continuous improvement?

When should a Pareto chart be used?

A Pareto chart is an excellent chart to use when the process you are evaluating produces data that are broken down into categories and you can count the number of times each category occurs. A Pareto diagram puts data in a hierarchical order, which shows the most significant problems to be corrected first. Making problem-solving decisions isn't the only use of the Pareto principle, since Pareto charts convey information in a way that enables you to see clearly the choices that should be made; they can be used to prioritize for many practical applications. They are excellent to use in presentations to management because they show the opportunities for improvement in a prioritized manner.

To create a Pareto chart:

To create on Excel®, go to Google and type "create a Pareto chart on Excel." It will give you immediate instructions. Also, there are companies that have tools available that will create them for a small fee after a short trial period.

To prepare for creating a Pareto chart, decide on the categories, then gather the frequency data, calculate the percentage, put the categories into descending order (highest to lowest) and then determine the cumulative sum.

The Pareto in Figure 7.2 shows that during a two-month period, the distribution line was interrupted 70 times. The most interruptions were from lightning (25) and second from trees. This analysis directed the utilities to look at the surge protection on the distribution lines and the grounding as well. For the trees, the utility looked at the lines and cut away any limbs close to the distribution lines. Each incident where the cables were cut to identify the root causes, an action plan to eliminate the causes was implemented. Lightning, trees, and cable cut interruptions accounted for 78.6% of all the interruptions.

Tools/Techniques #37: Pareto Analysis

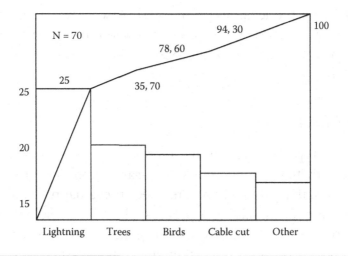

Figure 7.2   Pareto of electricity interruptions.

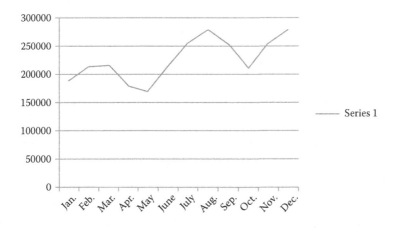

Figure 7.3   Metrics: kWh used by month.

7.6.3 Metrics

Metrics are excellent tools to track how well you are doing presently and toward meeting goals. Metrics are a graphical representation that drives us to action and improvement (Figure 7.3).

7.6.4 Criterion Matrix and Ranking

Remember, when you have a long list from brainstorming, affinity diagram, or nominal group technique, use multivoting down to the top three choices. Then develop the criteria, such as acceptable, feasible, suitable, timely, quality, cost, and others that you desire to achieve. Assign a scale 1 to 5 with 1 being the least and 5 the best. Also, Low, Medium, and High can work in a lot of cases. Measure each of the top three versus the criteria to guarantee that you have the best choice with the highest rated choice possible.

7.6.5 Flow Chart

A flow chart is a type of diagram that represents a process, showing, in sequence, the activities and decisions necessary to produce a product, service, or information. Flow charts are used in evaluating, analyzing, documenting, designing, or managing a process. Flow charts help us visualize a process by showing us specifically what is going on within. They help us identify bottlenecks, delays, duplication, and other waste. They are an essential tool in Lean and Six Sigma and helpful to us in managing the processes applicable to ISO 50001 EnMS (Environmental Management System). The flow process chart was introduced by Frank Gilbreth in 1921. There are other titled flow charts, such as strategic, data flow, etc., that have other specific uses, but the flow process chart is the one most beneficial to a team. Teams establish objectives. What is the process? See Figure 7.4.

Tools/Techniques #38: Flow Chart

7.7 Analyzing

7.7.1 Fishbone Diagram

In January 2012, the kWh usage for year 2011 had only decreased by a little over 1%. The team realized that only the conservation program had been fully implemented, but expected more reduction than what occurred. They went back and reviewed their past findings. In developing the electricity conservation program, the energy team wanted to know why conservation had not worked in the past. The team decided that a fishbone diagram may help to identify the potential root causes. The fishbone diagram is the most used cause and effect diagram.

The fishbone diagram can be used for identifying potential root causes or opportunities. Most of the time it is for identifying potential root causes. The effect or problem is placed in the box on the right. Next, major bones, usually four, but can be five or six depending on the complexity of the problem are placed in boxes. The bones can be selected from a list of possibilities. The list is people, process, policy, procedures, manpower, money, methods, management, technology, and environment. Once the major bones are selected, draw the fishbone with the effect to the right; the major bones split above and below a center line. The small bones are possible root causes and they are placed on either side of the major bone that it most closely associates with, and an arrow points toward the major bone. The flow is from the potential root cause to the major bone down to the center line and into the effect (Figure 7.5).

The potential root causes can be determined through brainstorming, NGT, or having the team place its possible ones onto a Post-it® note and then placing them on a whiteboard with the effect and major bones drawn onto it. The JUSE counselors state there are two things to remember. First, the fish always swim to the right. Second, a skinny fish is not good. In other

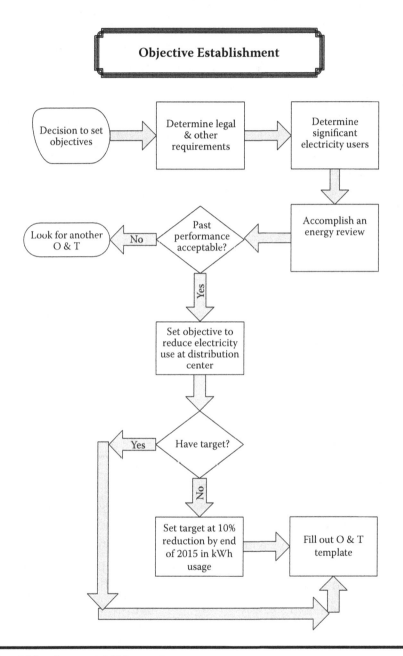

Figure 7.4 Objectives establishment process.

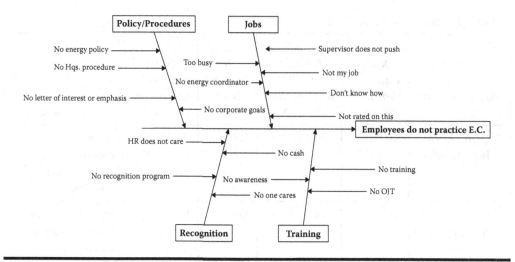

Figure 7.5 Fishbone diagram: Employees do not practice energy conservation.

words, identify as many potential root causes as you can, then the probability of having the root cause listed on the fishbone has increased.

Once the potential causes have been identified, the team should circle the ones that seem possible root causes and place and evaluate using a root cause matrix. After the root cause evaluation method, use data to verify the root cause. Paretos, double Paretos, histograms, and frequency diagrams are the most popular in verifying a root cause.

The team found several root causes. Lack of training and leadership in this area were the biggest root causes. If these were fixed, the problem would go away and an energy conservation program would be in place. This fishbone is a skinny one, but still helpful. When the team did it, it was fat, but made skinny to include in this book.

7.7.2 Root Cause Matrix

First, have the team review the fishbone and circle the ones they feel are the most probable of being a root cause. The next step is to bring the circled ones and place onto a root cause matrix (Table 7.4).

Tools/Techniques #39: Root Cause Evaluation Matrix

Next, the selected root causes need to be verified, if possible, with data or research. Paretos, double Paretos, graphs, histograms, and frequency diagrams are often used to verify a root cause. Many times just research can

Table 7.4   Root Cause Matrix

Potential Root Cause	Root Cause or Symptom (RC or S)	Eliminates or Minimizes Large Part of the Problem (Yes or No)	Under Our Control (Yes or No)	Is Feasible (Cost Is Not Excessive?) (Yes or No)	Remarks
1. Don't know how to save	RC	Yes	Yes	Yes	Need an electricity conservation training
2. No management emphasis	RC	Yes	Yes	Yes	Training can be sent by management. A policy letter can be sent by management.
3. No awareness	S	Maybe	Yes	Yes	#1 above will correct this
4. Personal electric items considered a benefit	S	Yes	Yes	Yes	#2 above can solve this situation if this is covered in a management policy letter
5. IT power management not practiced	RC	Yes	Yes	Yes	IT power management is one of the solutions
6. No energy policy or procedures	RC	Yes	Yes	Yes	Should be done
7.					
8.					
9.					
10.					
11.					
12.					
13.					
14.					

verify the root cause. For example, checking the policy book and not finding a management policy on electricity conservation and on personal electric items that can be used in the workplace would verify these two.

7.7.3 Benchmarking

The PDCA **(Plan–Do–Check–Act)** model for benchmarking looks a little bit different than the Deming wheel due to the specific process and steps necessary to be successful. Like the Deming wheel, it can be turned again and again for continuous improvement (Figure 7.6).

The Plan is the same, but the Do portion, you are collecting data about their company or organization and about your targeted process for improvement. In this step, you also select the performance measure to be improved and set a target for improvement. Analyze is necessary because seldom are the processes benchmarked exactly the same. You must determine what is it that makes their process perform better than yours. Then, you must adapt these improvements to your process. Also, ensure all who need to know are informed and training, if needed, is given. And, you should monitor performance for a while to make sure that it is improving as expected. Top management commitment, teamwork, measurement, coordination, process analysis, selling solution(s), action plans, implementing, monitoring, and taking action are all needed to make benchmarking a success and not just a tour of someone's facility.

The U.S. Department of Energy has a Commercial Building Energy Consumption Survey (CBECS) that enables benchmarking against other facilities of a similar type. They include office buildings, distribution centers, retail stores, grocery stores, and others. They do not presently include plants. Let's benchmark QVS's headquarters building to determine its energy units

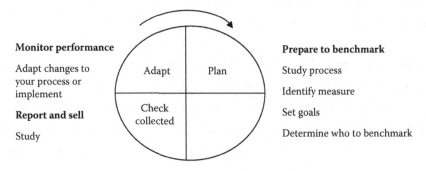

Figure 7.6 Benchmarking model.

or EUIs (energy use intensities) that is the energy intensity indicator (kWh/ square feet). The benchmark data also gives you an indication of the numerous variables that impact energy consumption. (See buildingsdatabook.eren. doe.gov/CBECS.aspx)

Benchmarking Data into the CBECS

Location: West–Southcentral
    Climate: Mild
Building Type: Office

Characteristics:

Building Vintage: 1980 to 1989
Square Footage: 50,000–100,000 sq. ft.
    Ownership: Corporation
Floors: 4 to 5
In a Multibuilding Complex: No

HVAC System:

Main Cooling Equipment: Packaged Units, Chillers
Main Heating Equipment: Boilers
Building Envelope: Percent Class: 11 to 25%
Building Shape: Rectangle with courtyard
Main Roof Construction: Buildup
Operations: Hours per week: 61 to 84
Number of computers: 1,000 to 2,499
Number of Servers: 500 to 999
Use of Generator: Backup
Laundry: Offsite

The CBECS requires 18 variables (in italics) to benchmark with other similar facilities. The QVS headquarters building electricity intensity is 48.76. An intensity of 100 (kWh/55,000 square feet) would be very high. The QVS intensity is good and projects costing many dollars will need to be spent to reduce it. An electricity conservation program alone will not reduce it 10% in five years.

Tools/Techniques #40: Benchmarking

7.8 Selling Your Solution

7.8.1 Rate of Return or Payback Period

Rate of return is very useful. You pay money to purchase something and then you get cash flow back—The gain or loss on your investment over a period you predetermine, usually shown as a percentage increase over your initial investment cost. This is an excellent indicator of how well you invested your money. However, for projects, payback period is more commonly used because it shows whether you should make the investment in the first place.

Let's take the change from T-12 lights to T-5s in a facility. First, what is the cost? Next, what will it save each year? How many years and months does it take with the projected savings to pay back the cost of doing this? This is known as the payback period. Let's look at this example further. The cost is $110,000 to replace all of the old T-12 lights. Lighting amounts to 22% of our total electricity cost. It is estimated that the T-5s are 10% more efficient. Then, $9 \times .22 = .198$ or for each year, 22% − 19.8% = 2.2% savings. Checking this: $.22 \times .10 = .022 = 2.2\%$ each year. The facility's annual electricity cost is $227,221.08. A 2.2% annual savings will result in a savings of $4,998.86 a year. The payback is simply calculated as $110,000/$4,998.86 per year = 22 years. In other words, it would take a company 22 years to pay back the investment. Fortunately, the payback period is much smaller because the T-5s are much more efficient.

What is an acceptable payback period? In most cases, company or organization heads are willing, without much hesitation, to support projects with payback of three years or less. The federal government for environmental or energy reductions are allowing up to 10 years payback. If you have a corporate goal of achieving a certain percent reduction, management will normally be more willing to fund projects over a three-year payback and usually up to seven or eight years.

Tools/Techniques #41: Payback Period

7.8.2 The Solution Matrix

The solution matrix is designed so that you can place possible solutions in a simple matrix and evaluate them as the most effective (Table 7.5).

Tools/Techniques #42: Solutions Evaluation Matrix

Table 7.5   Solution Evaluation Matrix

Possible Solution	Easy to Implement? Yes or No	Cost? High, Medium, or Low	Effective? Yes or No	Minimizes Root Cause? Yes or No	Management Will Support? Yes or No	Solves a Large Part of Problem or Opportunity? Yes or No
1. Develop an energy awareness training and send to all employees	Yes	Low	Yes	Yes	Yes	Yes
2. Energy team develops an energy policy, gets management to approve, and communicates to everyone	Yes	Low	Yes	Yes	Yes	Yes
3. Implement an IT power management program	Yes	Low	Yes	Yes	Yes	Yes
4.						
5.						

7.9 Facilitator Exercises

1. What technique is not used for collecting data or information?
   __ A. Brainstorming
   __ B. Force Field Analysis
   __ C. Affinity Diagram
   __ D. Nominal Group Technique
2. Which of these techniques is used to develop data for an abstract subject of whom you know little about?
   __ A. Brainstorming
   __ B. Force Field Analysis
   __ C. Affinity Diagram
   __ D. Nominal Group Technique

3. Which tool or technique would you use to measure customer satisfaction?
   __ A. Brainstorming
   __ B. Flowchart
   __ C. Surveys
   __ D. Nominal Group Technique
4. Which tool helps us identify process and output metrics?
   __ A. Brainstorming
   __ B. Flowchart
   __ C. Surveys
   __ D. Nominal Group Technique
5. Which tool helps us sell our solutions to management?
   __ A. Brainstorming
   __ B. Force Field Analysis
   __ C. Root Cause Evaluation Matrix
   __ D. Nominal Group Technique

(*See answers in Appendix 1.*)

Chapter 8

Objectives and Targets Development and Action Plans

8.1 Objectives and Targets

Objectives are something that all of us set so we can accomplish something better in either our personal or work life. The objective is simply a desired state or condition that is intended to be achieved by someone or a team, group, or organization. Often people use goals and objectives interchangeably, but they are not. Goals are long range, from 5 to 20 years out. They are written in very broad terms. Goals usually support an organization's vision or policy. Objectives are short range, usually one to two years in duration. They are more specific and support the organization's goals.

Examples include:

Goal 1
Increase Sales Objective 1: Increase sales in each of our five divisions by 10% each year for the next five years.

Goal 2
Increase Customer Satisfaction Objective 2: Develop a customer's satisfaction measurement system.

Goal 3
Be in Compliance with all Legal Requirements Objective 3: Maintain the Environmental Management System and evaluate compliance at least annually.

The three objective statements represent the three possible types of objectives. Objective 1 is to "**improve**" something (sales, in this example). Objective 2 is to "**develop or research**" something. In this case, a customer satisfaction measurement system. This type of objective can be a feasibility study to determine the need for something. An example would be determining the feasibility of using surveys to measure customer satisfaction versus focus groups or interviews. Study or research something could be an objective in this category. Objective 3 represents the third objective, which is to "**maintain**" something. In this case, it is compliance with all legal requirements. Organizations make improvements and then they should put in place actions to maintain these improvements or gains. Often objectives are developed to identify what actions are needed and then implemented. Normally, all business objectives are for one of these three types.

Targets are helpful with objectives in that they tell specifically what is to be addressed or needs to be done to achieve the objective. It is helpful when the targets are written to tell "how much is going to be achieved." Targets for the three objectives could look like this:

Goal 1
Increase Sales Objective 1: Increase sales in each of our five divisions by 10% each year for the next five years. **Target 1**: Using 2% increase in staff, achieve 10% annual increase in sales by more clients' and potential clients' onsite visits.

Goal 2
Increase Customer Satisfaction Objective 2: Develop a customer's satisfaction measurement system. **Target 2**: Formulate a customer's satisfaction survey by a specific date that measures both the customer's satisfaction and importance of several vital critical performance areas.

Goal 3
Be in Compliance with all Legal Requirements Objective 3: Maintain the Environmental Management System (EMS) and evaluate compliance at least annually. **Target 3**: Keep the EMS team in place, meet quarterly, and complying with the ISO 14001 EMS standards.

The targets should be measurable and actions to achieve them should be outlined in an action plan. The targets specifically tell what is to be done or the focus for the objective. It is often that the objectives and targets (O&Ts) are mentioned together, such as in ISOs standards.

8.2 Making Targets SMART

SMART is an acronym that means specific, measurable, actionable, relevant, and time framed.

Specific: Great goals or objectives are well-defined, specific, and focused. Focus creates a powerful action. The moment you focus on a goal, your goal becomes like a magnet, pulling you, your team, and the organization's resources toward it. The more focused your goals, the more team and organizational power you generate.

Measurable: An objective or goal without a measurable outcome is like a basketball game without a scoreboard or scorekeeper. Numbers are an essential part of our business. Keep the key performance indicators current and visible to all.

Actionable/Attainable: Far too often teams establish objectives and targets beyond their reach. Teams should dream big, but keep one foot firmly based in reality. Make them stretch, but make them realistic. Ensure that the objective, target, and/or goals are actionable. Ensure there are actions that can be done to achieve them.

Relevant: Achievable objectives, targets, and/or goals are based on the current conditions and realities. To be relevant means to be needed to achieve and further the team or organization's goals.

Time Framed/Time-Based: The objectives, targets, and goals should be time-based to ensure they are achieved in a reasonable time period.

Objective, target, and goal setting is the process of deciding what you want to accomplish and devising a plan to achieve the result you desire.

Target 1: Set the temperature thermostat to 76 degrees instead of 72 degrees in the summertime. It is **Specific** (tells one exactly what to do). **Measurable**? Yes. One can look at the thermostat to determine the setting to see if it is on 78 degrees or not. **Attainable/Actionable**? Yes, one only has to change the degrees. However, prior to this action, it would be important to explain to everyone why you are doing this, what you hope to achieve, and the importance of them in supporting and achieving the objective. Otherwise you will have a rebellion. **Relevant**? Absolutely. This change will save a lot of kWhs and lower the electricity usage. **Time-Based/Time Framed**: No, it is not. There is no indication of when this will be done and how long. To make it time framed, add a date to change the thermostat on a specific date or period of time, for example, "during Fiscal Year 2014."

Tools/Techniques #43: Making Objectives SMART

8.3 Objective and Target (O&T) Template and Developing Action Plans

It is a best practice to develop an objective and target template that can be filled in for each new established objective and target. An objective and target template similar to one that several government organizations used is shown in Figure 8.1. It has the O&T information at the top and an action plan at the bottom.

8.3.1 Explanation on How to Fill out the O&T Template

Follow these basic steps:

Facility Name: Enter the name of the facility and number and address.

Document Number: Place the objective and target number here. The number starts with OT for objective and target, the calendar year (last two digits), and then the no. 1 for the first one and then numbered in sequence for each new objective and target. For example, the third O&T developed for 2014 would be numbered OT-14-03.

Objective: Type the objective as developed.

Target: Type the target as developed.

Initiation Date: The date the O&T was developed.

Anticipated Completion Date: The date you expect the actions below to all be accomplished.

Actual Completion Date: The actual date all of the actions below were completed.

Use the appropriate title depending on whether this is energy, environmental, or safety O&T:

FACILITY NAME			DOCUMENT #:		
OBJECTIVE:					
TARGET:					
INITIATION DATE:					
ANTICIPATED COMPLETION DATE		ACTUAL COMPLETION DATE	<Enter actual date>		
ELECTRICITY HIGH USERS ADDRESSED:					
BASELINE:			MONITORED or MEASURED:		

Energy Action Plan:

#	Required Action	Person Responsible	Target Date	Status	Comment
	List each step needed to ensure O&T is met.	Enter a name.	Enter the date the team expects THIS step to be done.	Enter Red, Yellow or Green.	Enter the status of this step and record date of this status beside it. (4/4/11) Completed on (4/4/11) Management has not yet responded, extending target date by 10 days to 4/18/11.
1					
2					
3					
4					
5					
6					
7					
8					
9					
10					
11					
12					

Figure 8.1 An object and target (O&T) template.

Energy–Electricity High Users: The significant electricity users addressed by the O&T, such as heaters, boilers, air conditioners, motors, computers, servers, etc.

Environmental–Significant Aspects: List the significant aspects that this will address, such as chemicals, oxygen, oil, hazardous materials, etc.

Safety–Hazards: List the significant safety or health hazards that this O&T will impact or address.

Baseline: A year's worth of data that current situations can be compared to determine, if and how much improvement, if any, has been achieved. (The baseline does not have to be last year, it can be farther away if deemed appropriate.)

Monitored or Measured: After the O&T has been completed, check if this needs to be measured periodically. Examples include such items as recycling, calibration, etc.

Action plans tell **What** is going to be done, **Where**, by **Whom**, and **When**. They do not specifically tell why or how. The stoplight measures can be added to the action plan so, at a glimpse, one can tell if the objective is on target or track or if some action needs to be taken.

The first column is Required Action. These are the actions or steps of what is needed to be done. The **What**.

The second column is Person Responsible. Add the name of the person who is going to do this step. The **Who**.

The third column is Target Date. Add the date you desire and expect this action to be completed. The **When**.

The fourth column is Status. Enter Red if this activity is behind schedule (target date) or is not going well due to lack of resources or some other situation causing delays, such as lack of approval. Enter Yellow if the activity is a little behind schedule (target date), but you feel you can catch up in the near future. Enter green if the activity is on or ahead of schedule (target date).

The fifth column is Comments. Add any pertinent comments that you deem important that explain any problems or actions to be taken in the near future.

8.4 Establishing Objectives and Targets

Prior to establishing an objective or target, other preparations or information and data gathering have been done. In strategic planning, the customer's voice has been reviewed and analyzed, the mission statement established along with a vision that shows where the company or organization wants to be in 20 years, a strengths–weaknesses–opportunities–threats (SWOT) analysis and an environmental scan conducted, values and/or guiding principles for guiding everyone's daily actions, key result areas determined, and goals established. Now the Strategic Council or Top Management Council is ready to establish objectives. How about an energy team? What do they need to know prior to establishing objectives?

The team needs to know that management is committed to reducing energy and following ISO 50001 EnMS (Environmental Management System) standards. What is the scope of our EnMS, the energy policy and goals established by management, what are our major energy users, and what are the legal and other requirements. With this knowledge, the team can start establishing objectives and targets. Remember, the O&Ts can be of three types of objectives discussed above.

To reach an energy reduction goal, several improved O&Ts will be needed. To ensure latest technology or techniques are being used, research or feasibility studies will be needed.

After the team is mature and in the performing stage, O&Ts to maintain the processes and to continuously improve will need to be established and implemented.

Examples of objectives include:

Category 1: Improve
1. Install occupancy sensors in the bathrooms, break rooms, and other areas of infrequent use.
2. Install T-5 lights in the distribution center replacing the T-13 lights.
3. Design and implement an IT power management program.
4. Plan and implement an office paper-reduction program.
5. Install large ceiling fans to reduce natural gas usage from running the heaters in the distribution center.

Category 2: Research/Feasibility/Study/Develop O&Ts
1. Determine the feasibility of using solar energy applications for each facility.

2. Determine the feasibility of adding additional electric meters to increase our knowledge of electricity users.
3. Determine the benefits for keeping the hot air from joining the cold air in the data center on the way back to the air conditioner to be recooled.
4. Develop a training plan for all personnel to meet the ISO 50001 EnMS standard.
5. Develop an energy awareness training for management, employees, and contractors.
6. Develop a communications plan.
7. Develop an emergency preparedness and response plan.

Category 3: Maintain
1. Ensure EnMS team meets at least four times a year and has an agenda using PAL (purpose, agenda, limited).
2. Perform a self-inspection this year and use a CAR for any nonconformance items.
3. Maintain at least six EMS team members and ensure all have received EMS awareness training.
4. Perform a Legal Requirements Compliance Evaluation in October 2014.
5. Develop at least one O&T each year and implement.
6. Monitor the items requiring review each quarter at an EMS team meeting.

Let's now develop an O&T and action plan.

Facility Name: Enter the name of the facility and number and address—***Distribution Center, QVS Inc., Gun Barrel City, Texas***

Document Number: Place the O&T number here. The number starts with OT for objective and target, the calendar year (last two digits), and then the no. 1 for the first one and then numbered in sequence for each new objective and target. For example, the third O&T developed for 2014 would be numbered OT-14-03—*OT-114-011*.

Objective: Type the objective as developed. Develop a training plan for all personnel to meet the ISO 50001 EnMS standard.

Target: Type the target as developed—***Complete a coordinated and approved training plan for 2015 by December 15, 2014***

Initiation Date: The date the O&T was developed—***February 7, 2014***

Anticipated Completion Date: The date you expect the actions below will all be accomplished—***December 15, 2014***

Actual Completion Date: The actual date all of the actions below were completed—***Complete after it has been done.***

Use the appropriate title:

XXXEnergy–Electricity High Users: The significant electricity users addressed by the O&T, such as heaters, boilers, air conditioners, motors, computers, servers, etc.—***Training plan would include an energy awareness training for all employees and competency training for the employees that need the training in order to perform their jobs in a safe, competent manner.***

Environmental–Significant Aspects: List the significant aspects that this will address, such as chemicals, oxygen, oil, hazardous materials, etc.—***N/A***.

Safety–Hazards: List the significant safety or health hazards that this O&T will impact or address—***N/A***.

Baseline: A year's worth of data that current situations can be compared to determine if and how much improvement, if any, has been achieved—***Baseline is that there is no present training plan.***

Monitored or Measured: After the O&T has been completed, check if this needs to be measured periodically. Examples include such items as recycling, calibration, etc.—***The training plan execution including keeping training records for all employees will need to be accomplished.***

Action plans tell **What** is going to be done, **Where**, by **Whom**, and **When**. They do not specifically tell why or how. The stoplight measures can be added to the action plan so, at a glimpse, one can tell if the objective is on target or track or if some action needs to be taken.

The first column is the Required Action: These are the actions or steps of what is needed to be done—The **What**

Required Action				
1. Identify the people who need awareness training				
2. Develop the awareness training				
3. Send the PowerPoint training to all employees				

4. Track the participants who completed the awareness training				
5. Identify who needs competence training & what type of training or education				
6. Develop the competence training				
7. Schedule and give the competence training				
8. Keep current employees' training records				

The second column: Person responsible. Add the name of the person who is going to do this step—The **Who**

Required Action	Person(s) Responsible			
1. Identify the people who need awareness training	John Brown, EnMS team leader			
2. Develop the awareness training	John Brown, EnMS team leader			
3. Send the PowerPoint® training to all employees	John Brown, EnMS team leader			
4. Track the participants who completed the awareness training	John Brown, EnMS team leader			
5. Identify who needs competence training & what type of training or education	Jim Jones, Shop supervisor			
6. Develop the competence training	Jim Jones, Shop supervisor			

Required Action	Person(s) Responsible			
7. Schedule and give the competence training	Jim Jones, Shop supervisor John Brown, EnMS team leader			
8. Keep current employees' training records	Barbara Woods, Training manager			

The third column: Target date. Enter the date you desire and expect this action to be completed—The **When**

Required Action	Person(s) Responsible	Target Dates		
1. Identify the people who need awareness training	John Brown, EnMS team leader	April 15, 2014		
2. Develop the awareness training	John Brown, EnMS team leader	July 12, 2014		
3. Send the PowerPoint® training to all employees	John Brown, EnMS team leader	July 31, 2014		
4. Track the participants who completed the awareness training	John Brown, EnMS team leader	Dec. 15, 2014		
5. Identify who needs competence training & what type of training or education	Jim Jones, Shop supervisor	Aug. 15, 2014		
6. Develop the competence training	Jim Jones, Shop supervisor	Oct. 5, 2014		

7. Schedule and give the competence training	Jim Jones, Shop supervisor John Brown, EnMS team leader	Dec. 5, 2014		
8. Keep current employees' training records	Barbara Woods, Training manager	Dec. 15, 2014		

The fourth column: Status. Enter Red if this activity is behind schedule (target date) or is not going well due to lack of resources or some other situation causing delays, such as lack of approval. Enter Yellow if the activity is a little behind schedule (target date), but you feel you can catch up in the near future. Enter Green if the activity is on or ahead of schedule (target date).

Required Action	Person(s) Responsible	Target Dates	Status (Red, Yellow, or Green)	
1. Identify the people who need awareness training	John Brown, EnMS team leader	April 15, 2014	Green	
2. Develop the awareness training	John Brown, EnMS team leader	July 12, 2014		
3. Send the PowerPoint® training to all employees	John Brown, EnMS team leader	July 31, 2014		
4. Track the participants who completed the awareness training	John Brown, EnMS team leader	Dec. 15, 2014		
5. Identify who needs competence training & what type of training or education	Jim Jones, Shop supervisor	Aug. 15, 2014		

6. Develop the competence training	Jim Jones, Shop supervisor	Oct. 5, 2014		
7. Schedule and give the competence training	Jim Jones, Shop supervisor John Brown, EnMS team leader	Dec. 5, 2014		
8. Keep current employees' training records	Barbara Woods, Training manager	Dec. 15, 2014		

The fifth column: Comments. Enter any pertinent comments that you deem important that explains any problems or actions to be taken in the near future.

Required Action	Person(s) Responsible	Target Dates	Status (Red, Yellow, or Green)	Comments
1. Identify the people who need awareness training	John Brown, EnMS team leader	April 15, 2014	Green	John has completed required action no. 1 on Feb 8, 2012
2. Develop the awareness training	John Brown, EnMS team leader	July 12, 2014		Not completed yet, but in progress
3. Send the PowerPoint® training to all employees	John Brown, EnMS team leader	July 31, 2014		
4. Track the participants who completed the awareness training	John Brown, EnMS team leader	Dec. 15, 2014		

5. Identify who needs competence training & what type of training or education	Jim Jones, Shop supervisor	Aug. 15, 2014		
6. Develop the competence training	Jim Jones, Shop supervisor	Oct. 5, 2014		
7. Schedule and give the competence training	Jim Jones, Shop supervisor John Brown, EnMS team leader	Dec. 5, 2014		
8. Keep current employees' training records	Barbara Woods, Training manager	Dec. 15, 2014		

All of the information for the O&T Template has been completed and can be copied and pasted into the template. Individuals and teams can implement objectives and targets through a relatively new technique introduced during the past few years in Japan (Toyota kata). The action plan is a part of the problem-solving process.

Tools/Techniques #44: Action Plan

8.5 Achieving Team Results Using Toyota Kata

A kata is a routine or pattern that one takes to go from where he/she is to a targeted and desired condition. We have a starting point and know where we want to go, but don't know the way or steps we need to take to get to the target condition. We have to experiment and take small steps and then evaluate how well we have done and then, if needed, modify our approach. One does this as an individual, not part of a problem-solving team. We keep doing this experimenting, taking an iterative approach until we finally achieve the targeted condition. We did not make it in a giant leap, but in small steps along a path. This is shown in a simple flowchart in Figure 8.2.

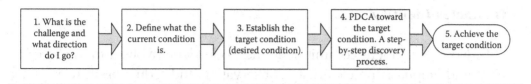

Figure 8.2   Toyota kata flow.

The above diagram shows that kata is a routine you practice until it becomes a habit. Once established as a habit, you will do it correctly without thinking about it. In other words, the practicing is done so one develops a mindset and the skill. There are two katas—one for coaching covered in Chapter 2 and one for improvement by a team. The latter is addressed below.

The problem or opportunity and approach can be simply shown as:

What do we want to improve?
What are the obstacles we need to overcome?
What is the desired condition?
What do we want to improve?

The team wanted to create an electricity reduction culture at QVS Corp facilities.

What are the obstacles we need to overcome? The energy team brainstormed the obstacles that need to be overcome so that the desired condition could be achieved.

What is the desired condition? The desired condition is to have an organizational culture whose attitude and habits are those of reducing electricity usage whenever possible and fully supporting the organization's goal of reducing electricity usage by 10% by end of 2015.

Focus: What is the focus process? Creating a culture that everyone wants to help reduce electricity use.

Challenge: What is the challenge? The desired culture does not exist now. People consider electricity use as a right and no consideration of saving consumption occurs.

Target Condition: What is desired? That all management personnel, supervisors, employees, and contractors desire to reduce electricity use and help make this a reality.

Current Condition: What is the current situation? Electric use is increasing. There is no plan for reduction. Employees do not know how or even why they should reduce electricity use.

Obstacles Identify:

1. No management commitment and no leaders involved in introducing and emphasizing electricity conservation and reduction in use.
2. Employees are not aware of how to reduce electricity use. There is no electricity conservation program, including no employee and contractor training.
3. Electricity usage is not monitored by management, supervisors, employees, or contractors.
4. There is no communication between management, the energy team, and the employees and contractors on electricity use. No one has communicated that it is important to reduce electricity consumption and cost.
5. Power management for IT (Information Technology) has not been identified as a priority.
6. No electricity reduction measures have been identified. There is no plan on how to reduce electricity use.

PDCA Cycle: Each time that the team practices is a Plan–Do–Check–Act (PDCA) cycle. The team tries to practice and overcome one obstacle at a time.

In practice, you may work on the same obstacle for several PDCA cycles with the cycle being defined as when you stopped and had to start again. For larger projects, you should develop a PDCA cycle sheet to record each cycle.

Date: **Process Metric:**
Process:
Step: What do you expect?   Result (observe closely) What did we learn?

Step 1

Step 2

Step n

For our example, this sheet would look like this:

Date: April 4, 2013 **Process Metric**: kWh used in 2013 by QVS Corp.
Process: Gaining management commitment
Targeted Condition: Top management is supportive, engaging in communicating why we need to reduce electricity
Current Condition
Step: What do you expect? **Result** (observe closely) **What did we learn?**

Step 1. Develop presentation and present to Strategic Council by management. — Strategic Council set a goal saving money to reduce kWh use by 10% goal by end of 2015.

Step 2. Identify how employees can save electricity:
    a. Turn off lights when they leave the room.
    b. Engage IT in identified power management program.
    c. Turn off appliances when not in use.
    d. Don't mess with the thermostats.

Step 3. Develop a PowerPoint electricity conservation plan. — Employees reviewed and started practicing the ways outlines.

Step 4. Develop a graph of kWh to maintain momentum. Management, supervisors, employees & contractors were informed and kept current with reductions. Must keep everyone informed monthly and make it visible.

Step 5. Develop a communications plan that identifies how to contact (telephone number and e-mail) the energy champion and energy team leader. Their roles and responsibilities should be included. Send to all employees and on site contractors.

Step 6. Energy team leader needs to communicate to the energy champion the need to get the IT director's approval and action. The director needs to assign the right people to this project and have them develop an action plan and coordinate it with the energy team leader. Together, they should then start implementing the coordinated actions plan.

Improvement, some innovation, and increased effectiveness occurred. This technique is systematic, scientific, and activates and motivates our creativity and solution development capabilities. Of course, this example is oversimplified and the team would probably not use kata to develop the actions. However, the above shows how the team can use the process and overcome obstacles to achieve results.

Tool/Techniques #45: Toyota Kata

8.6 Facilitator Exercises

1. O&Ts can be a feasibility study with a target. T __ F __
2. A target is a metric. T __ F __
3. Toyota kata has a trial and error component. T __ F __
4. An action plan tells how the activities can be accomplished. T __ F __
5. EnMS means Energy Management System. T __ F __
6. O&T and action plans are usually on the same page. T __ F __
7. What are the three types of objectives?
    a. __
    b. __
    c. __
8. What are the two parts of an O&T Template?
    a. __
    b. __
9. What does the R stand for in making objectives SMART? __
10. What does the T stand for in making objectives SMART? __

(See Appendix 1 for answers.)

Chapter 9

Projects and Project Management

9.1 What Is a Project and Project Management?

A project is simply a sequence of tasks or work that, when accomplished, creates a desired state, product, or condition. It is temporary; has a beginning and an end state. Once completed, the project is over and it no longer exists. Project management is the discipline of planning, organizing, managing, leading, and controlling resources to achieve the project's specific goal. The scope can be as small as a simple objective and target action plan to a large construction project. Each needs resources to accomplish and manage it for completion on time. The key results areas (KRAs) are shown in Figure 9.1.

Tool/Technique #46: A Bubble Chart

To be successful, the project should be completed on or ahead of schedule, a quality job or condition achieved, within the labor and time resources, and at or under budget or cost estimate.

Projects are defined by five features:

They have a beginning and an end.
They use resources.
They have specific goals, such as timely completion, on or under budget, Six Sigma level, etc.

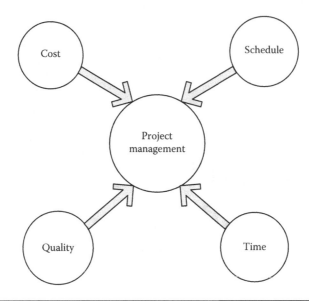

Figure 9.1   Project management key results areas.

Projects follow a plan.
Usually involve a team.

However, a single individual can have a project, such as building a patio or installing a patio cover.

Projects use resources, such as time, people, money, equipment, and facilities. Project management helps us balance these and use the least resources possible. You manage projects and lead people. This enables you to achieve the KRAs of project management.

Successful projects seem to have some common characteristics. They are well planned and organized. The project team is committed to the project's success. There is a balance among time, resources, and results. Finally, they achieve high customer satisfaction. Projects should have a well-defined goal. The time commitment must be understood. All costs should be known. A defined plan should be developed that when completed, the project is completed. Risks in the project's execution should be known and contingencies outlined if needed. Metrics should be in place that show the project's success, such as cost, schedule progress, milestones completion, and quality of product and performance. These factors comprise both the critical success factors and key results areas for a project.

9.2 Project Phases

The project phases are:

1. Planning
2. Design
3. Execution
4. Review
5. Closeout

A project manager should be appointed to manage each of these phases even if matrix management has to be applied. In this case, the project manager is responsible even when those performing the different functions, such as design, do not directly report to him or her, but to their functional manager. The project manager has implied authority and reports to the boss to whom all the functional managers report. The boss has given the project manager the authority to make decisions and manage the overall project. All of the phases must be completed and some can be ongoing with more than one phase being executed. For example, construction or execution (in an emergency) can be started prior to the entire design being completed.

Tools/Techniques #47: A Life-Cycle Chart

QVS project life cycle is shown in Figure 9.2. The RFI (request for information or input) is issued to get input and information from bidders or potential bidders. SOW (statement of work) describes what QVS wants done. The contractor uses this, plus a walk-through or meeting with QVS to develop its bid or cost estimate. The project approval, if an improvement project, will depend on the rate of return or payback period. The payback period is determined by dividing the cost of the project by the estimated savings or cost avoidance. If the cost can be paid back or recaptured in three years or less then the project will most probably be approved. If a longer payback is required, then other factors will normally be considered. For example, the president's executive order allows government energy projects to be funded up to 11 years payback.

The different project functions can range from one person accomplishing all or most of them to up to several hundred on a large construction project, such as a nuclear power plant. If a project is not good, then the energy reduction effort or any improvement effort will not be successful. Being

A Project's Life Cycle

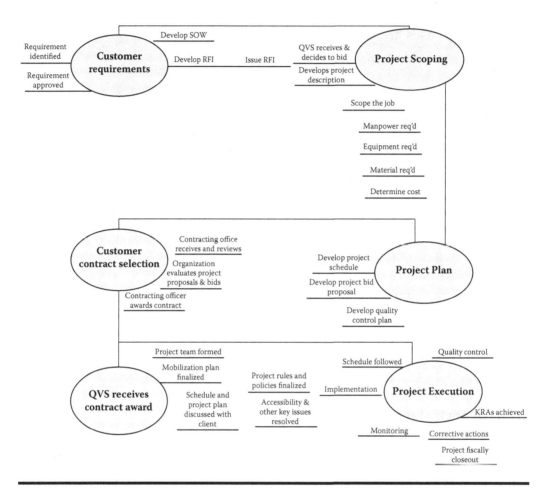

Figure 9.2   A project's life cycle.

good means it can be completed in a reasonable time and have an expected rate of return on investment. Objectives and targets action plans can be considered and called a project. They are normally accomplished by in-house resources. Projects that are contracted need a SOW and a schedule for completion, which is also an action plan. These projects are normally contracted. Therefore, objectives and targets and contracted projects are both called projects by the teams. A contracted project also could have an objective and target and an action plan. For energy projects, the cost, payback, and kWh saved when finished all should be calculated.

Tools/Techniques #47: Project Payback Period

The energy team will participate in the planning phase with facilities managers at each facility. Determining what is going to be done, arranging for the funding, developing the statement of work, and writing the contract and arranging with contracting to advertise the projects, and reviewing the bids and assisting in vendor selection are the major actions that will be involved. The design will be accomplished by the vendor and approved by the facilities manager. The contractor or vendor will do the project and facilities will inspect during the construction or execution. Facilities will either approve or not approve if there are any discrepancies. Of course, the project is never approved until the paperwork is complete. The closeout includes acceptance of the work by the contractor and final payment. Government projects start with the Energy Conservation Measure (ECM) and are tracked using this form until funded, and then project documents are managed until closeout.

Items that the facilitator needs to ensure include:

1. Identify the players in setting objectives and assist them where needed.
2. The project receives the necessary resources before commencement or an acceptable schedule and commitment for the resources.
3. Communicate the project's goals and/or objectives to ensure everyone is working on the same project, schedule, and budget.
4. Assist in accomplishing CPM (critical path method) if project schedule is critical and numerous activities in tandem or otherwise needs accomplishment.
5. Be ready to motivate all participants over the long haul so momentum is not lost.
6. Hold regular meetings using stoplight metrics to focus on results and to keep project on schedule.
7. Be sure proper controls are in place that will keep the project on schedule, within budget, and meeting objectives.
8. Be prepared for problems and changes; you can count on them occurring.

Of course, the project manager and project team (if project is large enough in scope) also will be responsible for the above eight. However, the results facilitator must be ready to assist and ensure the momentum and focus on the project's success is not lost.

9.3 Facilitator Exercises

1. The project phases are Planning, Design, Execution, Review, and Closeout. True __ False __
2. Even contracted projects may have an organizational objective and target. True __ False __
3. May an action plan also be called a project plan. True __ False __
4. An Energy Conservation Measure is used by the federal government to track energy or water projects. True __ False __
5. Projects have life cycles and sometimes life-cycle costing is used to determine the total cost of the project over its lifetime. True __ False __
6. What are the KRAs for a large project?

    __
7. What is matrix management?

    __

(See answers in Appendix 1.)

Chapter 10

Facilitator's Professional Behavior and Continuing Education

10.1 IAF Core Competencies

This IAF (International Association of Facilitators) Readiness to Perform model is in congruence with our model of continuous learning: Learn–Practice–Evaluate–Act.

Experience + Additional Training & Research + Reflection + Application = Facilitator's Continued Readiness

10.1.1 IAF Facilitator's Core Competencies

E. Build and Maintain Professional Knowledge
   1. Maintain a base of knowledge
   - Knowledgeable in management, organizational systems and development, group development, psychology, and conflict resolution
   - Understand dynamics of change
   - Understand learning and thinking theory

In facilitation, like other professional areas, it is extremely important to maintain an excellent base of knowledge. Facilitators need to know how to handle many different types of facilitation situations ranging from problem solving, process improvement, reengineering processes, Kaizen events, large groups identifying opportunities for improvement, and cost reduction adventures to many other facilitated events. Facilitators should understand Lean manufacturing, Six Sigma, Lean Six Sigma, strategic planning, vision establishment, action planning, measurement theory, statistical methods, seven quality control (QC) tools, seven management and planning tools, and organizational theory. In the facilitation area of expertise know what are Tuckman's five stages of team development, the various adult learning models, mutual learning model, skilled facilitator approach, critical success factors and measures for progress and results, the numerous facilitator tools and techniques, managing conflict, meeting effectiveness tools, critiquing, coaching, and numerous other topics. Additional training and research will add to your experience. Reflection of both your experience and training and asking: "How can I improve? Could I have used a different tool or technique at a session I did in the past? Have I managed conflict effectively? Do I intervene too quickly when conflict surfaces?" These types of questions are helpful in increasing your learning and body of facilitation knowledge. Applying new as well as proven techniques and knowledge and future facilitation efforts will help you maintain and improve your facilitation skills.

3. *Maintain professional standing*
- Engage in ongoing study/learning related to our field.
- Continuously gain awareness of new information in our profession.
- Practice reflection and learning.
- Build personal industry knowledge and networks.
- Maintain certification.

Advanced facilitators are always eager to learn new tools or techniques to help them better facilitate meetings and improvement teams. They are interested in learning new ideas and information about ways to facilitate, new tools, and industry information, such as who is best in class. Reflecting on what they have learned gives them the information of what additional items or research would increase their skills and abilities.

10.2 Certification

Certification is recommended; however, it is a personal choice. If you are a full-time facilitator, then becoming certified could help you in obtaining new business and maintaining what business you have. All of us should have personal development goals and becoming certified would fulfill that goal. After certification, you will want to continue your facilitation knowledge. The International Institute for Facilitation (INIFAC) and the International Association of Facilitation (IAF) are the two known organizations to certify facilitators. A comparison between the two for certification requirements is shown in Table 10.1.

The IAF certification cost is $1,500. The headquarters is located at 14985 Glazier Ave, Suite 550, St. Paul, Minnesota 55124. You can contact them at 1-800-281-9948 or http://www.iaf-world.org/issue3front.htm to learn when and where the next assessment event(s) will be held.

The INIFAC is located at 16913 SE 25th Street, Bellevue, Washington 98008. You can contact them at 703-909-8810 or ifo@inifac.org. The INIFAC certification fee is $1,400. The INIFAC certification is for a master facilitator, which is at a higher level than the facilitator certification level at IAF. INIFAC was created in order to certify a higher or top level of facilitator called certified master facilitator (CMF).

10.3 Model Positive Professional Attitude

10.3.1 IAF Facilitator Core Competencies

F. Model Positive Professional Attitude
2. Act with integrity
- Demonstrate a belief in the group and its possibilities.
- Approach situations with authenticity and a positive attitude.
- Describe situations as facilitator sees them and inquire into different views.
- Model professional boundaries and ethics (as described in ethics and values statement).

Trained facilitators show, through their actions, that they believe in the group and use every opportunity to communicate this to the organization's management and to the group or team. Any facilitator that the team will call "excellent" will most probably have a positive attitude, perseverance, patience, and call it as she or he sees it.

This requirement of a professional facilitator can best be said by identifying the values for a facilitator and then following them. Following your

Table 10.1 INIFAC versus IAF Certification Process

Certifying Organization	International Association of Facilitators www.iaf-world.org	International Institute for Facilitation www.inifac.org
Facilitator Certification	CPF Certified Professional Facilitator	CMF Certified Master Facilitator
Intention	IAF web site: "Qualified to design and provide *basic* group facilitation services"	Assess a candidate's ability to meet basic and higher level skills for advanced facilitation
Target Audience	Competent facilitators with experience in the field	Advanced facilitators with significant or moderate experience *(CPF not required)*
Cost	US $1,500	US $1,400
Experience	Seven sessions prior three years	30 sessions 3 years (10 session credit for CPFs)
Organization/ Sponsors	No minimum	Minimum 5 organizations/10 sponsors
Degree of Proficiency	Evidence of proficiency	Grading system: Scoring minimum 80% in six of six competencies
Written Assessment	Candidates provide examples of how they applied the core competencies in their work	Candidates provide written examples of knowledge and specific experiences in response to 30 questions related to the competencies
Facilitation Assessment	Candidate facilitates at a scheduled onsite assessment event, with assessor interview and immediate feedback	Candidate submits video of facilitated simulated session based on assigned topic and specific role plays

(Continued)

Table 10.1 INIFAC versus IAF Certification Process (Continued)

Recertification	• Every three years	• Every three years
	• List of seven facilitated workshops	• Document 15 facilitations
	• Listing of professional development undertaken since original certification date	• Three references
		• 40 hours personal development related to facilitation
	• Short essay (1,000–1,500 words), linking lessons learned since becoming a CPF, demonstrating changes in facilitation style/behavior, and indicating what growth has occurred during the period since CPF certification	• Renewal fee is US $300
	• Recertification fee US $500	

values and meeting the core competencies will be extremely helpful in obtaining continued business or requests for your facilitation assistance. The values for a facilitator include many, but the "must" ones are integrity, respect for others, and sensitivity to others' opinions, efficient, and mission-oriented.

Integrity: Adherence to moral and ethic standards including honest and sound character.

Respect for Others: Treat all people's opinions or comments with respect. Do not say, "That is a bad idea" or "That is stupid" or any downgrading comment.

Sensitive: Be sensitive to others' needs, problems, and objectives.

Efficient: Be organized, plan the facilitation session and then carry it out on time, within resources allotted, and with quality and enthusiasm.

Mission-Oriented: Keep focused on the purpose, objectives, and deliverables, and always achieve them.

It is a best practice to obtain critiques after each session and include questions about how well did the facilitator do his/her job, including making things clear, keeping the meeting on track, providing focus on the purpose, and accomplishing the deliverable(s).

In addition, do a self-assessment at times by reflecting on past experiences, what others have told you, and what you think you can improve. Little things like improving your writing on a whiteboard to demonstrate a tool or a finding, knowing when to use an icebreaker or not, selecting the best facilitator tool for a particular application, knowing how to motivate people, improving your listening skills, and a million other possibilities. If you follow these values and do a self-assessment or self-awareness exercise, you will meet the core competencies outlined in "E" above.

Facilitation is one of the most important skills you as a consultant bring to the table in helping your client solve problems collaboratively. Keep the 10 tips from Table 10.2 in mind when you are about to help your client solve its next tough problem.

10.4 Self-Assessments

F. Model Positive Professional Attitude
1. Practice self-assessment and self-awareness
* Reflect on behavior and results.
* Maintain congruence between actions and personal and professional values.
* Modify personal behavior/style to reflect the needs of the group.
* Cultivate understanding of one's own values and their potential impact on work with clients.

Facilitators, through their success with groups and teams, may become over confident and sometimes arrogant or even cocky. The best way to prevent this is to practice self-assessment and self-awareness. Remember, a facilitator is only as good as the last facilitation role he/she did. Goof up on a future one and your reputation could become tarnished. Always be aware of how you look and perform with the group or team. Ask yourself after each major event, how you can improve. Include in the critiques and analyze them and take corrective action if needed.

Be truthful. For the ones you are not sure of, you probably need to address and improve your skills in that area. It is recommended that each facilitator fill this out at least quarterly and then try to improve between the assessments. Another self-assessment is to make the left-hand column the

Table 10.2 Facilitator's Self-Assessment

Facilitator's Skills	Present Capability: Poor–Satisfactory–Okay–Good–Excellent	What Can I Do to Improve? How Am I Going to Improve?
1. Ability to influence		
2. Facilitate excellent meetings		
3. Management conflict		
4. Team building and achieving teamwork		
5. Know the technical area or processes to follow		
6. Able to use the facilitator's tools & techniques		
7. Development of good objectives and targets and action plans		
8. Able to manage projects		
9. Good at developing meaningful measures or metrics		
10. Excellent coach on a variety of subjects		

IAF's or INIFAC's Facilitator Core Competencies. It will be longer and a little more difficult to distinguish between the questions due to some overlapping and commingled competencies and some "politically correct" statements that are not truly facilitator's core competency areas.

Tools/Techniques #48: Facilitator's Self-Assessment Technique

10.5 Facilitator Exercises

1. Experience + Additional Training and Research + Reflection + Application = Facilitator's Continued Readiness is IAF's model for continuous readiness. Does it conflict with the continuous improvement model of Learning–Practice–Evaluate–Act? Yes ___ No ___
2. A facilitator's reputation from his/her last job often is the reason he/she gets or does not get the next job opportunity. True ___ False ___
3. Self-reflection or evaluation, if done objectively, can help a facilitator continue to improve. True ___ False ___
4. Facilitators becoming certified is recommended, but not mandatory. True ___ False ___

(*See Appendix 1 for answers.*)

Chapter 11

Evaluation of IAF Facilitator Core Competencies for Certification

11.1 The IAF Facilitator Core Competencies

The initial work on the competencies for facilitators began in 1991. IAF published "**Facilitator Competencies**" in *Group Facilitation: A Research and Applications Journal* in Winter 2000 (vol. 2, no. 2). Also published at that time were several commentaries by IAF members with suggestions for further refinement. This revision, for the purpose of certification, was completed in February 2003.

IAF's work has identified the following six areas of core competency (www.iaf.world.org.certification):

A. Create Collaborative Client Relationships	B. Plan Appropriate Group Processes	C. Create and Sustain a Participatory Environment	D. Guide Group to Appropriate and Useful Outcomes	E. Build and Maintain Professional Knowledge	F. Model Positive Professional Attitude

A. Create Collaborative Client Relationships
  #### 1. Develop working partnerships
   • Clarify mutual commitment
   • Develop consensus on tasks, deliverables, roles, and responsibilities

- Demonstrate collaborative values and processes, such as in co-facilitation

2. ***Design and customize applications to meet client needs***
   - Analyze organizational environment
   - Diagnose client need
   - Create appropriate designs to achieve intended outcomes
   - Predefine a quality product and outcomes with client

3. ***Manage multisession events effectively***
   - Contract with client for scope and deliverables
   - Develop event plan
   - Deliver event successfully
   - Assess/evaluate client satisfaction at all stages of the event or project

B. *Plan Appropriate Group Processes*
1. ***Select clear methods and processes that***
   - foster open participation with respect for client culture, norms, and participant diversity;
   - engage the participation of those with varied learning/thinking styles; and
   - achieve a high-quality product/outcome that meets the client needs.

2. ***Prepare time and space to support group process***
   - Arrange physical space to support the purpose of the meeting
   - Plan effective use of time
   - Provide effective atmosphere and drama for sessions

C. *Create and Sustain a Participatory Environment*
1. ***Demonstrate effective participatory and interpersonal communication skills***
   - Apply a variety of participatory processes
   - Demonstrate effective verbal communication skills
   - Develop rapport with participants
   - Practice active listening
   - Demonstrate ability to observe and provide feedback to participants

2. ***Honor and recognize diversity, ensuring inclusiveness***
   - Encourage positive regard for the experience and perception of all participants
   - Create a climate of safety and trust
   - Create opportunities for participants to benefit from the diversity of the group

- Cultivate cultural awareness and sensitivity

3. *Manage group conflict*
- Help individuals identify and review underlying assumptions
- Recognize conflict and its role within group learning/maturity
- Provide a safe environment for conflict to surface
- Manage disruptive group behavior
- Support the group through resolution of conflict

4. *Evoke group creativity*
- Draw out participants of all learning and thinking styles
- Encourage creative thinking
- Accept all ideas
- Use approaches that best fit needs and abilities of the group
- Stimulate and tap group energy

D. *Guide Group to Appropriate and Useful Outcomes*
1. *Guide the group with clear methods and processes*
- Establish clear context for the session
- Actively listen, question, and summarize to elicit the sense of the group
- Recognize tangents and redirect to the task
- Manage small and large group process

2. *Facilitate group self-awareness about its task*
- Vary the pace of activities according to needs of group
- Identify information the group needs, and draw out data and insight from the group
- Help the group synthesize patterns, trends, root causes, frameworks for action
- Assist the group in reflection on its experience

3. *Guide the group to consensus and desired outcomes*
- Use a variety of approaches to achieve group consensus
- Use a variety of approaches to meet group objectives
- Adapt processes to changing situations and needs of the group
- Assess and communicate group progress
- Foster task completion

E. *Build and Maintain Professional Knowledge*
1. *Maintain a base of knowledge*
- Knowledgeable in management, organizational systems and development, group development, psychology, and conflict resolution

- Understand dynamics of change
- Understand learning and thinking theory

2. *Know a range of facilitation methods*

- Understand problem-solving and decision-making models
- Understand a variety of group methods and techniques
- Know consequences of misuse of group methods
- Distinguish process from task and content
- Learn new processes, methods, and models in support of client's changing/emerging needs

3. *Maintain professional standing*

- Engage in ongoing study/learning related to our field
- Continuously gain awareness of new information in our profession
- Practice reflection and learning
- Build personal industry knowledge and networks
- Maintain certification

F. Model Positive Professional Attitude

1. *Practice self-assessment and self-awareness*

- Reflect on behavior and results
- Maintain congruence between actions and personal and professional values
- Modify personal behavior/style to reflect the needs of the group
- Cultivate understanding of one's own values and their potential impact on work with clients

2. *Act with integrity*

- Demonstrate a belief in the group and its possibilities
- Approach situations with authenticity and a positive attitude
- Describe situations as facilitator sees them and inquire into different views
- Model professional boundaries and ethics (as described in ethics and values statement)

3. *Trust group potential and model neutrality*

- Honor the wisdom of the group
- Encourage trust in the capacity and experience of others
- Vigilant to minimize influence on group outcomes
- Maintain an objective, nondefensive, nonjudgmental stance

11.2 Evaluation of the IAF Facilitator Core Competencies

Today, these facilitator core competencies are one of the most accepted ones. In this book, the author uses them, explaining when they were a part of the subject matter. Are they perfect? Are they correct? Can facilitators benefit from using them as a guide to develop their abilities?

Perfect? Absolutely no! Are they correct? In some areas, yes. In a few, no. Can facilitators use them as a guide to improve their capability? Absolutely.

The author has been a facilitator for over 30 years. He has facilitated groups, teams, and events on many different occasions. He was trained in early 1980s by Florida Power & Light (FPL) to be one of their original quality facilitators to help lead the company in its successful pursuit of the Deming prize. The FPL Facilitation Course was one of the most popular at that time and many of America's best companies' employees received this training as part of their quality journey.

11.3 INIFAC Core Competencies

In a research project, the International Institute for Facilitators (INIFAC) sought to identify the core competencies (knowledge, skills, and experiences) essential to a certified master facilitator (CMF). They received input from 450 facilitators. They developed the following list of six general core competencies with a total of 30 subcompetencies. They described them by an innovative and easy to remember acronym shown below.

Master facilitators bring "PAC³E" (presence, assessment, communication, control, consistency, engagement) to every engagement.

Presence
Master facilitators bring compassion and authority to the room. Through their verbal and nonverbal expression, they exude confidence, energy, and self-awareness, while also conveying a high level of warmth and caring. They make adjustments in their style to better serve the group.

Assessment
Master facilitators know and ask the questions necessary to accurately assess a client's needs. Based on their learning from past experiences, they create processes designed to address the client's specific

requirements. They carefully plan and prepare sessions. They recognize when a planned process is not working effectively and are able to define alternative processes quickly to reach the desired outcome.

Communication
Master facilitators are skilled communicators. They actively listen, making sure to play back and confirm important points. They have highly tuned analytic skills that allow them to process information quickly, differentiate various content issues, and isolate critical points in a discussion. They ask questions that help groups to engage effectively. They deliver instructions that are accurate, clear, and concise. They effectively identify and verbally summarize agreements.

Control
Master facilitators create and maintain a productive and safe environment in which participants with diverse styles and culture can engage in interactions that stay focused on achieving the goal. They maintain control of the session and an appropriate pace. They understand causes of disagreement and can effectively guide a group through conflict. They consciously take action to prevent, detect, and resolve dysfunctional behavior.

Consistency
Master facilitators understand and consistently apply best practice techniques for such activities as starting the session, focusing the group, recording information, and closing the session.

Engagement
Master facilitators know and use multiple techniques for engaging a group, problem solving, decision making, promoting creativity, and raising energy.

11.3.1 The Subcompetencies

A. Presence
  A1. Facilitator projects confidence in own skills and own ability to lead the group.
  A2. Facilitator demonstrates warmth and caring.
  A3. Facilitator understands the impact of energy on participants and facilitates in a style appropriate for the audience and the session topic.

A4. Facilitator makes adjustments in own style and language to adjust to the group.

A5. Facilitator demonstrates awareness of own strengths and weaknesses.

B. Assessment

B1. Facilitator asks the questions to assess a client's need and gains agreement with the client on the relevant scope and products.

B2. Facilitator plans and prepares for the session effectively and collaboratively.

B3. Facilitator develops customized processes to meet the specific requirements of clients.

B4. Facilitator recognizes when a planned process is not working effectively and is able to diagnose the cause, and defines alternative processes to reach desired outcomes.

B5. Facilitator evaluates experiences, identifies learnings and applies learnings to new situations.

C. Communication

C1. Facilitator actively listens, making sure to play back and confirm important points.

C2. Facilitator demonstrates the ability to process information quickly, differentiate content issues, and isolate critical points in a discussion.

C3. Facilitator asks appropriate focusing questions that help groups to engage effectively.

C4. Facilitator asks appropriate follow-up questions that clarify, probe, and redirect.

C5. Facilitator delivers instructions that are accurate, clear, and concise.

C6. Facilitator effectively identifies and verbally summarizes agreements.

D. Control

D1. Facilitator creates and maintains a productive environment in which participants engage in interactions that stay focused on achieving the goal.

D2. Facilitator creates and maintains a safe environment for people to speak openly without fear of retribution.

D3. Facilitator creates and maintains an environment that takes into account and fosters respect for diverse cultures and styles.

D4. Facilitator maintains an appropriate pace and manages the group's time during the session.

D5. Facilitator demonstrates techniques for effectively guiding a group through conflict to consensus.

D6. Facilitator takes action to prevent, detect, and address dysfunctional behavior.

E. Consistency

E1. Facilitator understands and consistently applies best practice techniques for starting the session.

E2. Facilitator understands and consistently applies best practice techniques for focusing and controlling the group.

E3. Facilitator understands and consistently applies best practice techniques for recording information.

E4. Facilitator understands and consistently applies best practice techniques for closing the session.

F. Engagement

F1. Facilitator knows and uses multiple techniques and tools for keeping a group engaged in the work and interacting.

F2. Facilitator knows and uses multiple techniques and tools for problem solving and decision making.

F3. Facilitator knows and uses multiple techniques and tools for promoting creativity.

F4. Facilitator knows and uses multiple techniques and tools for impacting energy.

It is interesting to note that, at first reading of the IAF and INIFAC core competencies, they do not appear to be similar. A closer look does show a number of similarities. The core competencies were designed to reflect knowledge, skills, and experiences. They, in many respects, do this. However, no specific tools and techniques are mentioned and mostly the emphasis is on the facilitator's behavior.

11.4 IAF and INIFAC Core Competencies Comparison

Let's compare the two sets of core competencies directly and see what it may show (Table 11.1).

Table 11.1 IAF and INIFAC Core Competencies Comparison

IAF	INIFAC	Comments	Recommendations
A. Create Collaborative Client Relationships **1. Develop working partnerships** • Clarify mutual commitment • Develop consensus on tasks, deliverables, roles, & responsibilities • Demonstrate collaborative values and processes such as in co-facilitation	C.6. Facilitator effectively identifies and verbally summarizes agreements.	IAF more detailed.	
A.2. Design and customize applications to meet client needs • Analyze organizational environment • Diagnose client need • Create appropriate designs to achieve intended outcomes • Predefine a quality product & outcomes with client	B.1. Facilitator asks the questions to assess a client need and gains agreement with the client on the relevant scope and products. B.3. Facilitator develops customized processes to meet the specific requirements of clients. F.3. Facilitator knows and uses multiple techniques and tools for promoting creativity.	Both focus well on the client's requirement.	
A.3. Manage multisession events effectively • Contract with client for scope and deliverables • Develop event plan • Deliver event successfully • Assess/evaluate client satisfaction at all stages of the event or project	B.1. Facilitator asks the questions to assess a client need and gains agreement with the client on the relevant scope and products. C.6. Facilitator effectively identifies and verbally summarizes agreements.	Both are good.	

(Continued)

Table 11.1   IAF and INIFAC Core Competencies Comparison (Continued)

IAF	INIFAC	Comments	Recommendations
B. Plan Appropriate Group Processes **1. Select clear methods and processes that:** • Foster open participation with respect for client culture, norms, and participant diversity • Engage the participation of those with varied learning/thinking styles • Achieve a high-quality product/outcome that meets the client needs	B.2. Facilitator plans and prepares for the session effectively and collaboratively.	A toss-up.	
B.2. Prepare time and space to support group process • Arrange physical space to support the purpose of the meeting • Plan effective use of time • Provide effective atmosphere and drama for sessions	B.2. Facilitator plans and prepares for the session effectively and collaboratively. D.4. Facilitator maintains an appropriate pace and manages the group's time during the session.	Both are satisfactory.	

(Continued)

Table 11.1   IAF and INIFAC Core Competencies Comparison (Continued)

IAF	INIFAC	Comments	Recommendations
C. Create and Sustain a Participatory Environment **1. Demonstrate effective participatory and interpersonal communication skills** • Apply a variety of participatory processes • Demonstrate effective verbal communication skills • Develop rapport with participants • Practice active listening • Demonstrate ability to observe and provide feedback to participants	C.3. Facilitator asks appropriate focusing questions that help groups to engage effectively. C.4. Facilitator asks appropriate follow-up questions that clarify, probe, and redirect. C.5. Facilitator delivers instructions that are accurate, clear, and concise. C.6. Facilitator effectively identifies and verbally summarizes agreements. E.2. Facilitator understands and consistently applies best practice techniques for focusing and controlling the group.	Both are good.	
C.2. Honor and recognize diversity, ensuring inclusiveness • Encourage positive regard for the experience and perception of all participants • Create a climate of safety and trust • Create opportunities for participants to benefit from the diversity of the group • Cultivate cultural awareness and sensitivity	D.2. Facilitator creates and maintains a safe environment for people to speak openly without fear of retribution. D.3. Facilitator creates and maintains an environment that takes into account and fosters respect for diverse cultures and styles. D.5 Facilitator takes action to prevent, detect, and address dysfunctional behavior. F.3. Facilitator knows and uses multiple techniques and tools for promoting creativity.	Both are good and focused.	

(Continued)

Table 11.1   IAF and INIFAC Core Competencies Comparison (Continued)

IAF	INIFAC	Comments	Recommendations
C.3. Manage group conflict • Help individuals identify and review underlying assumptions • Recognize conflict and its role within group learning/maturity • Provide a safe environment for conflict to surface • Manage disruptive group behavior • Support the group through resolution of conflict	D.2. Facilitator creates and maintains a safe environment for people to speak openly without fear of retribution. D.4. Facilitator demonstrates techniques for effectively guiding a group through conflict to consensus. E.2. Facilitator understands and consistently applies best practice techniques for focusing and controlling the group.	Both are good.	
C.4. Evoke group creativity • Draw out participants of all learning and thinking styles • Encourage creative thinking • Accept all ideas • Use approaches that best fit needs and abilities of the group • Stimulate and tap group energy	D.2. Facilitator creates and maintains a productive environment in which participants engage in interactions that stay focused on achieving the goal. F.1. Facilitator knows and uses multiple techniques and tools for keeping a group engaged in the work and interacting. F.4. Facilitator knows and uses multiple techniques and tools for impacting energy.	Both are general and vague.	

(Continued)

Table 11.1 IAF and INIFAC Core Competencies Comparison (Continued)

IAF	INIFAC	Comments	Recommendations
D. Guide Group to Appropriate and Useful Outcomes **1. Guide the group with clear methods and processes** • Establish clear context for the session • Actively listen, question, and summarize to elicit the sense of the group • Recognize tangents and redirect to the task • Manage small and large group process	C.1. Facilitator actively listens, making sure to play back and confirm important points. C.2. Facilitator demonstrates the ability to process information quickly, differentiate content issues, and isolate critical points in a discussion. C.3. Facilitator asks appropriate focusing questions that help groups to engage effectively. C.4. Facilitator asks appropriate follow-up questions that clarify, probe, and redirect. C.5. Facilitator delivers instructions that are accurate, clear, and concise. D.1. Facilitator creates and maintains a productive environment in which participants engage in interactions that stay focused on achieving the goal. E.2. Facilitator understands and consistently applies best practice techniques for focusing and controlling the group. F.1. Facilitator knows and uses multiple techniques and tools for keeping a group engaged in the work and interacting.	INIFAC is clearer.	

(Continued)

Table 11.1 IAF and INIFAC Core Competencies Comparison (Continued)

IAF	INIFAC	Comments	Recommendations
D.2. Facilitate group self-awareness about its task • Vary the pace of activities according to needs of group • Identify information the group needs, and draw out data and insight from the group • Help the group synthesize patterns, trends, root causes, frameworks for action • Assist the group in reflection on its experience	C.2. Facilitator demonstrates the ability to process information quickly, differentiate content issues, and isolate critical points in a discussion. C.5. Facilitator delivers instructions that are accurate, clear, and concise. E.2. Facilitator understands and consistently applies best practice techniques for focusing and controlling the group.	Both are okay.	
D.3. Guide the group to consensus and desired outcomes • Use a variety of approaches to achieve group consensus • Use a variety of approaches to meet group objectives • Adapt processes to changing situations and needs of the group • Assess and communicate group progress • Foster task completion	A.4. Facilitator makes adjustments in own style and language to adjust to the group. B.4. Facilitator recognizes when a planned process is not working effectively and is able to diagnose the cause, and defines alternative processes to reach desired outcomes. B.5. Facilitator evaluates experiences, identifies learnings, and applies learnings to new situations. C.2. Facilitator demonstrates the ability to process information quickly, differentiate content issues, and isolate critical points in a discussion. C.6. Facilitator effectively identifies and verbally summarizes agreements.	IAF is clearer on reaching consensus.	

(Continued)

Table 11.1   IAF and INIFAC Core Competencies Comparison (Continued)

IAF	INIFAC	Comments	Recommendations
D.3. (Continued)	D.1. Facilitator creates and maintains a productive environment in which participants engage in interactions that stay focused on achieving the goal. D.5. Facilitator demonstrates techniques for effectively guiding a group through conflict to consensus. E.2. Facilitator understands and consistently applies best practice techniques for focusing and controlling the group. F.2. Facilitator knows and uses multiple techniques and tools for problem solving and decision making. F.3. Facilitator knows and uses multiple techniques and tools for promoting creativity.	IAF is clearer on reaching consensus.	
E. Build and Maintain Professional Knowledge **1. Maintain a base of knowledge** • Knowledgeable in management, organizational systems and development, group development, psychology, and conflict resolution • Understand dynamics of change • Understand learning and thinking theory	B.5. Facilitator evaluates experiences, identifies learnings and applies learnings to new situations.	Both are not descriptive enough in what the base of knowledge should contain. Leaves it up to the facilitator.	

(Continued)

Table 11.1   IAF and INIFAC Core Competencies Comparison (Continued)

IAF	INIFAC	Comments	Recommendations
E.2. Know a range of facilitation methods • Understand problem-solving and decision-making models • Understand a variety of group methods and techniques • Know consequences of misuse of group methods • Distinguish process from task and content • Learn new processes, methods, & models in support of client's changing/ emerging needs	B.4. Facilitator recognizes when a planned process is not working effectively and is able to diagnose the cause, and defines alternative processes to reach desired outcomes. B.5. Facilitator evaluates experiences, identifies learnings and applies learnings to new situations. D.6 Facilitator takes action to prevent, detect, and address dysfunctional behavior. F.2. Facilitator knows and uses multiple techniques and tools for problem solving and decision making.	Both are good.	
E.3. Maintain professional standing • Engage in ongoing study/learning related to our field • Continuously gain awareness of new information in our profession • Practice reflection and learning • Build personal industry knowledge and networks • Maintain certification	F.2. Facilitator knows and uses multiple techniques and tools for problem solving and decision making.	IAF clearer on maintaining professional standing.	INIFAC should add something on maintaining certification and belonging and participating in a professional society.

(Continued)

Table 11.1 IAF and INIFAC Core Competencies Comparison (Continued)

IAF	INIFAC	Comments	Recommendations
F. Model Positive Professional Attitude 1. Practice self-assessment and self-awareness • Reflect on behavior and results • Maintain congruence between actions and personal and professional values • Modify personal behavior/style to reflect the needs of the group • Cultivate understanding of one's own values and their potential impact on work with clients	A.4. Facilitator makes adjustments in own style and language to adjust to the group. A.5. Facilitator demonstrates awareness of own strengths and weaknesses.		
1. Act with integrity • Demonstrate a belief in the group and its possibilities • Approach situations with authenticity and a positive attitude • Describe situations as facilitator sees them and inquire into different views • Model professional boundaries and ethics (as described in ethics and values statement)	D.1. Facilitator creates and maintains a productive environment in which participants engage in interactions that stay focused on achieving the goal.		

(Continued)

Table 11.1   IAF and INIFAC Core Competencies Comparison (Continued)

IAF	INIFAC	Comments	Recommendations
3. Trust group potential and model neutrality • Honor the wisdom of the group • Encourage trust in the capacity and experience of others • Vigilant to minimize influence on group outcomes • Maintain an objective, nondefensive, nonjudgmental stance		Not sure this is a good core competence.	
	A.1. Facilitator projects confidence in own skills and own ability to lead the group.	The author likes these A core competences because they should be an outcome judged in a certification process.	
	A.2. Facilitator demonstrates warmth and caring.	The author likes these A core competences because they should be an outcome judged in a certification process.	
	A.3. Facilitator understands the impact of energy on participants and facilitates in a style appropriate for the audience and the session topic.	Impact of energy–Whose energy? The facilitator?	
	A.5. Facilitator demonstrates awareness of own strengths and weaknesses.	In front of participants, this is not a good idea. It is important though for the facilitator to know this. It will help him continuously improve.	INIFAC should include this as facilitators needing to perform self-inspections, evaluate what they did well and what they can do to improve.

(*Continued*)

Table 11.1 IAF and INIFAC Core Competencies Comparison (Continued)

IAF	INIFAC	Comments	Recommendations
	E.1. Facilitator understands and consistently applies best practice techniques for starting the session.	All meetings should have an agenda that states the purpose of the meeting, what subjects are going to be presented by whom, and the time allotment for each subject.	
	E.3. Facilitator understands and consistently applies best practice techniques for recording information.	Great. Documentation is extremely important, especially for ISOs, but also for all meetings.	
	E.4. Facilitator understands and consistently applies best practice techniques for closing the session.	Same comment for E.1.	

11.5 Summary of Comparison

Although it is not possible to have a one-to-one comparison of the core competencies, it is possible to see if the major areas have coverage of a core competency or several of them. Both of International Association of Facilitators (IAF) and INIFAC are to be congratulated on developing comprehensive core competencies and using them in their certification programs. It is possible to compare a facilitator's performance to either one of them. INIFAC has on their web page a free comparison where facilitators can measure themselves against their core competencies. The simple and easy text of INIFAC's core competencies is well done and the manner in which the competencies are written is very good. IAF's core competencies provide a little more detail or information on what is included in a particular core competency. IAF places more emphasis on meeting the client's requirements and on client satisfaction.

The core competencies, although useful, do not include what is needed for a young facilitator starting his or her facilitation career. If a core competency consists of knowledge, experience, and skills, then what knowledge specifically should we have and what skills are necessary? The core competencies can be confusing as written. To demonstrate this, let's examine a few of INIFAC core competencies.

A.5. Facilitator demonstrates awareness of own strengths and weaknesses. Question: Is it important for a facilitator to know their strengths and weaknesses? They should try to improve their weaknesses, but demonstrate your weaknesses in front of the team? No way should a master facilitator demonstrate his/her weaknesses in front of a team. Of course, they would show their strengths. This needs to be rethought and maybe rewritten.

F.1. A facilitator knows and uses multiple techniques and tools for keeping a group engaged in the work and interacting. Sounds good. However, what are the techniques? If a healthy, safe environment has been created, the team members are in either the "Norm" or "Perform" stage, did their homework prior to the meeting, and no conflict occurs, then you should meet this core competency providing the next three conditions are met. If you have an excellent agenda developed using PAL (purpose–agenda–limited) and the facilitator knows the process and tools to use to accomplish the purpose, then the team should be working and interacting.

D.4. Facilitator maintains an appropriate pace and manages the group's time during the session. This is good; it sends a clear message. This core competency is almost self-explanatory. Time management and a PAL agenda are the techniques/tools needed. Little is said in both organizations' core competency about agendas. Good agendas are probably the most important facilitative tool to assist any facilitator.

F.1. Facilitators know and use multiple techniques and tools for problem solving and decision making. Of course, this is a true statement. What kind of problem-solving process should the facilitator know? DMAIC (define, measure, analyze, improve, control) or a simple one, such as (1) What is the problem? (2) What is the current situation? (3) What are the root causes? (4) What countermeasures should we recommend? (5) Sell our solution and implement. (6) Check to see how we are doing, and (7) Take corrective action and develop future plans. What are the basic tools that we should possess that supply the knowledge of and that we are able to apply. This is not done, even though most facilitators would agree on many of these listed next.

– Brainstorming
– Nominal Group Technique
– Multivoting
– Flowcharting

- Metrics
- Pareto diagrams
- Histograms
- Cause and effect diagram
- Surveys
- Check sheet
- Control chart
- Affinity diagram
- Matrices, such as root cause evaluation matrix, ranking, and simple statistical analysis (mean, mode, median, standard deviation, range)

However, there are no instructions similar to this before you are measured against this core competency. Wouldn't it be nice to demonstrate minimum behaviors, tools, techniques, and other knowledge, such as managing conflict or understanding group dynamics, developed as a minimum qualification and then through continuous learning add to their core competency inventory.

E.4. The facilitator understands and consistently applies best practice techniques for closing the session. Question: How can a facilitator know what the best practices are if they are not outlined? The author would suggest first summarizing what was accomplished in the meeting today and then having the participants fill out a critique form or the facilitator should go round robin and ask each participant: "What did we do well?" And, then: "What can we do better?" If that is the best practice, then why don't we say that.

There are certain techniques, tools, knowledge, etc., that are missing, not implied, or called for in both IAF and INIFAC core competencies to cover those needed for a results facilitator. The modern facilitator, able to handle more than one event, such as facilitating an ISO team through planning, developing, implementing, maintaining, and sustaining stages, should be knowledgeable of how to coach individuals or a team. In addition, how to develop an action plan and manage a project is normally necessary in most facilitating assignments that last several months. The facilitator must know the process that the team needs to follow to achieve the mission. The facilitator needs to be able to use any tools or techniques that are required to achieve the meeting's purpose. Team building is another helpful tool that is not mentioned. Ability to influence and understand the team members is not mentioned. Using the DiSC® personality profile can help you understand yourself and your team members. Training has become a task normally done in conjunction with a facilitator. No longer does a facilitator facilitate one event and remain neutral throughout. Being sometimes held responsible for the outcome in ISO team facilitating relieves the long-time requirement of being neutral, thus, the results facilitator emerges. Therefore, the IAF and the INIFAC core competencies are an excellent start, but not sufficient to cover the results facilitator. Of course, neither IAF nor INIFAC have endorsed the results facilitator as of now. Their core competencies should be reviewed, evaluated, and brought up to date at least every two years. The core competencies for a results facilitator are shown in the next section. More about what the core competency means and includes should be developed and published in conjunction with the core competencies.

11.6 Results Facilitator Core Competencies

Figure 11.1 depicts (clockwise) how the facilitator should plan and arrange the meeting, have a professional presence, Focus on achieving the objective through effective communication, utilizing the right tools and techniques while engaging the group or team to deliver success. This is what a facilitator needs to do.

Table 11.2 uses the FOCUSED concept to enable evaluation of IAF Facilitator Core Competencies for Certification by completing the Focus, Communicate and Engage columns. The other columns can be used when appropriate.

The items mentioned in this section that are not presently included in the present IAF and INIFAC core competencies are shown in Table 11.3.

For coaches, there is the International Association for Coaching (IAC) that also has core competencies and a certification process (www.certifiedcoach. org). There are several international organizations for trainers (Google international organization for training).

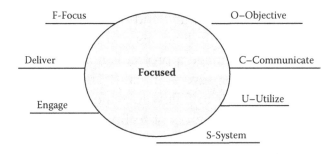

Figure 11.1   Focused (clockwise).

Table 11.2   Focused Approach

Focus	Objective	Communicate	Utilize	System	Engage	Deliver
Create a favorable impression while facilitating Create a climate of safety and trust Maintain congruence between actions, personal and professional values Modify personal behavior/style to meet the needs of the group or team Approach all situations with integrity and a positive attitude		Facilitator identifies properly and summarizes agreements verbally or in writing. Facilitator shows confidence in his or her skills and ability to lead the group. Use approaches that best fit needs and abilities of the group				
20. Range for physical space to support the purpose of the meeting and any meeting needs such as computer and easels with pads						
					Coach team and individuals when needed Use approaches that best fit needs and abilities of the group Know how to effectively engage the group	
5. Create a climate of safety and trust						
21. Maintain congruence between actions, personal and professional values						

Table 11.3 Results Facilitator Core Competencies

Skills	Core Competencies	S = Same for normal facilitator or R = for Results Facilitator only (Behavior–Skills–Education– Experience)
1. Ability to influence	1. Create a favorable impression while facilitating 2. Coach team and individuals when needed 3. Create a climate of safety and trust 4. Use approaches that best fit needs and abilities of the group 5. Maintain congruence between actions, personal and professional values 6. Modify personal behavior/style to meet the needs of the group or team 7. Approach all situations with integrity and a positive attitude 8. Facilitator identifies properly and summarizes agreements verbally or in writing 9. Facilitator shows confidence in his or her skills and ability to lead the group 10. Know how to effectively engage the group	S: The facilitator must be able to influence management and the team or group. When the management representative, the team leader or any team members need coaching on a technique or tool, the facilitator should do so using a coaching model or process. If the meeting is not going well, modify what you are doing until you get the team back on track. Always be honest and forthright. Summarization of points or issues discussed is always helpful to the team.

(Continued)

Table 11.3   Results Facilitator Core Competencies (Continued)

Skills	Core Competencies	S = Same for normal facilitator or R = for Results Facilitator only (Behavior–Skills–Education–Experience)
2. Possess effective meeting knowledge	11. Arrange for physical space to support the purpose of the meeting and any meeting needs such as computer and easels with pads 12. Plan effective use of time 13. Identify information and data the group needs, and draw out opinions, recommendations, and insight from the group 14. Use a variety of approaches to meet group objectives and/or purposes 15. Adapt processes and tools to changing situations and needs of the group or team 16. Maintain an objective, nondefensive, nonjudgmental stance, and a caring and professional attitude 17. Facilitator plans and prepares for the meeting effectively 18. Facilitator maintains an appropriate pace and manages the group's or team's time during the session 19. Facilitator knows and uses multiple techniques and tools for keeping a group or team engaged in the work, process, and interacting with each other	S: Perform the premeeting duties, the in-meeting tasks, and the after the meeting requirements per the facilitator checklist. Always notify the participants with an agenda using PAL (Purpose-Agenda-Limited), approved by the team or group leader. Get everyone involved in the discussion, manage any conflict or disruptive behavior, and summarize major points or issues as you proceed. Be sure everyone knows the meeting's objectives or purpose, use the appropriate tools and techniques to move the team or group toward meeting the objective(s), adapt processes if not working or determined inappropriate, and maintain a caring, professional attitude throughout the meeting, assign action items (with team leader's approval) and document the meeting within three days.

(Continued)

Table 11.3   Results Facilitator Core Competencies (Continued)

Skills	Core Competencies	S = Same for normal facilitator or R = for Results Facilitator only (Behavior–Skills–Education–Experience)
3. Manage conflict	20. Provide a safe environment for conflict to occur 21. Manage disruptive group behavior and individual difficult behavior 22. Support the group and individuals through resolution of conflict 23. Facilitator creates and maintains a safe environment for people to speak openly and freely without fear of retribution. 24. Facilitator understands and applies appropriate techniques for focusing and controlling the group.	S: Remember conflict can be constructive if it is not allowed to get out of hand. Be ready to handle and resolve conflict and disruptive behavior, but not too soon (be observant and patient before acting). Facilitator creates a safe environment with techniques, such as establishing team or group ground rules and reminding them of the rules when they are not being followed. Using the agenda to maintain focus and appointing subgroups when needed with the right personnel on each.
4. Team building ability	25. Encourage creative thinking of team members and use tools to help 26. Build team to work effectively together, do their individual responsibilities while supporting the others 27. Understand group dynamics and team development	S: Facilitator encourages creativity in the team or group members and uses tools, such as brainstorming or nominal group technique, that enables creativity. Build the team to work together through exercises that forces teamwork and recognizes each member's importance to the team or group. Recognize the team or group on any important accomplishment.
5. Know the technical area process	28. Know and keep the group engaged on the process to be followed from start to completion	S: Too often this technical area or process is thought to be the responsibility of the functional or cross-functional members on the team. It is not. The process from simply following the agenda, a problem-solving process, or predetermined process, such as achieving a construction partnering agreement, is the responsibility of the facilitator. Learn the process prior to the meeting and keep the team on process during the meeting.

(Continued)

Table 11.3   Results Facilitator Core Competencies (Continued)

Skills	Core Competencies	S = Same for normal facilitator or R = for Results Facilitator only (Behavior–Skills–Education–Experience)
6. Know the key facilitation tools and techniques	29. Understand problem-solving and decision-making models including root cause analysis 30. Understand a variety of group methods and techniques to generate ideas, analyze ideas, develop countermeasures, and sell to management, implementation, monitoring, and ensuring completion and success	S: Every facilitator should know at least two problem processes with DMAIC being one of them. Generation of ideas tools, such as brainstorming, nominal group technique, affinity diagram are a must. Learning to use multivoting helps you build consensus quickly even though it is not a true consensus. Developing a problem statement or objective statement should be easy following a given procedure or process. Metrics or performance indicators development with establishing targets or goals and a data collection plan should be a requirement and tool of every facilitator. Gather data using check sheets, surveys, interviews, and Internet research are tools needed by facilitators in their sessions. Analysis of data and determining root causes are a must. Fishbone diagram with a root cause matrix, structure tree, and relationship diagrams are often beneficial. Using matrices and assigning criterion and gauging the efficiency, suitability, and/or effectiveness of possible counter-measure should be a tool that a facilitator can use any time in a meeting when it is called for by the situation. Histograms and Pareto diagrams to show priorities, flowcharting to show a process and to identify process and outcome metrics and eliminate waste is a must to any facilitator. Barriers and aids or force field analysis are good tools to help prepare to sell your team's or group's ideas and countermeasures. Control charts and simple regression analysis are tools that cannot be ignored. A facilitator should follow the Learn–Practice–Evaluate–Act continuous learning model. Every tool or technique you learn could help you become an even better facilitator.

(Continued)

Table 11.3   Results Facilitator Core Competencies (Continued)

Skills	Core Competencies	S = Same for normal facilitator or R = for Results Facilitator only (Behavior–Skills–Education–Experience)
7. Objective development	31. Know considerations or requirements and be able to develop objectives, targets, and action plans	R: Although this is shown as a requirement of a results facilitator, all facilitators should know it. Goals are long range and written in brief statements. Objectives are for two years or less and are more specific. The facilitator should know what elements, such as the legal requirements, risks, and other important elements that are needed to be considered prior to establishing the objective(s). Once the objective is established, then how do you ensure it is SMART (specific, measurable, actionable, realistic or relevant, and time framed) should be in a facilitator's toolkit.
8. Project management	32. Assist the group or team in managing and monitoring objectives and targets or projects to ensure the project's purpose is achieved	R: Tools and techniques to ensure the project is achieved on time, within budget, and with quality are important. How to develop action or project plans that includes what is going to be done, by whom, and when are essential for results facilitators. Using Gantt charts and even Critical Path Scheduling or Method (CPM) could be needed to ensure this core competency is a successful one.

(*Continued*)

Table 11.3   Results Facilitator Core Competencies (Continued)

Skills	*Core Competencies*	*S = Same for normal facilitator or R = for Results Facilitator only (Behavior–Skills–Education–Experience)*
9. Communicate with management, employees, and team	33. Develop rapport with participants including team members 34. Practice active listening to be able to effectively communicate the right message 35. Facilitator actively listens and then makes sure to confirm important points by playing them back. 36. Facilitator demonstrates the ability to process information quickly, differentiating content issues and identifying critical points in a discussion. 37. Facilitator asks follow-up questions that clarify, probe, and refocus attention. 38. Facilitator presents instructions that are clear, concise, and accurate.	S: Communicate clearly. Give good, clear, and accurate instructions. Go over a tool or technique until everyone understands. Learn to ask probing questions to get at the issues or pertinent points. Summarize after a lengthy session and some points could be hazy. Remember to listen actively and don't interrupt someone else unless absolutely necessary.
10. Know your client	39. Know your client's organization, mission, vision, and culture	S: Study your client's organization. The mission, vision, values, culture, and their facilitation needs. Determine the requirements for your services, exactly what deliverables are expected and when, whether any other facilitators are going to be involved, and the pay and how and when it will be received. Keep your client informed of status, issues and achievements.
11. Reach agreement on client's needs	40. Reach consensus on tasks, deliverables, roles, & responsibilities including co-facilitation 41. Clarify mutual commitment 42. Contract with client for scope, deliverables, and price or payment 43. Achieve a high-quality product and outcome that meets or exceeds the client needs	S: Place the facilitation requirements in a contract after they are determined and consensus has been reached. Any time a requirement may not be reached on time due to any reasons, yours or the organization, be sure the client knows ahead of time.

11.7 Critical Success Factors (CSFs) for a Facilitated Session

What is the critical thing that must happen at a session that is facilitated to ensure success? First, we will say that the client's requirements must be understood and agreed upon by the facilitator. Next, the facilitator must prepare for the session using the facilitator's checklist making sure the room is reserved, the meeting materials are present, and that an agenda was prepared and sent ahead of the meeting to all participants letting them know the time, date, and place where the meeting is going to be held. If the items on the agenda are covered, then it is almost certain the meeting's objective will be met. During the meeting, the agenda is followed within the timeframes, any disruptions or conflicts are managed, everyone participates, the solution solves the problem or seizes the opportunity, and all are in consensus. Then the notetaker writes the minutes that also show action items that need to be done and who is designated to accomplish them, and distributes the minutes to the participants and other interested personnel in three days or less. At the end of the session, a critique of the participants was done and they felt it was an excellent meeting that met the meeting objective. The client was happy with the results and complimented both the team leader and the facilitator.

Reviewing this description, the CSFs categories include:

■ Client Requirements and Satisfaction
■ Managing and Controlling Disturbances and Conflict
■ Group Engagement, Participation, and Meeting Desired Outcome(s)
■ Communications
■ Facilitator's Performance, Before, During, and After

Not surprisingly, the CSFs look a lot like the main headings in both of the core competencies shown above. For a facilitator to be able to accomplish the above—session after session—is what this book is about. Continuous learning, commitment, dedication, and adherence to core competencies will enable a facilitator to accomplish this. Businesses and the government need experienced and competent facilitators. The technique used above is not often taught or even included in textbooks or on the Internet. However, it can be very useful to a team. Write down what has to occur to have a success. Then go in and pick out of the scenario what the CSFs or key results areas (KRAs) are. These can be your CSFs or corporate KRAs. From these goals can be made and metrics or actionable performance measures determined. The process is: 1. Determine key result areas. 2. What are the metrics to measure progress and results. 3. What is critical to make this happen?

11.8 Facilitators' Core Competencies Recommendations

Shouldn't there be just one list of core competencies for facilitators who are certified master facilitators or certified professional facilitators? The certification process has sufficient distinguishing differences to decide on a facilitator's level using the same core competencies. Their knowledge of them and their performance can still be judged, with the CMF requiring higher marks from the assessment.

INIFAC and IAF are not in competition. They are separate organizations, with some members involved in both, dedicated to the facilitation profession. This will allow for a joint task force, with members from IAF and INIFAC, to consolidate the core competencies for facilitators. For example, coaches have only one list of core competencies. Why should facilitators have two or more? The author likes the INIFAC format and name, but IAF has some elements that could add more meat to some of the items, such as client's requirements or needs. Comprehensive, feasible, and suitable facilitation core competencies could be developed. The results facilitator could aspire to the IAF and INIFAC core competency list, providing the skills in Chapter 3, Figure 3.2. Skill set of a results facilitator are a part of their skill set and the few areas mentioned above that were not covered.

11.9 Facilitator Exercises

1. The author believes the IAF core competencies are all inclusive and no additional competencies need to be added. True __ False __
2. The IAF core competencies creation was a major undertaking and overall the IAF did a respectable job. True __ False __
3. The IAF core competencies are used in the IAF facilitators' certification process. True __ False __

4. The INIFAC core competencies are clearer and simpler written than the IAF's. True __ False __

5. The INIFAC core competencies are called PAC³E. True __ False __

(See Appendix 1 for answers.)

Chapter 12

Facilitator's Offshoots and Questions from New Facilitators (39 Different Areas)

12.1 The 39 Areas

12.1.1 Subject Content

12.1.1.1 Is It a Must That the Facilitator Know the Subject Content?

Facilitators are expected to be the ISO 50001 EnMS and the Tools and Techniques authority, but what about the meeting's subject matter? If it is either of the two above, it is the facilitator's responsibility. If it is about the facility's problems or opportunities, then the team leader is responsible for the subject area. What if the team leader is new and doesn't know the subject, should the facilitator help? Absolutely, as the name of this book implies (*The Results Facilitator: Expert, Manager, Mentor*). If needed, and if the facilitator is knowledgeable, then assist the team leader so that the meeting's purpose and the goals are achieved. Remember, results are not about who gets the credit, it's about producing the deliverables and achieving the desired results as a team. If the task is for a one- or two-meeting facilitator job, then the facilitator is neutral and does not deal with subject content, but merely the process to lead to obtaining the objective.

12.1.2 Responsibility for Results

12.1.2.1 Is the Facilitator Held Responsible for the Results?

In those cases where a facilitator works for a staff group at the headquarters of a company and facilitates at its facilities, is he/she held responsible for the results whether that is spelled out or not? Unfortunately, the facilitator is held responsible. Should you change your method of facilitating? No, continue to facilitate to get results and alter your process or technique only when required. If you are facilitating an energy team, get familiar with the facility, equipment, electricity usage, and significant electricity users. This will help you answer questions from other staff members at the headquarters. Remember as a facilitator, you are not worried about who gets the credit, but that the team achieve its goal. If they do, you also will be recognized as a successful facilitator and as a team member. For the one or two meeting facilitation jobs, the team is held responsible for the results. The facilitator makes it easier for them to achieve the objective.

12.1.3 Team Composition

12.1.3.1 Is the Facilitator a Team Member?

This is an excellent question. It depends on the mindset of the team. If the facilitator has fit well into the team meetings, has helped them achieve their purposes, and moved them toward their goals, the team will most probably consider the facilitator as a part of its team. If the facilitator comes from another location, such as a headquarters, and facilitates at a facility that reports to the headquarters, then the team may not think of the facilitator as a team member, but someone from headquarters. The team has roles and responsibilities defined and facilitator is one of them. The author has always felt a part of the team, even often facilitating more than one team during the same time period. If an external facilitator is used, he or she may not feel part of the team, but more like an orchestrator.

12.1.3.2 What Is the Optimum Size for a Team?

A team should have at least two members other than the facilitator. If the team is cross functional, then it should have at least one team member for each major functional area. Trying to achieve the latter has driven some teams to have 12 or more members. This is unacceptable because it is so large that it is nonproductive. The reason can be that the number of possible communications between team members is so large that nothing gets done. An excellent team size is between five and seven including the team leader and the facilitator. In the past, when a team got behind, the 3M Company would reduce the team size by one. They definitely would not add another member as most corporations would.

12.1.4 *Team Momentum*

12.1.4.1 *How Many Objectives and Targets (O&Ts) Are Necessary to Maintain a Team?*

Objectives and targets drive the momentum of a team that is pursuing quality improvement, strategic planning goals and objectives, or ISO standards implementation. It is why teams need to meet on a periodic basis to see if the O&Ts are being progressed and eliminate any barriers to progress. The author has always felt comfortable with four to six O&Ts, except for task teams where they have only one O&T. However, once the objective is achieved, the task team is disbanded. The ISO teams continue on their continuous improvement journey. Several O&Ts are necessary to provide them momentum.

12.1.5 *Jumpstarting a Team*

12.1.5.1 *How Can You Jumpstart a Team if Needed?*

Teams can get mired down due to loss of key members, change in team leader or facilitator, change in top management and their support, had great success in the past but struggling now, objectives and targets not considered important, team has been in business for a long time, and for numerous other causes.

Jumpstarting can be accomplished in several ways depending on the team's individual circumstances. Replacing a team leader with a more dedicated and enthusiastic one or with a more experienced facilitator may do the job. Looking and finding a way to get management more involved in supporting the team, or having them reemphasize the importance normally is an excellent countermeasure. The jumpstarting process defined in Chapter 11 works.

12.1.6 *Facilitator's Skills*

12.1.6.1 *Are All Facilitators Equal?*

The answer is absolutely no. Often good team members with people skills are appointed as a facilitator and have received little or no training. Depending on the team type, purpose, and team leader and team members' experience, the newly appointed facilitator may be successful or not. However, for a facilitator not trained in the skills outlined in this book, teams with a major purpose and demanding issues would be most difficult. If the newly appointed facilitator receives the oval skill set, then his/her probability of success approaches 100%. Facilitator's experience, training, education, and personality all contribute to how good a facilitator can be.

12.1.7 *Seven Quality Control Tools*

12.1.7.1 *Is Life over for the Seven QC Tools?*

The seven QC tools initiated by the total quality consultants in Japan during the 1980s and 1990s were extensively used. The seven QC tools are graphs, check sheets, histograms, Pareto charts, fishbone diagrams, control charts, and scatter diagrams. These tools are still very useful in Lean and Six Sigma applications. Other statistical tools, different kinds of flow charts, Pugh matrixes, DMAIC problem-solving process, and several others have expanded the tool kit. For a simple problem or opportunities, these seven QC tools are still very useful.

12.1.8 *Listening*

12.1.8.1 *How Important Is the Ability to Listen for a Facilitator?*

Listening is extremely important. One good rule to remember is: It is hard to listen with your mouth moving (talking). There are numerous barriers to good listening that the facilitator must overcome such as: not listening to subject matter that is not interesting, writing and only partially listening, dreaming about something else while someone else is talking, and thinking of how you are going to do something while someone is explaining how they would do it. Everyone is guilty of this, so facilitators must keep their focus.

12.1.9 Training

12.1.9.1 Who Provides the Training to New Team Members?

Normally, the facilitator. It is a good practice to develop a new members' training PowerPoint® presentation to give to new members to help bring them up to speed. The facilitator is the one who also briefs the management on the process the team will use to accomplish their mission and goals or objectives. Of course, if an organization has a training department, they may accomplish the training.

12.1.9.2 Who Trains the Objective Champion or Strategic Council or Top Management in the EnMS?

Normally, the lead facilitator. However, facilities managers, environmental managers, energy consultants, or advisers (in-house or contractors) may do the training. The lead facilitator for EnMS or EMS is the energy team facilitator, adviser to the objective champion, and, if requested, facilitator to top management and/or their team, such as the Strategic Council.

12.1.10 Certification

12.1.10.1 Should I Become Certified?

This decision is a personal one. The author believes in certification if it will help one's career. The author became a registered professional engineer almost immediately after reaching four years of experience. The U.S. Air Force civil engineering encouraged that its officers become PEs (professional engineers). This was a motivating factor for the author, who facilitated some meetings while in the air force, but did not know what facilitation was at the time. Later at Florida Power & Light Company, he was selected as one of the original facilitators in the company's successful bid for the Deming prize. (FPL was the first company outside Japan to win the coveted Deming Prize for Quality). The author facilitated many teams at all levels including a company-wide, corporate cross-functional strategic team to improve electrical distribution reliability. Next, with the author's own industrial engineering and quality improvement company, he facilitated many military and civilian teams on multiple subjects from strategic planning, process improvement, and conflict resolution in organizations and problem solving. In the past seven years, the author as a contractor (senior associate environmental and energy consultant) facilitated eight major government facilities' environmental teams (some included energy) and a headquarters energy team. Because he had already become an experienced facilitator at FPL and trained as a facilitator, he did not feel it was essential for him to become certified. However, if it will help you by providing credentials, by all means, go for it.

12.1.11 Communications

12.1.11.1 How Can You Improve Communications?

In every organization where the author has surveyed the employees, this is always a major concern. All of us have heard the statement that 10% never get the word. In constructing a large nuclear plant, plant management ran into this situation. The site manager desired that all personnel be informed of certain information. He recommended that the site staff communicate with as many media of communications necessary to ensure 100% were informed. Media is any form of unique communications, such as handing out a letter at the gate, posting information on the official bulletin board, mentioning in staff meetings, mentioning at tail board meetings, and others. It took seven different media until the last person was informed.

There are several ways to enhance communications. Active listening, active understanding, caring, honesty, showing interest, and demonstrating respect are some characteristics the management, team leaders, and facilitators need to practice. Having hidden agendas, showing hostilities, becoming defensive, and stereotyping are conditions that hinder good communications.

12.1.12 Feedback

12.1.12.1 How Do You Ensure the Feedback You Give as a Facilitator Is Helpful?

Feedback from facilitators is so important in helping teams learn, adjust, improve, and grow. Sharing knowledge and experiences is an important skill of a facilitator. Prior to providing the feedback, it is a best practice for the facilitator to ask him/herself three questions. First question is: "Does it pertain to the matter or issue under discussion?" Secondly: "Does the team need to know this?" Third: "Will it help the team to do better?"

Feedback for feedback sake is not helpful to the team and often can become very distracting.

12.1.13 Group Stages

12.1.13.1 Can You Actually See a Team Go through the Four or Five Stages of Group Dynamics?

The answer is: Sometimes. Most of the time, you cannot, except when going from the Storm to the Norm stage since the meeting room will be less noisy. A team going from the Norm to the Perform stage can be validated in how the team produces deliverables and results. The fifth stage added by Tuckman (Tuckman Model of Team Development) is Adjourned. Of course, that one is recognizable.

12.1.14 Team Members

12.1.14.1 Has It Been Your Experience That the Team Leader, Facilitator, and One or Two Team Members Do Most of the Team Work?

In Quality, Lean, and Six Sigma teams, I have not found that prevalent. In Environmental Management System teams, I have witnessed that on several teams. In this case, you normally have a team leader and one or more team members who are greatly interested in improving the environment. The other team members are on the team as a part-time job and have busy regular jobs. Therefore, they just attend meetings and do as little as they can outside the team meetings. Energy teams are too new to make a judgment. It is a possibility that the team leader, facilitator, and facilities personnel will carry the burden for most outside the meeting work assignments. The facilitator should try to make the teamwork equitable and to get all the members involved at the meetings.

12.1.15 Team Members Replacement

12.1.15.1 On Permanent Teams, Do You Think That Team Members Should Be Replaced Periodically, for Example, Every Year?

Some supervisors and managers push for this. As long as new members are interested and receive some training, this policy will work. There is normally attrition due to transfers, promotions, and retirements that provides some turnover or change in team members. The author does believe if a member wants to stay on the team, then he/she should be allowed to do so. Changing the team leader is another subject. Any change should ensure the new leader is interested, motivated, and ready to take the challenge.

12.1.16 *Team Leader/Facilitator Coordination*

12.1.16.1 *Should the Team Leader and Facilitator Meet before Each Meeting?*

A person-to-person meeting may not be necessary, but a telephone call or email communication is highly recommended. Together they need to develop the purpose of the meeting, the time, and a decision on who is going to notify the team and reserve a meeting room. Also, who is going to cover each item and if any guests are going to attend and participate in the meeting. When the team is notified of the time, date, and place for the meeting, a copy of the agenda should be given to each of them. Sometimes either the team leader or facilitator will need to contact all or certain team members to see if they can attend at certain times or dates prior to completing the agenda and team notification.

12.1.17 *Meeting Length*

12.1.17.1 *How Long Should Our Meetings Last?*

The answer really depends on what items are included in the agenda. If the team is reviewing, say, the monitoring and measurement plan or the communications plan, it will not take long. However, if they are developing it and putting it into words, then it will take much longer. It is a best practice to have one or two members draft something like these two examples and then bring them to the meeting for review.

Most EnMS or EMS meetings require an hour. At the beginning of the planning and development phase, an hour and a half can be beneficial. Some teams have reduced their meetings to 30 minutes. To do so takes a lot of planning to be sure everything that needs to be done is covered and documented. Training sessions normally vary from one to four hours.

12.1.18 Document Control Manager

12.1.18.1 Is It a Good Practice to Have the Team Leader for an ISO Team Be the Document Control Manager?

Yes. The teams where the team leader is the document control manager have managed their documents better than teams that had a separate document control manager. No one knows what should be documented better than the team leader and facilitator. Using the facilitator as the document control manager is not usually done if he/she facilitates other teams.

12.1.19 Award and Recognition

12.1.19.1 When a Company or Organization Has an Awards Program, Does It Motivate Teams?

Absolutely. Having both team and individual awards programs are motivating. The awards do not have to be expensive to be effective. A plaque, watch, and gift certificate are three examples that are well received and not expensive. Recognition and awards should be *timely*, *sincere*, and *appropriate*.

12.1.20 Energy Team

12.1.20.1 Does a Company Only Need to Have One Energy Team or Are Others Recommended?

This depends on the size of the company, the distance between facilities, and the number of facilities. Naturally, you must have the corporate energy or EnMS team. Next, it is logical to have one team at each facility that works with the corporate team. In addition, task teams that are temporary and focus on one task, such as improving the HVAC or lighting system, could be beneficial.

12.1.21 Lead Facilitator

12.1.21.1 How Do You Define a Lead Facilitator?

If an organization has multiple teams, then each should be facilitated. A full-time facilitator can facilitate 8 to 10 teams. The lead facilitator is the one that facilitates the corporate energy or EnMS team or quality councils, works with the organization's top management and keeps the other facilitators informed on major issues and plans. Each facility should have at least one facilitator. Often, staff directorates have facilitators for their teams. Facilities could have a facilitator for operations, one for procurement, one for inventory, etc. The number will be determined by the need for teams. Having a facilitator just for the sake of having one is not recommended.

12.1.22 *Lean and Six Sigma*

12.1.22.1 *Do Lean and Six Sigma Efforts Need Facilitators?*

Absolutely. Often the black belt or green belt will do the facilitation and sometimes lead the meetings. The team leader has some facilitator training and may be thought of as the facilitator.

12.1.23 *Objective and Target Responsibilities*

12.1.23.1 *Is It Good to Have Most, If Not All of the Team Members, Be Responsible for an Objective and Target on an ISO Team?*

Yes. Each team leader and facilitator should, over time, have each team member either assigned as the responsible person for an objective and target or have completed one or more in the past.

12.1.24 *O&T Responsible Person*

12.1.24.1 *What Are the Responsibilities of an Objective and Target Responsible Person?*

The responsible person is responsible for the action plan for the objective and target. He or she either accomplishes the listed tasks on time or ensures, if others are listed, that they accomplish their assigned tasks. He or she reports status or any problems to the team at their regular meeting or to the team leader if any assistance is required in between meetings.

12.1.25 *O&T Time to Completion*

12.1.25.1 *How Long Should an Objective and Target Take to Finish or Complete?*

Objectives and targets can take as long as two years or they can be done in 30 minutes or less, depending on the scope and complexity. To place a sign saying "turn off the lights" may take 30 minutes or less, but to monitor and measure the EnPIs will take as long as the organization is pursuing energy reduction and savings. Installing a boiler would take some time, whereas putting different belts on an air handler would not.

12.1.26 *Coaching Effectiveness*

12.1.26.1 *How Do You Know Whether the Coaching You Have Been Doing Was Effective?*

The real key is: Can they do what the coaching focus was on better now than before? Ask yourself, "What behavior or action should they now be able to accomplish?" If possible, observe and provide meaningful feedback.

12.1.27 *kWh Intensity*

12.1.27.1 *Why Is kWh/sq. Footage Used as an EPI When kWh Usage Tells You How Well You Did?*

True. kWh usage does, over time, tell you how well your countermeasures have worked. Facilities are of different sizes and it is not possible or feasible to compare them if not normalized. This is done by dividing by the number of people, number of computers, or total gross square footage. This EnPI now can be benchmarked with similar facilities to see how well you are doing. The trend for both kWh usage and electricity intensity (kWh/sq. ft.) will be identical.

12.1.28 Team Types

12.1.28.1 What Are the Different Kinds of Teams That Exist in Today's Organizations and Companies?

Any attempt to list them will most probably fail by leaving several out. However, let's try.

- Tiger Team: Team formed to handle quickly relatively small tasks.
- Natural Working Group: Team in the same functional or subfunctional area formed to work on problems that arise in their area.
- Functional Team: Similar to the Natural Working Group in that they address problems in their functional area. A little more formal and they often use a problem-solving process.
- Task Team: Formed to address one major task problem or opportunity, completes it, and then disbands.
- Process Improvement Team (PIT): Addresses a key support or operational process to make improvements in performance or customer satisfaction. Sometimes called a Process Action Team (PAT).
- Strategic Improvement Team: A cross-functional team that addresses a strategic objective or goal.
- Headlight Team: A high-level, cross-functional team that is looking at fuzzy areas to bring focus on items that organization should address.
- EnMS Team: A cross-functional team that addresses energy issues and problems.
- EMS Team: A cross-functional team that addresses environmental problems.
- Safety Team: A cross-functional team that addresses safety issues.
- Self-Directed Work Team: A group of people with different skills and talents who work together to achieve a goal or purpose without supervision.
- Kaizen Event: Normally lasts one or two days with focus on improving a key process. Process participants and Kaizen facilitator are in attendance.
- Quality Circle: Similar to the functional team.
- Quality Improvement Team: A group of people assigned to improve a process or solve a problem.
- Quality in Daily Work Team: A team assigned to improve quality satisfaction on daily issues or a process.
- Lean Team: A team assigned to take the waste out of a process and improve its performance.

■ DMAIC Team: A team assigned to solve a problem or improve a process using Six Sigma.

12.1.29 Facilitator Benefits

12.1.29.1 What Are the Benefits of Having a Facilitator?

The author could write several chapters to answer this question, but the benefits are very apparent if you now have facilitators. Meetings are started and finished on time. Every meeting has an agenda. Most meetings achieve their purpose. Team goals and corporate goals are achieved. The corporate mission is enhanced and vision is achieved.

Meetings expend several resources: the rooms, equipment, and team members' or participants' time. It saves the company considerable money if the meetings are effective. Complex issues can be worked out by teams in a smooth and productive fashion.

Trained facilitators are excellent people to have for career advancement in the organization. They make excellent supervisors, managers, directors, and executives.

12.1.30 Neutrality

12.1.30.1 Should a Facilitator Be Neutral and Not Participate in the Meeting Contents?

In some group events, the facilitator must remain neutral because participants may think he/she is bias. A facilitator will know when this is the case depending on the event. If the facilitation is an ongoing team, the facilitator has some responsibility for the results, the facilitator is knowledgeable of the contents topic, then he or she can engage in content discussion. Implementing an ISO 14001 EMS or ISO 50001 EnMS are examples of Results Facilitators if the facilitator is a part of the organization either as an employee or contractor, then they can enter the contents discussions.

12.1.31 Team's Success

12.1.31.1 When Is a Team Considered Successful?

A team is considered successful when it achieves its objective, providing it was met in a timely and quality manner.

12.1.32 In-House versus Outside Facilitator

12.1.32.1 When Is it Best to Use an Outside Facilitator Instead of an In-House Facilitator?

It is best, in most cases, to use an outside facilitator for special events, such as a Kaizen event or introducing a new strategy where the in-house facilitator, as of yet, has not received any training.

Often a mixture of outside or contract facilitators with in-house facilitators is best to start a new strategy, such as an ISO standard implementation.

Some organizations develop a "super star" facilitator that through his or her experiences, successes, and personality is well respected. This facilitator can be used when normally you would hire one from the outside. However, this type of facilitator is rare, especially since most would not have the training or education to implement new strategic initiatives.

12.1.33 LeBron James as NBA's Best Results Facilitator

12.1.33.1 Why Is LeBron James Called the Best Facilitator Ever in the NBA?

How about Michael Jordan? Michael had more than six assists per game in only 3 of his 15 years. Kobe Bryant, only in one year. LeBron continues to do so year after year.

12.1.34 Results Facilitator Name Acceptability

12.1.34.1 Will the Facilitator World, including the National Organizations, Accept the Term Results Facilitator?

Probably not. They have entrenched in their minds that a facilitator should be neutral to subject content or topics. Results facilitation is now a reality and they all will have to deal with it eventually. Many teams are on journeys with no destination. These teams foster the results facilitators.

12.1.35 Things a Facilitator Can Do Badly

12.1.35.1 What Are Some of the Things You Noticed That Facilitators Do Badly in Some Meetings?

Some facilitators push their own agenda items instead of the team's, do not control the talking that goes on that is not on subject, do not effectively handle disagreements, and do not adequately know the tool or technique that the team is using.

12.1.36 *Process Observers*

12.1.36.1 *In My Last Organization, the Facilitator Used Process Observers to Help Monitor the Team Meetings. Do You Think They Are Useful?*

In my experience, a trained facilitator does not need additional process observers. The facilitator is the best one to observe how well the process is going. The process observers can throw the team progress off track in some of their observations and critiques. However, if it works for you, use them.

12.1.37 *Exit Interviews*

12.1.37.1 *Should the Team Have Exit Interviews with Team Members Who Resigned or Ask to Be Excused from the Team?*

Absolutely. The team leader and one member of the team or the facilitator should interview them. Why are they leaving? What could the team do to improve? Are the meetings too long? Too boring? Not effective? Contain wrong members from the wrong functional areas? This is a good opportunity to get information on how to improve the team's effectiveness.

12.1.38 *Team Closure*

12.1.38.1 *Should There Be Specific Activities Accomplished When a Team Is Closing?*

Yes. Ensure that team's recommendations are presented to management and include all affected personnel. Determine how improvements will be maintained. Develop a list of lessons learned to include any functional areas that would be helpful to add to a future team with a similar problem or opportunity. Complete all required reports and documentations.

12.1.39 Facilitators Phased out

12.1.39.1 Don't Most ISO Standards Implementation Teams Phase out Facilitators When They Reach the Maintenance Stage?

Yes, many do. The facilitating duties are learned by the team leader or some team members and they perform them when the facilitator is no longer assigned to the team. This is the development style of facilitation described earlier.

Tools/Techniques #50: Questions and Answers

12.2 Facilitator Exercises

1. Can a facilitator sometimes be the team leader, if the team leader is absent? Yes __ No __
2. Which is the most important, a caring attitude or a confident attitude or both? Caring __ Confident __ Both __
3. If you have the skills to be an inside facilitator, do you have the skills to be an outside facilitator? Yes __ No __
4. Which type of facilitator—normal or results—should you encounter the most? Normal __ Results __
5. Can you have a lousy team leader and an excellent facilitator and the team will be successful? Yes __ No __ Depends __
6. Can you have an excellent team leader and an inexperienced facilitator and the team will be successful? Yes __ No __ Depends __
7. Will a team of 20 people normally be successful? Yes __ No __

(See Appendix 1 for answers.)

Chapter 13

Conclusions

Whether you are a normal or a results facilitator or both, facilitating is a very interesting and rewarding experience. To be the best, learning must be a continuous endeavor to keep up with the latest techniques, tools, and concepts that can help achieve future jobs and missions. The facilitator's continuous learning model should be followed and become a way of life (Figure 13.1).

Learning is continuous. This book helps the journey because it includes techniques and tools helpful to facilitators. Of course, you will not use all of them at each facilitation session, but, over time, you will probably employ all of them. Included in this book is over 75 exercise questions or problems to complete to help you remember important points or information. Gain the skills of a results facilitator and practice them in your facilitating efforts.

Practice is the best way to make these tools and techniques become your own. You will like some tools and concepts better than others and will use them often. In the author's case, the nominal group technique, multivoting, metrics, Paretos, flowcharting, surveys, and the fishbone diagram are the ones that he often uses in his facilitating efforts. Prepare before each facilitation effort so you are ready to go immediately when the meeting starts. Using the comprehensive facilitator's checklist can help in this endeavor. Be ready to use the right tools and techniques, and facilitator's meeting and group dynamics abilities to manage and to assure that the climate is safe and pleasant.

Evaluate how you did after each facilitation effort. Self-assessments can identify areas for improvement and then taking actions to achieve the improvements can make you a better and more effective facilitator.

Figure 13.1 Facilitator's continuous learning model.

Consider becoming certified. It will accelerate your improvement focus and provide you with professional recognition. This will enable you to increase your résumé and advertisement for future facilitation business.

Both the IAF and INIFAC did an excellent job in identifying the core competencies for facilitators. However, as pointed out in Chapter 11, there are several that should be considered for addition for the challenging facilitating jobs of the twenty-first century. We recommend that IAF and INIFAC review their list and update where needed. Preferably, they will consolidate into just one official facilitator's core competencies list. Notably missing are coaching, establishing objectives, developing action plans, and project management skills. These are absolute if IAF and INIFAC agree to the results facilitator concept and accept it as a valid facilitator type.

Bruce Tuckman did an exceptional job in identifying the stages for team development in the 1960s. Because we have teams, such as those needed for ISO 14001 EMS and 50001 EnMS, and OHSMS 18000 Safety, a sustainment stage should be considered. These teams do not meet and solve a problem and then dismantle. They are on a journey without a destination.

Use DiSC® Profile or some personality profile to know yourself, your team members and, your team leader. This practice also will help you improve your abilities and capabilities. Use the coaching process to help your team members or workgroups. If the problem being addressed does not have a clear path to a conclusion and solution, consider the trial and error approach of Toyota kata.

Meetings are the platform for facilitators. Become masterful in how to conduct meetings including developing agendas using PAL and finishing the meetings using PAPA. Use the techniques to handle difficult behaviors and conflicts while achieving meeting objectives. Use team building to change your team to a high performing one.

Prior to any meeting that you are going to facilitate, know the technical process. You will be called on to keep the team on the process, otherwise the members can stagger off to a nonproductive venture. Prior to the meeting, prepare what tools and techniques will be most appropriate to use. However, be competent in the tools and techniques so you can switch to a new one if conditions call for it.

Use the CSFs for ongoing meetings to achieve a system. This gets the team focused on improvement by showing progress and highlighting what the team can do to improve prior to the next measurement session.

Always conduct yourself as a professional—prepare–be patient–summarize–correct–coach–teach–assist–manage–encourage–recognize–innovate— so you can be the best facilitator possible. Good luck in your journey. It should be an interesting and rewarding one. Remember, continuous learning, along with new experiences, are how you grow in professionalism, knowledge, and effectiveness.

Appendix

Facilitator Exercises

Chapter 1

1. Facilitators do not have a chance to be certified. **False**
2. In a process outputs and outcomes are the same. **False**
3. INIFAC means International Association of Facilitators. **False**
4. Open space technology is one of the 20 facilitation engagement processes. **True**
5. Effective critiques can be done in person at end of meeting or by filling out a critique form and giving to facilitator when the participant leaves the meeting room. **True**
6. Ground Rules should be established in the Engagement part of the process. **False**
7. The process major activities include
   d. Introductions–Engagements–Tools and Techniques–Critiques
8. At the beginning of the meeting (if it has not already been done), the facilitator should get the participants to agree on:
   d. Objective–Output–Outcome

Chapter 2

1. It is a best practice to evaluate each meeting soon after it was held. **True**
2. TOTs is an excellent technique to keep children happy. **False**
3. A facilitator only has responsibility for conducting or orchestrating the meeting and no duties before or after the meeting. **False**
4. Either using PAL or OAR is okay. **True**
5. It is okay for the facilitator to help write the meeting minutes. **True**

6. Meeting minutes should be completed and distributed to the participants within three business days. **True**
7. The facilitators' continuous learning model is:
   d. Learning–Practice–Evaluate–Act
8. Jumpstarting can help regain lost team/system momentum. **True**
9. It is best if the team solves its own problem(s). **True**

Chapter 3

1. The result facilitator is a new kind developing over the last 10 years. **True**
2. Most of the skills of a normal facilitator are also applicable to the results facilitator. **True**
3. IAF is the only organization that certifies facilitators. **False**
4. What is the facilitator's model for continuous improvement?
   Learning–Practice–Evaluate–Act
5. Which one of the possible skills is not appropriate for a facilitator?
   B. Stubborn
6. What is the difference between a skill and a core competency? **Core competency includes skill, training, and education**
7. What is the single largest difference between a results facilitator and a normal facilitator? **Neutral and not neutral**
8. What is the best process for a facilitator to continuously improve?
   Learning–Practice–Evaluate–Act

Chapter 4

1. Toyota kata can be done by an individual or a team. **True**
2. Facilitators are born because they have the desired influence personality. **False**
3. Toyota kata has a scientific base. **True**
4. A person who is dominant should not be a facilitator. **False**
5. Five Ss are a Lean tool/technique. **True**
6. The first S stands for Shine. **False**
7. Lean's primary focus is to eliminate waste. **True**
8. For presentations, when using the guide for a 30-minute presentation, you should not have more than 30 slides. **True**
9. Six Sigma's focus is on reducing variation of a process. **True**

10. Coaching should be provided to a team or team member only when everything else has not worked. **False**

Chapter 5

1. Tuckman's four stages of team involvement are:
   D. Form, Storm, Norm, & Perform
2. Name two of the most difficult behaviors that a facilitator must be able to deal with at meetings: **Side discussions and argumentative behavior**
3. The skilled facilitator approach stems from the same purpose as the mutual learning model. **Yes, both have some purpose.**
4. The same teaching approach for adults does not vary much from that for middle school children. **No. Adults need to participate more and not just listen.**
5. What are two ground rules set for meetings that should always be included? **Turn off cell phones and invoke the 100 mile rule**
6. What new stage does the author recommend to be added to the present four? **Sustain**
7. Flash cards are sometimes called "Cheat Cards". **True**
8. The engagement process called "tag" is similar to the game we played as kids. **True**
9. Why don't you hear the word GroupBuilding? **Because of their large numbers, it can become very difficult and wieldy to try to build a group.**
10. The main thrust of team building is to get the team to work and complete something together. **True**
11. Is it possible to have a "team of one"? **False**
12. Which is more difficult to facilitate, a group or a team? **Group**
13. If a team is performing in a manner that a facilitator says they have teamwork, would it be visible if you observe the meeting? **Yes**

Chapter 6
1. Using DMAIC, where would the problem definition be? (Please check correct one.) **D**
2. When using DMAIC, where would the control chart be included? (Please check correct one.) **C**

3. When using DMAIC, where would the metric be located? (Please check correct one.) **M**
4. When using DMAIC, where would a cause and effect diagram most probably be included? (Please check correct one.) **A**
5. What are the seven QC Tools? **(1) Graph (Indicator), (2) Flowchart, (3) Pareto, (4) Histogram, (5) Fishbone diagram or Cause and Effect diagram, (6) Scatter diagram, and (7) Control chart**
6. Which tool of the seven QC tools is used to prioritize what should be worked on next? **Pareto**
7. Which tool of the seven QC tools is used to show whether a process is in or out of control? **Control Chart**
8. Which tool of the seven QC tools is used to show if there is any correlation between two variables? **Scatter Diagram**
9. When would you use CAPDO instead of Plan–Do–Check–Act? **When you are addressing an existing process.**

Chapter 7

1. What technique is not used for collecting data or information? **B. Force Field Analysis**
2. Which of these techniques is used to develop data for an abstract subject of which you know little about? **C. Affinity Diagram**
3. Which tool or technique would you use to measure customer satisfaction? **C. Surveys**
4. Which tool helps us identify process and output metrics? **B. Flowchart**
5. Which tool helps us sell our solutions to management? **B. Force Field Analysis**

Chapter 8

1. O&Ts can be a feasibility study with a target. **True**
2. A target is a metric. **False**
3. Toyota kata has a trial and error component. **True**
4. An action plan tells how the activities can be accomplished. **False**
5. EnMS means Energy Management System. **True**
6. O&T and action plans are usually on the same page. **True**

7. What are the three types of objectives? **Improve–Feasibility–Maintain**
8. What are the two parts of an O&T template? **O&T and action plan**
9. What does the R stand for in making objectives SMART? **Either Realistic or Relevant**
10. What does the T stand for in making objectives SMART? **Time-framed**

Chapter 9

1. The project phases are Planning, Design, Execution, Review, and Closeout. **True**
2. Even contracted projects may have an organizational objective and target. **True**
3. May an action plan also be called a project plan. **True**
4. An Energy Conservation Measure is used by the federal government to track energy or water projects. **True**
5. Projects have life cycles and sometimes life-cycle costing is used to determine the total cost of the project over its lifetime. **True**
6. What are the KRAs for a large project? **Cost, Schedule, Time, and Quality**
7. What is matrix management? **A person has implied authority over a function where the people work functionally for someone else.**

Chapter 10

1. Experience + Additional Training & Research + Reflection + Application = Facilitator's Continued Readiness is IAF's model for continuous readiness. Does it conflict with the continuous improvement model of Learning-Practice-Evaluate-Act? **No**
2. A facilitator's reputation from his/her last job often is the reason he/she gets or does not get the next job opportunity. **True**
3. Self-reflection or evaluation, if done objectively, can help a facilitator continue to improve. **True**
4. Facilitators becoming certified is recommended but not mandatory. **True**

Chapter 11

1. The author believes the IAF core competencies are all inclusive and no additional competencies need to be added. **False**
2. The IAF core competencies creation was a major undertaking and overall the IAF did a respectable job. **True**
3. The IAF core competencies are used in the IAF facilitators' certification process. **True**
4. The INIFAC core competencies are clearer and simpler written than the IAF's one. **True**
5. The INIFAC core competencies are called PAC^{3}E. **True**

Chapter 12

1. Can a facilitator sometimes be the team leader, if the team leader is absent? **Yes**
2. Which is the most important, a caring attitude or a confident attitude or both? **Both**
3. If you have the skills to be an inside facilitator, do you have the skills to be an outside facilitator? **Yes**
4. Which type of facilitator—normal or results—should you encounter the most? **Normal**
5. Can you have a lousy team leader and an excellent facilitator and the team will be successful? **No**
6. Can you have an excellent team leader and an inexperienced facilitator and the team will be successful? **No**
7. Will a team of 20 people normally be successful? **No**

Facilitator Exercise 1

You are a facilitator on a strategic improvement team. Your team has been chartered to develop a plan to reduce paper use in your company by 20% by end of December 2014.

1. Prepare an agenda for the meeting using PAL.

Strategic Planning Improvement Team Meeting Agenda		
Purpose: Reduce paper use in our company by 20% by end of December 2014.		
Date/Time: Jan 14, 2014 10 a.m.–12 noon		
Agenda:		
10–10:30	Develop a name for the initiative or program	*Team*
10:31–11:30	Brainstorm possible ways to reduce office paper use; select the most suitable ways	*Team*
11:31–12 noon	Develop the objective, target, and action plan	*Team*

2. What tools or techniques would you use? **Brainstorming, multivoting, and an objective and target with an action plan template**.
3. Develop an objective and target for this task and an action plan.

What	*Who*	*Where*	*When*	*Remarks*
1. Prepare a PowerPoint® presentation to train all employees on the new office paper reduction	Facilitator and team leader	In the main conference room	Jan 15, 2014	Training program will include program name (PRIDE-Paper Reduction in Daily Effort) and suggested way to save paper
2. Gather paper use statistics	John Miller	In the accounting office	Jan 17, 2014	Get past two years data
3. Prepare a metric to show progress and results	Jim Trout	In his computer using Excel®	Jan 18, 2014	Metric will show benchmark: Last two year's paper use and by quarters how much used in 2014
4. Implement Duplex Printing: Announce to everyone by email, set copying elements on the machine to duplexing, develop & place signs near the copying machines	Louise Moore	Place signs on computers and set machines for duplexing	Jan 25–Feb 4, 2014	Duplexing is one of the best methods to reduce office paper use. The other best practice is to use electronic files and get rid of paper duplicate copies.
5. Track paper use and communicate to the team and to all employees	Jim Trout	In his computer and communicate by company-wide email and placing metrics on bulletin board	Beginning of second quarter in 2014	Do after each quarter until goal is achieved.

Facilitator Exercise 2

An energy team identified four possible O&Ts:

1. Set thermostat to 68°F (winter) and 78°F (summer).
2. Put in place 28 occupancy sensors in hallways, restrooms, break rooms, and mechanical rooms.
3. Change out the T-12s lights in the old office area to T-5s.
4. Implement a power management program in the office areas.

Questions:

1. What information do you need to prioritize these four O&Ts? Answer: How much kWh each would save or reduce and the cost in dollars for the action or project?
2. What type of prioritization technique would you use? Answer: Several techniques are possible, such as payback period, criterion matrix, and least cost per kWh reduced are the three most commonly used.

Chapter 13 Facilitator Exercise

An improvement team selected (1.) Leadership/Management Involvement, (2.) Employee Involvement, (3.) Resources, (4.) Objectives and Targets, and (5.) Communications as their Critical Successes Factors. They have been meeting for three months. The maximum score a CSF can achieve is a 5 and the highest score for the five CSFs is 25 (5 × 5 = 25). The scores received so far have been:

Meeting Date	1. Leadership 1–5	2. Employee Involvement 1–5	3. Resources 1–5	4. O&Ts 1–5	5. Communications 1–5	Total Score
Oct 14, 2013	2	1	1	1	1	6
Nov 17, 2013	2	2	1	1	1	7
Dec 10, 2013	2	3	1	3	1	10

1. Is the team improving? **Yes**
2. Do you think the team has O&Ts now? **Yes, 3 score shows progress.**
3. What CSFs do you need to address right away? **3. Resources and 5. Communications**

4. Name two things you could do to improve the leadership score? **Have management send out awareness training, hold a management review, send a commitment letter to all employees, showing what you are doing supports corporate goals, emphasize in staff meetings**

5. Name two things you could do to improve the communications score? **Send out PowerPoint training, develop a newsletter and distribute, put signs on bulletin board, hand out promotional material as employees enter the facilities**

6. What could be causing the low resources scores? **Poor conference rooms, some team members not available for meetings, promotional material requests not approved and funded**

You are a facilitator of a team of five people plus yourself, all from the same functional area. Your meeting tomorrow is to decide how to spend $500 for the summer party or picnic. The team's job is to reach consensus on what type of party, activities, and how to spend the money. If you need to assume anything, write it down as an assumption.

1. Write an agenda
2. Write the minutes using PAPA.

(Don't forget the actions items.)

Meeting Agenda: Functional Team		
Purpose: Team is to decide how to spend $500 for the summer party or picnic.		
Date/Time: June 22, 2014, 10–11 a.m.		
Agenda:		
10–10:10	Our purpose and decisions we need to make	*Team Leader*
10:10–11:20	Decision to have a summer picnic or a party	*Team*
10:20–10:50	Brainstorm a list of possibilities for purchasing	*Team*
Prioritize possibilities and select one		
Add and ensure it does not exceed $500		*Team*
10:50–11	Assign responsibilities	*Team Leader*

Assumptions: Date and time for the meeting and individual meeting items. No alcohol beverages.

PAPA

Meeting Agenda: Functional Team
Purpose: Team is to decide how to spend $500 for the summer party or picnic.
Date/Time: June 22, 2014, 10–11 a.m.
Agenda Results:

The functional team decided to have a picnic. Action Item #1: Elvin and Louise were selected to obtain the location by June 30, 2014.

The team brainstormed the possibilities of spending the $500. They selected:

- A clown for the children. Action Item # 2: Mary will obtain the clown for the picnic at or below $120.00.
- A small band. Action Item #3: Jack will hire the band at $150 or below to play at the picnic.
- Have BBQ plate with rolls and sodas for everyone. Action Item #4: John and Veronica will arrange for the food and drinks to be brought to the picnic by 11 a.m. on July 4, 2014. Cost $200.
- Hire an umpire for the softball game. Action Item #5: George will arrange for a qualified umpire to be at the picnic for the softball game between the accountants and the customer service personnel. Cost not to exceed $30.

Approved
John Lucky, Team Leader

Comment: Of course, your minutes will be different, but using the PAPA concept will save you in preparation time.

Chapter 3: Exercise 2

The management representative for energy, your boss, stated the energy team never starts on time or ends on time. I would like for you to find out why and determine what we can do to turn that around. Please advise me on this after the next meeting. The meetings data are listed below:

Meeting Number	Start Time = early/late (in minutes)	Finish Time = early/late (in minutes)
1	−15	−30
2	−05	−22
3	−12	−02
4	−42	−52
5	−07	−14
6	−17	−10
7	−22	−45
8	−09	−36
9	−13	−62
10	0	−12
11	−13	−26
12	−14	−34
13	−03	−15
14	−54	−45

1. What tool would you use to discover why meetings did not start on time? **A cause and effect diagram. A fishbone diagram would be very appropriate.**
2. What is the metric you would use to determine how bad the situation is? **Percentage of meetings that started on time and percentage of meetings ending on time. The data points would be for each six months. The first six months, six out of six started late. For the second six months, five of six started late. The first data point is "0" because all six were late. The second six months, one of six meetings was started on time (1/6 = .166 or 16.6%).**
Figure A1.1 and Figure A1.2 are two different charts. First, the bar chart and then the line chart or graph. Both are appropriate, but the line chart or graph is better at showing trends and the bar chart is better at doing or showing comparisons. Calculate percent of meetings starting on time for both the first and second six months and plot on a line

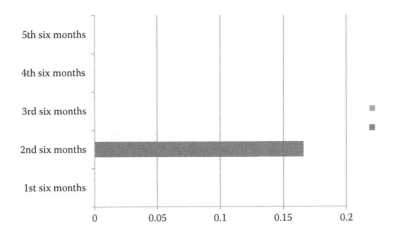

Figure A1.1   Bar chart.

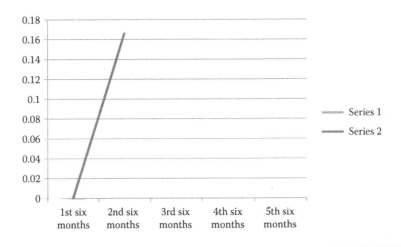

Figure A1.2   Line chart or graph.

graph. As the team improves, these graphs will show the improvement. You could combine the two with the metric being percent meetings started and ended on time.

3. What other tools/techniques would you use in finding the root causes and identifying corrective actions or countermeasures? **Fishbone diagram, root cause evaluation matrix, force field analysis or barriers and aides analysis, and a solution matrix**.

Bibliography

Alpaugh, P. K., V. J. Renner, and J. E. Birren. 1976. Age and creativity: Implications for education and teachers. *Educational Gerontology* 1: 17–40.

Beckett, D., Jr. Six tips for being a good facilitator. Online at: www.dannybeckettjr.com

Bens, I. 2000. *Facilitating with ease!: A step-by-step guidebook with customizable worksheets on CD-ROM.* San Francisco: Jossey-Bass.

Boynton, A. C. and R. W. Zmud. 1984. An assessment of critical success factors. *Sloan Management Review* 25 (4): 17–27.

Cameron, E. 2001. *Facilitation made easy,* 2nd ed. Milford, CT: Kogan Page.

Camp, R. C. 1989. *Benchmarking: Finding and implementing best practices that lead to superior performance.* Milwaukee: ASQC Quality Press.

Caralli, R. A. 2004. *The critical success factor method: Establishing a foundation for enterprise security management.* Pittsburgh: Carnegie Mellon Software Engineering Institute.

Chang, R. Y. and M. Morgan. 2000. *Performance score cards: Measuring the right things in the real world.* San Francisco: Jossey-Bass.

Chung, K. H. 1987. *Management: "Critical success factors.* Weiston, MA: Allyn and Bacon.

De Bono, E. 1985. *Six thinking hats: An essential approach to business management.* New York: Little, Brown & Company.

Denning, S. 2011. How do you change an organizational culture? Online at: www. Forbes.com

Digman, L. A. 1986. *Strategic management: Concepts, decisions, cases.* Plano, TX: Business Publications, Inc.

Drucker, P. F. 1964. *Managing for results.* New York: Harper and Row.

Facilitation checklist. Job performance situations 3-c: Building essential skills in facilitation, decision-making, and communication. head start moving ahead competency-based training program. HHS/ACF/ACYF/HSB. 1998.

Hackman, J. R. 1987. The design of work teams. In *Handbook of organizational behavior,* ed. J. Lorsch (pp. 315–342). Englewood Cliffs, NJ: Prentice-Hall.

Hackman, J. R. 2002. *Leading teams: Setting the stage for great performances.* Boston: Harvard Business School Press.

Hackman, J. R. and M. O'Connor. 2004. *What makes for a great analytic team? Individual vs. team approaches to intelligence analysis.* Washington, D.C.: Intelligence Science Board, Office of the Director of Central Intelligence.

Hackman, J. R. and R. Wageman. 2005. A theory of team coaching. *Academy of Management Review*, 269–287.

Hackman, J. R. and R. E. Walton. 1986. Leading groups in organizations. In *Designing effective work groups*, ed. P. S. Goodman (pp. 72–119). San Francisco: Jossey-Bass.

Heron, J. 1999. *The complete facilitator's handbook.* Milford, CT: Kogan Page.

Hogan, C. F. 2002. *Understanding facilitation.* London: Kogan Page.

Hogan, C. F. 2003. *Practical Facilitation.* London: Kogan Page.

Hogan, C. F. 2007. *Facilitating multicultural groups: A practical guide.* London: Kogan Page.

Hogan, C. F. 2013. *Facilitating cultural transitions and change, a practical approach.* Stillwater, OK: 4 Square Books.

Howell, M. T. 2005. *Actionable performance measurement: A key to success.* Milwaukee: ASQ Quality Press.

Howell, M. T. 2010. *Critical success factors simplified: Implementing the powerful drivers of dramatic business improvement.* New York: Taylor & Francis Group.

Howell, M. T. 2014. *Effective implementation of ISO 50001 energy management system.* Milwaukee: ASQ Quality Press.

Hunter, D., A. Bailey, and B. Taylor. 1998. *The facilitation of groups.* Brookfield, VT: Gower.

James, B. 1982–1988. The Bill James abstract. New York: Ballantine Books.

Johnson, J. A. and M. Frieson. 1995. *The success paradigm: Creating organizational effectiveness through quality and strategy.* New York: Quorem Books.

Justice, T., et al. 1999. *The facilitator's fieldbook: Step-by-step procedures, checklists and guidelines, samples and templates.* New York: AMACOM.

Leidecker, J. K. and A. V. Bruno. 1984. Identifying and using CSFs. *Long Range Planning* 17 (1): 23–32.

Mears, P. 1995. *Quality improvement tools and techniques.* New York: McGraw Hill.

Mizuno, S., (ed.). 1988. Management for quality improvement. In *The 7 new QC tools.* Cambridge, MA: Productivity Press.

Owen, H. 1997. *Expanding our now: The story of open space technology.* San Francisco, CA: Berrett-Koehler.

Owen, H. 2012. *Open space technology: A user's guide.* Sydney, Australia: ReadHowYouWant.

Pollalis, Y. A. and I. A. Freze. 1993. A new look at CSFs. *Information Strategy* Fall: 24–34.

Prahalod, C. K. and G. Hamel. 1990. Core competency of the corporation. *Harvard Business Publishing* May.

Rockart, J. F. 1986. A primer on critical success factors. In *Rise of managerial computing.* Homewood, IL: Dow Jones Irwin.

Rockart, J. F. 1979. Chief executives define their own data needs. *Harvard Business Review* 57.2 (March-April).

Rockart, J. F. and C. V. Bullen. 1981. *A primer on critical success factors.* Cambridge, MA: MIT, Center for Information Systems Research, Sloan School of Management.

Rother, M. 2009. *Toyota kata: Managing people for improvement, adaptiveness, and superior results.* New York: McGraw-Hill Professional.

Schuman, S. (Ed.). 2005. *The IAF Handbook of Group Facilitation: Best Practices from the Leading Organization in Facilitation.* San Francisco: Jossey-Bass/ Wiley.

Schwarz, R. 2002. *The skilled facilitator: A comprehensive resource for consultants, facilitators, managers, trainers and coaches,* 2nd ed. San Francisco: Jossey-Bass.

Shih, J. 2013. Business processes impacts in shaping organizational culture. *The Quality Management FORUM,* 38 (4).

Steiner, G. A. 1979. *Strategic planning.* New York: MacMillan.

Web Sites

Facilitation Company: Information, ideas, and references

www.facilitationcompany.com
http://www.openspaceworld.org/
http://lists.openspacetech.org/pipermail/oslist-openspacetech.org/2012-
September/028385.html (Owen, H. 2008. *Open space technology: A
user's guide*, 3rd ed. San Francisco: Berrett-Koehler.) http://www.open-
spaceworld.org Open Space Institute
http://www.openspaceworldscape.org

International Facilitation Association

http://www.iaf-world.org/issue3front.htm
IAF core competencies for certification: www.iaf.world.org.certification

Diagnosis Intervention Model

www.cdbanational.com

Difficult Behaviors

facilitoru.com/blog/meetings/dealings-with-difficult behaviors www.
masterfacilitatorjournal.facilatoru.com/archives/skill223.html

Facilitator's Checklist

www.uncher.org/4371d7c92.pdf Facilitators Toolkit-UNHCR
www.baruch.cunhy.edu/hr/documents/Facilitatorsskills-checklist.doc
www.edjj.org/training/pdf/Facilitator's%20checklist.pdf
www.ucop.edu; Facilitator's Checklist/ucop
www.uspto.gov/web/offices/com/oqn-oldFacilitation.pdf; Facilitator's Toolkit
www.fni.se/Documents/ICMI/checklist-for-facilitators.pdf
www.6cafn.ca/toolkit/tools2.2; Facilitator's Checklist
www.msduua.org/wp-content/12/TJDEEEffective Group Facilitation.pdf
www.ask.com/Facilitation Checklist

Group Effectiveness Model

Physlogy.wikia.com/wiki/Hackman's_group_effectiveness_model

Managing Organizational Climate

A Rahim, TV Bonoma - Psychological reports, 1979 - amsciepub.com

Mutual Learning Model

www.schwarzassociates.com/what-is-the-mutual-learning-model

PAL (Purpose-Agenda-Limited)

http://www.mannersmith.com/resources/issue.cfm?id = 6

Team Stages

Tuckman's teamwork questionnaire: www.nwlink.com/~donclark/leader/
teamsuv.html
Tuckman's theory of forming, norming, storming, performing:

The Management Assistance for Nonprofits:

http://www.mapnp.org/library/grp_skll/theory/theory.htm

The Skilled Facilitator's Approach

www.schwarassociates.com The skilled facilitator's approach

Tuckman's Four Stages of Group Development

*en.wikipedia.org/.../***Tuckman's_stages_of_group_development**

Others

www.nwlink.com/~donclark/leader/leadtem2.html
www.google.com
www.ask.com
http://www.iso.org/energy_management_system_standard
http://www.sei.ie/energymap/
Learn@coreexcel.com (for DISC booklet information)

Index

A

ability to influence
  client understanding, 58–60
  coaching, 62–74
  collaborative client relationships, 58–60
  facilitator/team leader interface, 60–61
  feedback, 63, 64–65
  final steps, 63, 64–65
  guidelines, 63–70
  IAF core competencies, 58–60
  keeping focused, 61
  Lean, 65–66
  meeting client needs, 59
  method, 68–70
  multisession events management, 59–60, 184
  overview, 55–56
  performance area for development, 63, 64
  player engagement, 63, 64
  presentations, 68–69
  self-understanding, 56–57
  shared responsibility, 60
  Six Sigma, 65, 66–67
  team members, knowing, 61–62
  Toyota kata, 70–74
  working relationships, 58–59, 61
acting, perform stage, 80
actionable/attainable goals, 153
action plans, 156, 158–164
active facilitator type, 39
adjourn stage, 80
affinity diagrams, 130, 132–133
analysis

benchmarking, 145–146
  fishbone diagram, 141, 143
  root cause matrix, 143–145
appropriate group processes, 192
appropriate outcomes
  consensus, 196–197
  groups, 95
  overview, 185, 195
argumentative behavior, 84, 87
assessment, 187–189
assumptions, surfacing, 7
awards, 223

B

barriers and aids analysis, 116
becoming/sustaining an excellent facilitator
  after the meeting, 18–19, 24–26
  continuous learning, 13–14
  facilitator's checklist, 15–26
  ground rule establishment, 23–24
  INIFAC's core competency B Assessment, 15, 19
  jumpstarting team, 30–33, 217
  just before meeting, 17, 22
  during the meeting, 17–18, 22–24
  OAR, 20–21
  PAL, 20–21
  prior to meeting, 15–16, 19–21
  process, 22–23
  self-evaluation after each meeting, 27–28
  TOTs, 28–30
behavior, 83–85, 238
benchmarking, 145–146
benefits

of facilitators, 227
neutrality, 9–10
brainstorming, 126–129
bubble chart, 169
building teams, 102, *see also* Teams and
    team members
business facilitator type, 36

C

CAPDO (Check–Act–Plan–Do), 117–119
cause and effect diagram, 81
certification, 176–177, 219–220
check sheets
    gathering data, 133
    idea generation, 123
    overview, 134
client relationships
    collaborative, 58–60, 191
    overview, 183–184
client understanding
    collaborative client relationships, 58–60
    IAF core competencies, 58–60
    IAF/INIFAC comparison, 184, 191
    multisession events management, 59–60,
        184, 191
    working relationships, 58–59
coaching
    effectiveness, 225
    feedback, 63, 64–65
    final steps, 63, 64–65
    guidelines, 63–70
    method, 68–70
    overview, 62
    performance area for development, 63,
        64
    player engagement, 63, 64
    presentations, 68–69
    Toyota Kata, 70–74
    type of, 63, 64
collaborative client relationships
    client understanding, 58–60
    IAF/INIFAC comparison, 191
    overview, 183–184
comments, action plans, 163–164
communication
    INIFAC facilitator core competency, 188

INIFAC subcompetencies, 189
participatory environment, 184, 193
skills, 51, 52, 220
company information systems, 134
comparison table, 44
complainers, 85
composition of team, 216–217, *see also*
    Teams and team members
concluding, 7
confidence, 55
conflict management, 88–90, 185, 194
conflict resolution facilitator type, 37
consensus, 185, 196–197
consistency, 180, 188
construction partnering example, 113
content facilitator type, 39
continuous learning, 13–14
control, 188–190
core practices and competencies, 6–7, *see*
    also IAF (International Association
    of Facilitators)
countermeasures, 124
creativity, 185, 194
criterion matrix, 128, 140
critical incident, 97
critical success factors (CSFs), 212–213
CSF, *see* Critical success factors (CSFs)
culture
    awareness and sensitivity, 83
    managing, 239

D

data
    gathering, 133–137
    toolkit, 122–124
debate, 97
decision making, 4
development facilitator type, 39
development of objectives, 157–158
Diagnosis Intervention Model, 238
differences, facilitator types, 40
DiSC profile, 57
diversity, inclusiveness, 184–185, 193
DMAIC
    overview, 67, 81
    problem-solving, 114–115

team, 227
document control manager, 223
double Pareto analysis, 143

E

effectiveness, coaching, 225
efficiency, 179
EMS team, 226
enabler, facilitators, 5
energy of team, 223
engagement, 180, 188, *see also* Facilitation
    engagement processes
EnMS team, 226
environmental scan, 129
evaluation
    ideas, 137–141
    perform stage, 80
events management, multisession, 59–60,
    184, 191
exit interviews, 229

F

facilitation
    problems, 10, 228
    process, 2–4
    structure, 1–2
    unwanted events/occurrences, 10
facilitation engagement processes
    cartoons, 98
    critical incident, 97
    debate, 97
    flash cards, 97
    games, 97
    gap analysis, 99
    group projects, 97
    interviewing partners, 97
    movement, 98
    open space technology, 98–99
    performance, 97
    polling, 97
    posting polarized views, 98
    questionnaires/quizzes, 97
    rating, 97
    role playing, 97
    stories, 98

SWAT/SWOT, 100
    tag game, 98
    World Café method, 100–101
Facilitation Network Singapore (FNS), 7
facilitation tools/techniques, *see also* Tools/
    techniques
    affinity diagrams, 130, 132–133
    analysis, 141–148
    benchmarking, 145–146
    brainstorming, 126–129
    check sheets, 133
    company information systems, 134
    countermeasures, 124
    data, 122–124, 133–137
    environmental scan, 129
    fishbone diagram, 141, 143
    flow charts, 140–141
    focus groups, 136–137
    headlight teams, 129
    ideas, 122–123, 126–129, 140
    implementation, 124
    Internet research, 134
    matrix, 147–148
    metrics, 140
    multivoting, 137
    nominal group technique, 126–129
    objective and problem definition, 122
    overview, 121
    Pareto analysis, 137–139
    payback period, 147
    rate of return, 147
    root cause matrix, 143–145
    solutions, 147–148
    strategic planning, 129–133
    surveys, 135
    SWOT analysis, 130
    toolkit, 121–126
facilitators
    benefits of having, 227
    checklist, 15
    core practices, 6–7
    decision making, 4
    defined, 1
    effective functioning, 4
    focused approach, 205–211
    group achievement, 5
    groups, 4

helper and enabler, 5
in-house *vs.* outside, 228
lead facilitators, 223–224
phase out, 230
roles and responsibilities, 6
subject content, 215
supporting others, 5
team composition, 216–217
team leader interface, 61, 222
Web sites, 238–239
facilitators, types
ability to influence, 49, 51
active, 39
business, 36
client organization knowledge, 51–52
communication, 51, 52
conflict resolution, 37
content, 39
deliverables, 51, 53
development, 39
differences, 40
facilitator tools/techniques, 50, 51
hendecagon model, 47–52
manage conflict, 50, 51
meeting, 39
meeting knowledge, 49–50, 51
objective and target development, 51
overview, 35–36
process, 39
project management, 51
results, 39, 44–46, 205–211
skill set, 47–52
small groups, 37–39, 41
team building, 50, 51
technical knowledge, 50, 51
training, 36
wraparound, 37
facilitators behavior and continuing
    education
acting with integrity, 177, 180, 186, 199
certification, 176–177
IAF core competencies, 175–176
IAF facilitator core competencies, 177,
    179–180
maintaining professional standing, 176
modeling positive attitude, 177–180, 186,
    199
professional knowledge, 175–176
facilitator's exercises, *see end of each
    chapter*
facilitators meeting checklist
after the meeting, 18–19, 24–26
just before meeting, 17, 22
during the meeting, 17–18, 22–24
prior to meeting, 15–16, 19–21
self-evaluation after each meeting, 27–28
TOTs, 28–30
feasibility of objectives, 157–158
feedback
coaching, 63, 64–65
FNS core practice, 7
helpful, 220–221
final steps, coaching, 63, 64–65
fishbone diagram
data analysis, 123
overview, 81, 141, 143
tools/techniques, 81
flash cards, 97
flexibility, 55
flowcharts, 70, 140–141
FNS, *see* Facilitation Network Singapore
    (FNS)
focus, facilitator/team leader interface, 61
focused approach, 205–211
focus groups
gathering data, 136–137
overview, 137
follow-up, 7
form stage, 78
frequency diagrams, 143
functional team, 226
functioning of groups, 4

G

games, 97
gap analysis, 99
gathering data
check sheets, 133
company's information systems, 134
focus groups, 136–137
Internet research, 134
surveys, 135
ground rule establishment, 23–24

Group Effectiveness model, 238
groups, *see also* Teams and team members
  achievements, 5
  appropriate outcomes, 95, 185, 195
  conflict management, 88–90, 185, 194
  consensus, 185, 196–197
  creativity, 185, 194
  dynamics, 90–94, 221
  facilitation engagement processes, 97
  facilitator, 4
  focus groups, gathering data, 136–137
  guidance, 95–96
  modeling positive professional attitude,
    95–96
  neutrality, 95–96
  observation, 90–94
  overview, 77
  planning appropriate processes, 184, 191
  self-awareness, 95, 185, 196
  stages, 221, 239
  supporting processes, 184, 192
  trusting potential, 95–96, 186, 200
  useful outcomes, 95, 185, 195
guidelines, coaching, 63–70

H

harvest, 101
headlight teams, 129, 226
helper, facilitators, 5
Hendecagon skill model, 47–52
high-performance results, 102–107
histograms, 124, 143
Howell, Marv, 253–254

I

IAF (International Association of
    Facilitators)
  appropriate and useful outcomes, 185,
    195
  client understanding, 58–60
  collaborative client relationships, 183–
    184, 191
  comparisons, 190–204
  cultural awareness and sensitivity, 83
  evaluation, 187

INIFAC, 187–204
  integrity, 180, 199
  modeling positive attitude, 177–180, 186,
    199
  overview, 7, 11, 183
  participatory environment, 82, 88–90,
    184–185, 193
  planning appropriate group processes,
    184
  professional knowledge, 175–176, 185–
    186, 197
  recommendations, 213
  results facilitator core competencies,
    204–211
  Web site, 238
ideas
  collecting, 7
  criterion matrix and ranking, 140
  evaluation, 122–123, 137–141
  flow charts, 140–141
  generation, 122–123, 126–129
  metrics, 140
  multivoting, 137
  Pareto analysis, 137–139
  synthesizing, 7
impacts diagram, 104
implementation, 124
improve as objective, 157
inclusiveness, 184–185, 193
indicator graph, 14
influence, *see* Ability to influence
information systems, 134
in-house facilitators, 228
INIFAC (International Institute for
    Facilitation)
  becoming/sustaining an excellent
    facilitator, 15, 19
  core competencies, 7, 11, 187–188
  facilitation engagement processes, 96–101
  IAF comparisons, 190–204
  subcompetencies, 188–190
integrity
  ability to influence, 55
  core competency, 180, 199
  facilitators, 177, 186, 199
  modeling positive attitude, 179, 186
Internet research, 134

intervention approaches, 86–87
interviewing partners, 97
introductions phase, 22
introduction to others, 100
Ishikawa diagram, *see* Fishbone diagram
ISO 14001 EMS example, 112
ISO 50001 EMS example, 110–112

J

James, LeBron, 228
jumpstarting team, 30–33, 217

K

Kaizen team, 226
kata, *see* Toyota kata
know-it-all behavior, 84
kWh intensity, 225

L

Lean methodology, 65–66, 176, 224
Lean team, 226
Learn–Practice–Evaluate–ACT model, 13, 56
life-cycle chart, 171
Likert type format, 135–136
listening, 7, 218

M

maintaining objectives, 158
maintaining professional standing, 176, 186,
    197
management, multisession events, 59–60,
    184, 191
Management Assistance for Nonprofits Web
    site, 239
matrix
    overview, 41
    solutions, 147–148
measurable goals, 153
meeting client needs, 59, 184, 191
meeting facilitator type, 39
meetings
    during, 22–24
    after, 24–26

facilitator neutrality, 227
just prior to, 22
length, 222
overview, 232–233
prior to, 15–21
self-evaluation after each, 27–28
methods
    coaching, 68–70
    selecting, 184
    TOTs, 29
metrics, 140
mission-oriented attitude, 179
modeling positive attitude
    core competency, 177, 179–180
    efficiency, 179
    facilitators, 177–180
    groups, 95–96
    integrity, 179, 186, 199
    overview, 186, 199
movement, 98
multisession events management, 59–60,
    184, 191
multivoting, 128, 137
Mutual Learning Model, 239

N

name acceptability, 228
natural working group, 226
NBA facilitator, 228
needs, meeting client's, 191
negative personality, 85
neutrality
    benefits, 9–10
    FNS core practice, 7
    groups, 95–96, 186, 200–201
    importance, 7, 9
    meeting contents, 227
"never-ending, on a journey" team, 80–82
new facilitators, 216, *see also* Questions,
    new facilitators
nominal group technique, 126–129
nontalkers, 85, 86
norm stage, 78

O

OAR (objective, agenda, restricted), 20–21
objectives and targets
    action plan development, 154–156
    establishment, 157–164
    number of, 217
    obstacles identification, 166
    overview, 151–152
    PDCA cycle, 166
    responsibilities, 224
    SMART, 153–154
    template, 154–156
    time to completion, 225
    toolkit, 122
    Toyota kata, 164–168
observation
    check sheet, 92
    group dynamics, 90–94
    perform stage, 80
    processes, 229
off subject talking, 84–85
open space technology, 98–99
outcomes
    consensus, 196–197
    groups, 95
    overview, 185, 195
outside facilitators, 228

P

PAL (purpose, agenda, limited), 20–21, 239
PAPA (purpose, agenda, points, action
    items), 24–26
paraphrasing, 7
Pareto analysis, 123, 137–139, 143
participatory environment
    IAF core competencies, 82, 88–90
    IAF/INIFAC comparison, 193
    overview, 184–185
patience, 55
payback periods, 147, 172
PDCA (Plan-Do-Check-Act) cycle
    benchmarking, 145
    CAPDO, 119
    continuous improvement, 112
    overview, 13–14

TOTs, 29
people management
    adjourning stage, 80
    argumentative behavior, 84, 87
    behavior, 83–85
    building teams, 102
    cartoons, 98
    complainer, 85
    critical incident, 97
    cultural awareness and sensitivity, 83
    debate, 97
    facilitation engagement processes, 96–101
    flash cards, 97
    form stage, 78
    games, 97
    gap analysis, 99
    group guidance, 95–96
    group projects, 97
    high-performance results, 102–107
    IAF core competencies, 82–83, 88–90
    intervention approaches, 86–87
    interviewing partners, 97
    know-it-all behavior, 84
    modeling positive professional attitude,
        95–96, 177–180, 186, 199
    movement, 98
    negative personality, 85
    neutrality, 95–96, 186, 200–201
    nontalkers, 85, 86
    norm stage, 78
    observing, 80, 90–94
    off subject, 84–85
    open space technology, 98–99
    participatory environment, 82, 88–90,
        193
    performance, 97
    perform stage, 79–80
    personality clashes, 84
    polling, 97
    posting polarized views, 98
    questionnaires/quizzes, 97
    rambling, 85, 86
    rating, 97
    role playing, 97
    self-awareness, 95, 185, 196
    side conversations, 84, 87
    stages of team development, 78–82, 239

stories, 98
storm stage, 78
sustain stage, 80–82
SWAT/SWOT, 100
tag game, 98
talkative, 84, 86
team members, 83–85
trusting group potential, 95–96, 186, 200
Web site, 238
World Café method, 100–101
perception, 56
performance
    areas for development, 63, 64
    facilitation engagement processes, 97
    indicators, 123
perform stage, 79–80
perseverance, 55
personality clashes, 84
phases, projects, 171–173
planning appropriate group processes, 184
player engagement, 63, 64
polarized views, 98
polling, 97
positive attitude, 177–180, 186, 199
posting polarized views, 98
potential of groups, trusting, 95–96, 186, 200
PowerPoint presentation, 69
presence, 187–189
presentations, 68–69
prioritization, 127
problems
    facilitation, 10, 228
    problem-solving example, 114–116
    toolkit, 122
process diagrams, 3
processes
    diagrams, 3–4
    IAF/INIFAC comparison, 191
    during meetings, 22–23
    overview, 2–4
    selecting, 184
    supporting group, 184, 192
process facilitator type, 39
process improvement team (PIT), 226
professional knowledge
    core competency, 175–176

overview, 185–186, 197
professional standing, maintaining, 176, 186, 197
project payback period, 172
projects and project management, 169–173
purpose, TOTs, 29

Q

QC tools, 116, 176, 218
Quality Circle, 226
quality improvement team, 226
quality in daily work team, 226
questionnaires/quizzes, 97
questions
    FNS core practice, 7
    perform stage, 79
    World Café method, 100
questions, new facilitators
    award and recognition, 223
    benefits of having facilitators, 227
    certification, 219–220
    closure, 229
    coaching, 225
    communication, 220
    composition of teams, 216–217
    document control manager, 223
    energy of team, 223
    exit interviews, 229
    facilitators, 218, 222, 227–228, 230
    feedback, 220–221
    groups stages, 221.239
    in-house facilitators, 228
    James, LeBron, 228
    jumpstarting a team, 217
    kWh intensity, 225
    lead facilitators, 223–224
    Lean, 224
    listening, 218
    meeting length, 222
    momentum, 217
    name acceptability, 228
    neutrality, 227
    objectives and targets, 224–225
    outside facilitators, 228
    phase out of facilitators, 230
    process observers, 229

replacement, team members, 221
responsibility for results, 216
seven quality control tools, 218
Six Sigma, 224
skills of facilitators, 218
subject content, 215
success, 227
teams and team members, 216–217, 221,
    223, 226–227, 229
time to completion, 225
training, 219

R

rambling, 85, 86
ranking, 127, 140
rate of return, 147
rating, 97
recognition, 223
recommendations, 213
relationship chart, 71
relationship diagram, 53
relationships, 58–59, 183–184
relevant goals, 153
replacement, team members, 221–222
research of objectives, 157–158
respect for others, 179
responsibilities, *see also* Roles and
    responsibilities
    objectives and targets, 224
    for results, 216
    shared, 60
results facilitators
    core competencies, 204–211
    overview, 39, 44–46
role playing, 97
roles and responsibilities, 6
root cause matrix, 143–145
round robin, 127

S

safety team, 226
scatter diagram, 123
self-assessment
    facilitators, 180–181
    modeling positive attitude, 180–181, 199

self-awareness
    facilitators, 180–181
    group guidance, 95, 185, 196
self-directed work team, 226
self-evaluation after each meeting, 27–28
self-understanding, 56–57
sensitivity, 179
setting, World Café method, 100
seven QC tools, 116, 176, 218
shared responsibility, 60
showing, perform stage, 80
side conversations, 84, 87
silent generation, 127
Six Sigma, 65, 66–67, 69, 176, 224
size of team, optimum, 216–217
Skilled Facilitator's Approach Web site, 239
skills, *see also* Becoming/sustaining an
      excellent facilitator
    ability to influence, 49, 51
    client organization knowledge, 51–52
    communication, 51, 52
    deliverables, 51, 53
    facilitator tools/techniques, 50, 51
    manage conflict, 50, 51, 185, 194
    meeting knowledge, 49–50, 51
    objective and target development, 51
    professional knowledge, 185–186, 197
    project management, 51
    questions about, 218
    team building, 50, 51
    technical knowledge, 50, 51
small group rounds, 100
SMART goals, 153–154
solutions
    matrix, 147–148
    payback period, 147
    rate of return, 147
specific goals, 153
stages of team development, 80–82, 221,
    239
status, action plans, 162–163
staying on track, 7
stories, 98
storm stage, 78
strategic improvement team, 226
strategic planning
    affinity diagrams, 130, 132–133

environmental scan, 129
headlight teams, 129
structure, 1–2
study objectives, 157–158
subcompetencies, INIFAC, 188–190
subject content, 215
success, 212–213, 227
summarization, perform stage, 79
supporting others, 5
surveys
gathering data, 135
overview, 136
sustaining, *see* Becoming/sustaining an
excellent facilitator
sustain stage, 80–82
SWAT/SWOT, 100, 130
synthesizing ideas, 7

T

tag game, 98
talkative team members, 84, 86
task team, 226
teaching, perform stage, 80
team coaching process, 69, *see also*
Coaching
team leader/facilitator interface, 61, 222
teams and team members, *see also* Groups
argumentative behavior, 84, 87
behavior, 83–85, 238
building, 102
closure, 229
complainer, 85
composition, 216–217
energy, 223
exit interviews, 229
facilitator interface, 61, 222
high-performance results, 102–107
jumpstarting, 30–33, 217
knowing, 61–62
know-it-all behavior, 84
momentum, 217
negative personality, 85
nontalkers, 85, 86
off subject, 84–85
overview, 77, 101
personality clashes, 84

rambling, 85, 86
replacement, 221–222
results, 164–168
sharing work, 221
side conversations, 84, 87
size, optimum, 216–217
success, 227
survey, 92–94
talkative, 84, 86
types, 226–227
technical area/processes knowledge
CAPDO, 117–119
construction partnering example, 113
ISO 14001 EMS example, 112
ISO 50001 EMS example, 110–112
overview, 109–110
PDCA, 119
problem-solving example, 114–116
tiger team, 226
time-frame/based goals, 153–154
toolkit
countermeasures, 124
data, 122–124
idea generation and evaluation, 122–123
implementation, 124
objective and problem definition, 122
tools/techniques, *see also* Facilitation tools/
techniques
action plan, 164
affinity diagrams, 133
barriers and aids analysis, 116
benchmarking, 146
brainstorming, 127
bubble chart, 169–170
CAPDO, 117
cause and effect diagram, 81
check sheets, 134
comparison table, 44
criterion matrix, evaluation, 128
DMAIC, 81, 114
environmental scan, 129
facilitator's checklist, 15
fishbone diagram, 81
flowcharts, 70, 141
focus groups, 137
ground rules, 24

Hendecagon diagram, 47
impacts diagram, 104
indicator graph, 14
life-cycle chart, 171
matrix, 41
meeting self-evaluation, 27
multivoting, 128
nominal group technique, 127
OAR, 20
observation check sheet, 92
PAL, 20
PAPA, 24
Pareto analysis, 139
payback periods, 147, 172
PDCA cycle, 14
PowerPoint presentation, 69
process diagrams, 3
project payback period, 172
QC tools, 116
relationship chart, simple, 71
relationship diagram, 53
root cause evaluation matrix, 143
seven QC tools, 116
Six Sigma, 69
SMART goals, 154
solutions evaluation matrix, 147
surveys, 136
SWOT analysis, 130
team coaching process, 69
team survey, 92
TOTs, 28
Toyota kata, 74, 168
Venn diagram, 41
TOTs (team objectives and targets), 28–30

Toyota kata
    achieving team results, 164–168
    coaching, 70–74
    overview, 74, 168
training, 219
trusting potential, groups, 95–96, 186, 200
Tuckman's stages, group development,
    78–82, 221, 232, 239

U

unwanted events/occurrences, 10
useful outcomes
    consensus, 196–197
    groups, 95
    overview, 185, 195

V

Venn diagram, 41

W

Web sites, 238–239
welcome and introduction, 100
What, action plans, 156, 159–160
When, action plans, 156, 159, 161–162
Where, action plans, 156, 159
Who, action plans, 156, 160–161
Whom, action plans, 156, 159
working relationships
    client understanding, 58–59
    facilitator/team leader interface, 61
World Café method, 100–101

About the Author

For the last eight years, Marv Howell worked as a contractor senior environmental associate for Analytical Services Inc., which provided environmental services to the Drug Enforcement Administration. Marv implemented environmental management systems and facilitated their monthly meetings at eight DEA facilities that included labs, division offices, intelligence center, and an air operations center. All eight facilities passed at least one second party audit.

In addition, he was instrumental in planning and designing several energy management system actions/efficiencies initiatives that resulted in saving more than $400,000 a year in electricity cost, reducing natural gas use at the air operation center by 32% a year, improving power factor at one facility from .70 to .996 thus saving $7,200 dollars a year, assisting in planning light upgrades from T-12s to T-8s and T-5s, planning advanced meters installation and build automation systems upgrades, and performing energy audits to include a data center that when his recommendation is implemented will reduce energy use by more than 30% annually.

Marv helped facilities develop energy conservation plans and communicate them to all the facilities' management, supervisors, employees and contractors.

Marv was the manager of distribution planning and reliability for FPL where early in 1982 he became one of FPL's original facilitators. He was instrumental in assisting FPL to become the first company outside of Japan to win the coveted Deming Prize for Quality. He was a lieutenant colonel in U.S. Air Force civil engineering where he was involved in energy reduction efforts, reliability, project management, construction, maintenance management, efficiency, productivity improvements, and facilitation efforts. From 1991 to 2003, Marv had his own quality improvement company in Miami, Florida where he helped many companies and organizations such as U.S. Air Force, Intel, and Oklahoma State University at Oklahoma City improve their quality improvements efforts, practice strategic management, control their processes and improve them, implement lean improvements and facilitate Kaizen events. He earned his bachelor's degree in mechanical engineering from Mississippi State University and a master's degree in industrial engineering from the University of Pittsburgh. His books that have been published are: *Effective Implementation of ISO 50001 Energy Management System* (2014) by ASQ Quality Press; *Critical Success Factors Simplified* (2010) by CRC Press; and *Actionable Performance Measurement—A Key to Success* (2006) by ASQ Quality Press.

E-mail address:

MHowellQMT@aol.com

Printed in the United States
by Baker & Taylor Publisher Services